WORKING WITH FOUCAULT IN EDUCATION

Working with Foucault in Education

By

Margaret Walshaw
Massey University, New Zealand

SENSE PUBLISHERS
ROTTERDAM / TAIPEI

A C.I.P. record for this book is available from the Library of Congress.

ISBN 978-90-8790-188-2 (paperback)
ISBN 978-90-8790-189-9 (hardback)

Published by: Sense Publishers,
P.O. Box 21858, 3001 AW Rotterdam, The Netherlands
http://www.sensepublishers.com

Printed on acid-free paper

For Martin

CONTENTS

	Acknowledgments	ix
	Foreword	xi
1	**Getting to grips with Foucault**	1
	The importance of theory	1
	A context for Foucault's ideas	3
	Foucault and poststructuralism	5
	A brief history of Foucault's counter-history	6
	Early work	8
	From archaeology to genealogy to ethics	9
	Key concepts	17
	Conclusion	25
2	**An archaeology of learning**	27
	Behaviourism	28
	Cognitivism	29
	Constructivism	31
	Sociocultural formulations	32
	Activity/Situativity/Social practice theory	34
	Conclusion	37
3	**Discourse analysis**	39
	Discourse	40
	Discourse analysis	44
	Subject positions and texts	45
	The policy text in context	46
	Conclusion	62
4	**The subjectivity of the learner**	65
	Subjectivity as constituted in discourses	66
	Power	67
	Knowledge	69
	Donna's mathematical performance	71
	Conclusion	77
5	**Students' identity at the cultural crossroads**	79
	Identity	80
	Colliding discourses	82
	Mothers and daughters and low socio-economic status	85
	Mothers and daughters and high socio-economic status	89
	Reflections on identity	93

6 **Learning to teach in context** 95
Teachers' identities' explained 95
Dividing practices 99
Exploring context in identity construction 102
Three moments of identity 103
Reflections on context in identity construction 109

7 **Subjectivity and regulatory practices** 111
Disciplinary power 112
Subjectification 114
An exploration into the constitution of teaching 115
Transitory positions 116
Regulatory practices 119
Technologies of surveillance and normalisation 124
Concluding thoughts on the constitution of teaching 127

8 **Girls disciplining others** 129
Normalisation 129
Stories about girls (and boys) in schooling 131
The study 133
Girls monitoring boys in the classroom 134
Girls monitoring other girls in the classroom 137
Closing comments about disciplining practices 140

9 **Research** 143
Knowing others 144
Research traditions 144
Rethinking research 146
Constructing reality 149
Breaking away from convention 152
Rachel's story 155
Reflections on research 163

10 **Endings marking new beginnings** 165
Looking back 166
Looking forward 168

Bibliography 171

Suggestions for further reading 177

Foucault's work: A selection 177

Index 181

ACKNOWLEDGMENTS

The book has been written particularly with students and educators in mind. The author's own students and colleagues have been a source of inspiration–through their curiosity about Foucault and in their enthusiasm to get a grip of his work. The greatest debt is to them.

The author would like to thank a number of people for their support and encouragement in the work:

Hilary Povey and Una Hanley have generously permitted the use of extracts from their work presented at the Psychology of Mathematics Education international conference in Prague 2006. To them, and all the presenters at the Discussion Group–Tansy Hardy and Heather Mendick–and to the many participants, thank you for your helpful conversations.

Special thanks are due to Wendy Osborne at Massey University, New Zealand, for graciously providing all the necessary secretarial assistance with the manuscript.

The author and publishers are grateful to the following for permission to reproduce extracts of the author's work: *British Journal of Sociology of Education; Cambridge Journal of Education; Journal for Research in Mathematics Education; For the Learning of Mathematics; Journal of Mathematics Teacher Education; New Zealand Journal of Educational Studies.* A full list of copyright permissions is provided at the end to the book.

FOREWORD

> I shall take as my starting-point whatever unities are already given...; but I shall not place myself inside these dubious unities in order to study their internal configurations...I shall make use of them just long enough to ask myself what unities they form...I shall accept the groupings that history suggests only to subject them at once to interrogation.
>
> (Foucault, 1972, p. 26)

This book is about new ideas. The title *Working with Foucault in Education* was chosen with two purposes in mind. First I emphasise theory. I set out to introduce readers to the scholarly work of Michel Foucault. The second purpose concerns the practical side of how those ideas might be useful. This aspect is given emphasis because many readers want to know what relevance Foucault's ideas actually have for education. By merging knowledge and application, *Working with Foucault in Education* allows readers to come to know and appreciate the significance of Foucault's ideas for the discipline—and at a level that is neither too demanding nor too superficial. Above all, the intent is that the personal, practical and intellectual challenge it presents will cultivate a new attitude towards education.

The book comes hard on the heels of widespread interest in Foucault's work and it is thanks to this interest that a great deal of published work has already become available. However, literature that draws on Foucault's ideas is generally organised around social and cultural analyses that stop short of education. As happens in relatively uncharted territory, many students and scholars in the educational field don't have the faintest notion about Foucault's work, let alone the uses that his work might be put to. Others have some understanding but have not had the opportunity, or the inclination, to date, to work with the ideas and apply them in their work. From the discipline's point of view, because changes in terms of purposes, content, and methods, are currently taking place, this is an opportune time to open up a different conceptual world.

Of course new conceptualisations and new explanations are far from new for education. The discipline has a long tradition of expanding its knowledge base and has a fine record of responsiveness to changes in society. Recent interest in alternative frameworks is by no means an exception. Think for a moment about the current interest surrounding activity theory. And think, too, about the push for evidence based practice. It wouldn't be stretching the truth to say that the discipline has, in its search for compelling understandings of people and processes, tended to become more receptive to influences outside its own roots. It has opened itself up to alternative ways of thinking.

The trend towards thinking in other ways has found its way into university degree and diploma courses. Whatever the discipline determines will be the next 'must have' in the pecking order, we can be sure that the concepts encapsulated within Foucault's theories, and the uses they are put to in the book, are diverse and relevant to not just students, but anyone interested in and working in education. You can be sure to find that the treatment given to his ideas is not a superficial gesture. That's because Foucault's 'system' of ideas is taken seriously. The ideas are made accessible from the mere fact that they are grounded in the concrete detail of particular people within particular situations in education. It's the application to everyday life within education where the ideas come into their own.

To put matters in perspective, *Working with Foucault in Education* is devoted in large part to critical interrogations relevant to the discipline. It reaches beyond conventional understandings to engage readers in issues relating to curriculum development, teacher education, research and classroom teaching and learning in contemporary society. The reason this is possible is that Foucault provides a language and the theoretical tools to deconstruct, as well as shift thinking about familiar concepts within the discipline.

This new line of investigation creates an awareness of the merits and weaknesses of contemporary theoretical frameworks within the discipline and the impact these frameworks have on the production of knowledge. Educators, policy makers, teachers, and scholars have the opportunity to question what drives their practices. To add to this, they have the opportunity to develop a new sensitivity to the diffusion of power. As can only happen with Foucault's framework, a space is opened for clarifying how a sense-of-self is caught up in regulatory practices and truth games. The good news is that this new awareness means readers will be better positioned to participate in educational criticism and be better placed to play a role in educational change.

OVERVIEW OF CHAPTERS

The volume consists of ten chapters. The first chapter gets to grips with Foucault. It sets the scene by providing a context for the development of Foucault's thinking. It emphasises that Foucault's scholarly work is to be read more as a conceptual interrogation, rather than a search for essentials and truth. One of the delights of new thinking is in seeing how that thinking can be put to use. The chapters that follow do just that. They take a thematic approach and include vignettes that explore ways by which Foucault's conceptual apparatus might be operationalised. Rather than applying key insights to the entire field, the chapters look at selected aspects of the discipline, in particular, curriculum, learning, learning to teach, and research. It is through those explorations that we develop an awareness of the cultural, economic, political and social factors that influence educational processes and practices.

Chapter 1 discusses the importance of theory and puts Foucault theoretical framework in a context that includes specific academic, social and cultural conditions. The chapter briefly outlines the main stages of Foucault's work, beginning with his early work through to his archaeological and genealogical phases and later to his return to ethics. The phases form a backbone to the way he deals with particular social issues and provide insights into his own theoretical development. They also highlight the sheer complexity of social practice and the difficulty in coming up with universal checklists for explaining what we do. Of course different kinds of analyses need different kinds of tools and a different use of language. We learn about the subject, discourse, governmentality, and technologies of the self.

Chapter 2 draws on Foucault's approach to history. His archaeological methodology helps us come to terms with how scholarly thinking about the concept of learning has moved in various directions over time. The archaeology allows us to unearth the assumptions that prop up various theories of learning and provides a refreshingly new way to think about concepts. It charts the development of how we understand learning and shows us how particular rules or discourses at particular times make it possible for certain understandings about learning to be entertained and legitimated in classrooms. It provides an arresting reminder that competing stories about learning reflect different versions of social life within different social conditions.

Alternative conceptions of learning lead to different views about what learners ought to do and the sort of thinkers they might become. We trace a range of theories to find out what kind of learner is proposed. Our analyses take us to behaviourism, cognitivism, constructivism and the sociocultural formations, including social constructivist, interactionist or participatory, enactivist and complexity theories, as well as activity/situativity/social practice theory. Each has something important to tell us about the shape and character of learning and each sets in motion new thinking about knowledge about learning as a discursive event.

Chapter 3 expands on Foucault's notion of discourse. It clarifies how discourses can only make sense within contexts. The reason is that discourses systematically constitute versions of the social world for us. They are historically variable ways of specifying truth and knowledge. To add to the tension, discourses position actual people. We use these ideas in an analysis of discourse. Critical discourse analysis is an approach, using Foucault's ideas, that allows us to explore the way people are positioned within spoken language and written texts. It specifically focuses on the use of language to show how meanings generated through discourses are produced as a social fact. They shape our viewpoints, our beliefs and our practices.

In trying to get a grasp of the method of discourse analysis, we look at how a curriculum policy text positions, locates, defines and regulates people, in different ways. Curriculum policies set agendas, enforce priorities, minimise or elevate particular knowledges and subject positions. This is a thought-provoking proposal, and we explore how this happens by looking at a specific policy text. Through the analysis we trace the underlying values that shape what appear to be commonsense understandings of its key terms, the logic of reason, development and the pedagogical relations it promotes, and its imperatives of 'difference' and strategies for gender and race.

Chapter 4 works with Foucault's understanding of subjectivity to explore how learners are constituted in discourses. Students are caught up within discursive practices within the classroom just as they are caught up in the subject positions established for them within a policy text. We reintroduce power to develop an understanding of how integral it is to our personal and public lives. Even in classrooms that look, on the surface, equitable and inclusive, we discover that power seeps right through its social structure. We come to an understanding in the chapter of the close relationship that power has with knowledge. We explore that relationship through intersubjective relations and the discourses that make them possible within a classroom.

Our analysis of classroom life examines the way power infuses itself within, and operates through, the discourses and practices of classroom life. We use Foucault's conceptual tools of discourse, subjectivity and power to investigate the methods of regulation operating through practices within the classroom. They help us explore the role that power has in the constitution of subjective experience. Through the analysis we notice the effects of teacher, peer- and self-regulatory practices on one student, and how such practices impinge on her thinking and acting. It is then possible to see how thinking is produced within discourses and practices, and how power infuses the 'reality' of classroom life.

Chapter 5 explores subjectivity at the cultural crossroads. Subjectivity is the central concept and the chapter provides us with the resources to explore its constitution in discourses. But the discourses that act upon us are many and varied. We all end up taking up multiple identities as different discursive formations are made attractive to us. Yet the discourses offer us competing ways of organising and giving meaning to what we do and think. Gender and class are cultural discourses and we perform them by negotiating through a wide range of discursive formations that are often beyond our comprehension.

Cultural discourses bring a powerful dimension to the way we take up our identity. Our analyses explore the role that social categories play in the production of subjectivities. Our focus is specifically on social class and on people and relationships. Girls from all socio-economic backgrounds contend with issues associated with femininity, family, academic progress, and history, and their schooling cannot be viewed in isolation from them. From the spoken texts we get an understanding of the complex ways that disadvantage and privilege work in inequitable ways in shaping gendered subjectivities.

Chapter 6 works with Foucault in teacher education. The focus is on understanding how pre-service teachers construct an identity for themselves as teachers. We find out that identities are created through complex structural processes and historical events. Like it or not, there is no such thing as a 'born teacher'. Because of the complexity of discourses that demand their attention in the different sites within which they participate, pre-service teachers' ways of understanding themselves as teachers will always be in a state of flux. We draw on Foucault's notion of dividing practices to drive this point home.

In our exploration into the construction of teaching identity we will observe the political and strategic nature of *modes of operating*, *knowledges*, and *positionings* that are central to identity construction. Learning to teach is a distinct social activity with particular social relationships, knowledge forms, and associated pedagogic modes. Our analysis is focused on three moments: educational biography, teacher education programme, and teaching practice in schools. Each of these moments shows us how teaching identity is produced and reproduced through social interaction, daily negotiations, and within particular contexts that are always filled with other peoples' meanings.

Chapter 7 continues the exploration into the 'making' of teachers. It addresses the issue of conformity to regulatory practices found within institutions. The notion of disciplinary power provides background understanding to the idea of subjectification to explain why we might feel the need to self-regulate or discipline ourselves without any formal compulsion to do so. We look back to Bentham's Panopticon and its particularly novel approach to surveillance and regulation of a population. Bentham's design, incorporating invisible strategies and tactics, marked a new morality that opened itself up to new institutional practices and with them, the self-regulation of people within them.

We use the concept of regulatory disciplinary practices to explore how a group of pre-service teachers comes to conform to, and 'make their own', the specific practices in the classrooms within which they practise. We observe how they weigh up classroom practices in relation to what they have learned in their university courses. Practices and surveillance and normalisation within the classroom, however, also come into play. In the spaces shared by the pre-service and associate teachers, issues of privilege and subordination feature prominently. We see whose experiences and what knowledges count or are withheld during the process of establishing pedagogic authority

Chapter 8 develops Foucault's notions of normalisation and surveillance further. Surveillance affects the choices we make and tends to normalise our options. In fact, it normalises our thinking, being and doing to such an extent that we begin to 'watch ourselves'. The school and the classroom perform a normalising function and they do this by setting standards through a form of coercion that is disguised from us. Students' actions, interactions, and knowledges are under constant gaze by school officials. The surveillance not only politicises the work done in classrooms, it also contributes to a sense of self-in-schooling. The surveillance and normalisation comes from a variety of quarters, including other students within the classroom.

Our analysis is focused on the classroom and captures the dynamic between gendered subjectivity and schooling. The classroom is shown to be a place where norms, beliefs and actions are produced, monitored and regulated. At the heart of our exploration are everyday girls situated within wider social, institutional and educational practices. Integral to the discussion is powerful thread of female monitoring that runs through the social space of the classroom. The analysis will reveal how girls strategically normalise, by none-too-subtle means, behaviours that they deem characteristic of the gendered learner.

Chapter 9 works with Foucault in research. It raises questions about how we structure the conceptual categories in our research endeavours. It also raises issues about how we know one another. It considers how the traditions of the scientific model stake out certain spaces for establishing credibility. Objectivity is discussed in relation to Foucault's ideas on truth and knowledge claims. In a process in which cognitive resources and positions of authority and expertise are unevenly distributed, constructing reality gets tangled up in power games. The trouble is that it's not a matter of applying the correct method or of trying and looking harder.

Conventional research reporting portrays an orderly pathway and unproblematic decision making for the researcher. The chapter looks at first steps in doing research differently and flags the importance of a wide view of knowledge construction, all the while registering the limits of knowing. These counterpoints to conventional research provide a way through which to capture non-linear 'lines of flight'. In the analysis put forward, the report signals the dilemmas involved in providing an accurate account of a student's narrative. The researcher attempts to come to terms with the difficulty in achieving a coherent and logical story, when the interviewee see-saws back and forth in talking of her experiences.

Chapter 10 works with Foucault to mark endings and new beginnings. The chapter pulls together the ideas developed and summarises the range of inquiries pursued in the book. It notes how the analyses account for multiple layers of engagement in educational settings, processes, and policy. It makes the important point that the inquiries have used language differently, have moved away from linear teleology, and do not promise total vision. Many of the analyses have explored lived experience, not in the sense of capturing reality and proclaiming causes, but of understanding the complex and changing discursive processes by which subjectivities are shaped. They showed us how meanings are validated, and whose investments they privilege.

Developing familiarity with Foucault's language and thinking is one thing: developing an awareness of how they might best be put to use is another. Working with Foucault and putting his ideas to use allows us to extend our 'what' questions about people, relationships, and systems into questions concerning 'how' and 'why'. Of course this does not mean that other approaches used in education have diminished in value. To the contrary, their intellectual concerns and convictions will be around for a long time yet. What it does mean, however, is that Foucault's system can be used as a key lever for critical interrogation of education's practices and processes. The final chapter alerts us to this potential and the ways in which Foucault's work might clear a space for new insight within the discipline and for imagining creative change.

A NOTE ON THE USE OF THIS BOOK

There are a number of ways you can use this text. The structure of the book is designed to help you come to terms with new knowledge and with new analytical skills in a systematic way. But let's be clear about one thing: this is not a 'how to' manual that gives you rules and steps to follow. In fact if you are looking for definitive solutions to long-standing issues, Foucault's work is not the place to begin. That's because Foucault never claimed to provide hard and fast answers to anything. So this book on Foucault's conceptual framework is more of a guide that will equip you with the know-how to think differently as you make your way through various aspects of education. Whether used for course work, research, or otherwise, you will first want to come to terms with Foucault's conceptual language and will find that information in the first chapter. In the chapter, rather than putting Foucault's work under critical interrogation, as some commentators have done, we use his work as a resource to stretch your mind as well as provide you with the tools for bringing critical inquiry to bear on education.

Readers using this text for course work will find the order of the chapters useful to developing new understanding and for exercising the imagination. Readers with particular interests and passions may prefer to be selective and may want to begin reading the chapters in the order that suits personal preference. Whatever order you read the book, it is there to be used iteratively, shaping and reshaping understanding, in response to your own continuing questions and pursuit of knowledge.

All chapters include activities. I hope that you will act upon them. They are there as opportunities to explore issues relating to the theme of the chapter, using either your own data or the data provided. After working with the data, take some time to reflect on how the use of Foucault's conceptual language on the data initiates a shift in your own thinking.

At the end of the book you will find suggestions for further reading. These are references to Foucault's original work and to a selection of other texts on Foucault. A full reference list of the sources used in the book is also provided towards the end of the book. You might want to follow up these sources for the purpose of extending your knowledge.

A NOTE ON THE DATA SOURCES USED IN THE BOOK

Working with Foucault in Education uses a number of data extracts to provide examples for putting Foucault's ideas to use. Most of the data comes from my own research. In a couple of cases, however, I have selected material from the ideas of other people working in education. Data not been attributed to any source has been collected in my own research projects. Although most are drawn from my work in mathematics education, they all have application across other educational fields. Following my ethical obligations to the research participants whose transcripts I have used, I have given the speakers fictitious names.

CHAPTER 1

GETTING TO GRIPS WITH FOUCAULT

IN THIS CHAPTER

- The importance of theory
- A context for Foucault's ideas
- Foucault and poststructuralism
- A brief history of Foucault's counter-history
- Early work
- From archaeology to genealogy to ethics
- Key concepts

THE IMPORTANCE OF THEORY

Have you ever thought seriously about the theories you use, and their usefulness to the work you do in education? Theorising is important. Although we often overlook the fact, theorising is a fundamental aspect of the fabric of our lives. So much of what we do depends on our theories—they allow us to make sense of things. In any social community the ways in which made sense of reality has profound implications for social progress and individual identity. We derive a sense of self and purpose from the way we put the world in focus. Let's put it this way: the theories we fashion out of concepts allow us to understand the world more acutely. Without them we would be unable to tell which aspects of reality are critical to us and which are unimportant. They allow us to develop a vision of what to work toward, and what sort of changes might be necessary. The same is true in education—what we understand, hope and strive for in the discipline depends on our conceptual schemes.

The important thing to remember is that every theory is simply a lens. Just as an optical lens improves our sight, in a similar way theories improve our insight. The conceptual frames we use to make sense of events and practices have consequences for how we go about our work within education. The kinds of questions that we might ask, even down to questioning itself, stem from the sort of theories that guide our understanding about how we claim to know what we know. But much as we would want to think to the contrary, no theory can bring everything into focus all at once. That is not to say that theories are not useful. It is simply to clarify that any theoretical lens that we have used or might use in the future in education puts boundaries around the scope of our vision. They blind us from seeing otherwise. As they zoom in on the foreground or fade out to capture the background, our theoretical lens glosses over, in turn, important distant or close-up views. In other words, by putting a positive spin on certain aspects of reality, theories cause us to ignore other details that lie nearer or farther away. They prevent us from thinking afresh, from imagining things differently and from asking other kinds of questions.

Let's see what views some of our theories in education have opened up for us. Some people who work in education are drawn to constructivism or socioculturalism. Others are using enactivism and symbolic interactionism. Still others are drawing on a range of other theoretical lenses that help them think, imagine and ask questions in a different way. These include distributed cognition, critical theory, and information-processing psychology. Figure 1 (adapted from Lather, 2006) shows some of the theories that inform work in education and reveals the ways in which these theoretical lenses shape the way we 'view' the world.

Table 1: Some Theoretical Frames

	POSITIVIST	**INTERPRETIVIST**	**EMANCIPATORY**
Theoretical Lens	Behaviourism	Constructivism Enactivism Hermeneutics Interpretivism Naturalism Phenomenology Situated Knowing Socioculturalism Symbolic interactionism Information-processing	Critical theory Feminist theory Critical race theory
Objective	To know	To understand	To liberate
View of 'reality'	Objective and found	Subjective and constructed	Subjective, constructed in a context of power
View of 'truth'	Truth is one	Truth is many	Truth is many and constitutes a socio-political system

Most scholarship today in education is situated within interpretivist frames. For most scholars in our discipline, the set of theoretical propositions that this frame offers, has the effect of defining the concepts through which data are to be understood. It's not so long ago that positivist propositions underpinned most work in the discipline. Certainty, order and clarity were the order of the day, and reality had the same qualities regardless of who was observing it. Naturally, it made a lot of sense to want to 'know', when truth was known to be absolute and final. In contrast, it makes more sense to 'understand' and 'explain', if truth claims are multiple and reality is subjective and constructed—as is taken to be the case in interpretivist conceptual frameworks. And it makes sense to strive from freedom when a desire for a just world is what drives your practice, as it does in the emancipatory framework. These different theoretical positions offer a way of understanding the world, in general, and of understanding knowledge, representation and subjectivity, in particular, and, hence, of interpreting information in education.

Foucault provides a different way of looking at things. For him, it is the *concepts* we develop, rather than the theoretical frame that we privilege, that become our starting points for interpreting information. Once you think along those lines, you develop a sensibility about how to explain the data. The fascinating thing about this alternative view is that theories can provide different and sometimes conflicting answers to our questions, even when the same concept is used. As an example, consider the concept of 'moving bodies'. As you will be aware, Einstein provided a contradictory theory to that offered by Newton. Even though the same concept of 'moving bodies' functioned in the formulations of both Newton and Einstein, the explanations offered by the theories differed markedly.

In a more general way, the distinction between the concepts that interpret data, on the one hand, and the theories that provide an explanation of them, on the other, proved immensely interesting to Foucault. He came to the conclusion that reality is ultimately unknowable. Having made that pronouncement, he went out of his way to stress that truth claims are socially constructed systems that bring with them their own contradictions. This led him to an interest in tracking the history of concepts, in preference to the convention of mapping out the development of theoretical formulations. The ideas he came up with and the methods he used were quite unlike anything that had been seen before. It was an accomplishment so extraordinary and novel, when compared with the trends in scholarship, that led him to be enormously influential in the social and human sciences. Clearly, this man's ideas are worth getting to know.

A CONTEXT FOR FOUCAULT'S IDEAS

> I do not conclude from this that one may say just anything within the order of theory, but, on the contrary, that a demanding, prudent, 'experimental' attitude is necessary; at every moment, step by step, one must confront what one is thinking and saying with what one is doing, with what one is...but, on the other hand, I have always been concerned with linking together as tightly as possible the historical and theoretical analysis of power relations, institutions, and knowledge, to the movements, critiques, and experiences that call them into question in reality.
>
> (Foucault, 1984, p. 374)

Foucault was born in 1926 near Paris and died in 1984. He was, by all accounts, quite a personality. A man of means and connections, he counted among his good friends, Derrida, Barthes, and Althusser. So it would come as no surprise that he lived and worked in the midst of vibrant intellectual, social and political times. What emerged within this era, beginning around the 1940s, was a different way of seeing and working. Understandings that people took for granted began to become more open to question and doubt. This is what 'postmodernism' is all about and it developed as a critical and self-reflective attitude, firstly, within literary criticism. During the early and mid-1970s it gained a much wider audience, and interest spread to include architecture, dance, theatre, painting, film and music, and then contemporary culture and society as a whole. The upshot was that it soon entered the full range of human sciences. Back in his state of origin, Michel Foucault was up there, along with Jacques Derrida, Julia Kristeva, Jean-Francois Lyotard, and others, taking up the 'postmodern sensibility'.

By the 1980s, postmodernism became a dominant 'structure of feeling' for many intellectuals across the world. For many others it was at least an emergent attitude. Yet, as is often the case when a new way of thinking and acting is introduced, postmodernism became controversial and brought on highly charged reactions across academic disciplines. You take my point. Those who did push the cause made sure that postmodernism developed right across the disciplines. The group's avowed aim was to express a loss of faith in the forms of knowledge that we have all inherited. What they were keen to get across, more than anything, was the idea that traditional values, assumptions and explanations are no longer adequate, nor even desirable, when we try to make sense of our contemporary social and cultural world.

Some commentators have argued that Foucault's work is a paradigmatic example of 'postmodern' thought (see Hartsock, 1990; Hekman, 1990; Hoy, 1986). Interesting enough, others (e.g., McNay, 1994) have noted that Foucault himself never saw his work as 'postmodern'. In fact, it is said (see Usher & Edwards, 1994) that he made out that he didn't know what the term 'postmodernism' (or 'poststructuralism') meant or what problems these terms were meant to address. There are many meanings and purposes in circulation, and we would be hard pressed to overlook that fact. To help our own understanding here, let's think of postmodernism as signifying a *mood* that captures the end of totality, holism and presence, and let's think of poststructuralism as *theorising* that ending. The interesting thing is that, despite Foucault's own resistance to both terms, most texts write about him as a thinker within this recent tradition. And this is the way we shall categorise him too.

FOUCAULT AND POSTSTRUCTURALISM

It might come as no surprise to learn that poststructuralism follows structuralism. That's usually the effect that the term 'post' has. I mention that fact because Foucault belongs to a group of French thinkers who were very keen to move structuralist (and Marxist) ideas forward. The group included Althusser (1971), Derrida (1973, 1976), Kristeva (1981, 1984, 1986), and Lacan (1977), and along with Foucault, they brought a breath of fresh air to conventional thinking. Let me explain. Although they all worked on different projects, what they were able to do was critically and sensitively overturn "inherited structures of belief and convention" (Wolin, 1992, p. 8). Their diverse set of initiatives in social and philosophical thought, helped crystallise ideas about knowledge and subjectivity for our contemporary world. In a nutshell, they each helped us think about and do things differently.

For many people, this is where the confusion begins, and so a few points of clarification would be in order. Poststructuralists all share some fundamental assumptions of language, meaning and subjectivity. They see language as fragile and problematic and as *constituting* social reality rather than *reflecting* an already given reality. For Foucault, and other poststructuralists, the approach taken with the structural analysis of signs, missed the mark in some respects. The argument that the *post*structural analysts make is that meaning is not absolute in relation to a referent, as had been proposed by de Saussure. But more than that: they reject the notion of knowing as an outcome of human consciousness and interpretation–as described by phenomenology. They also deny that knowing is an outcome of different interpretations–which is what hermeneutics claims. Instead, for them, reality is in a constant process of construction. What is warranted at one moment of time, may be unwarranted at another time. Their claim is that because the construction process is ongoing, we do not have access to an independent reality. There is no 'view from nowhere', no conceptual space not already implicated in that which it seeks to interpret. Put bluntly, there is no stable unchanging world, no realm of objective truths, to which anyone has access.

Objectivity is not the only concept that poststructuralists take issue with. They debate conventional understandings of **reason**. The terms of their objection are centred on three specific aspects of reason: its universality, *a priori* necessity, and its absolutism. They replace universality with 'local' determinants; in place of *a priori* necessity, they counterpose fallibility and contingency; and in place of absolutism they insist that rationality is always relative to time and place. What's more, poststructuralists also object to the notion of a disembodied **rational autonomous subject.** They deny that the self offers certainty and an apparent access to truth in its essential human nature. What they offer instead is a 'decentred' self–a self that is an effect of discourse which is open to redefinition and which is constantly in process.

These ideas are complex and take some time to absorb. Through the chapters we will develop them in more detail, allowing you to get a better grip of what they convey. Meanwhile, using an approach put forward by Carr (1995), in Table 2, we will summarise the alternatives that the ideas make possible, and contrast them with conventional ideas.

Table 2: Key differences between conventional and poststructuralist understandings

	Conventional understanding	**Poststructuralist Understanding**
Reason	universal	Local
	a priori	fallibility and contingency
	absolutist	relative to time and place
The subject	autonomous	Decentred
Interpretation	separation between knowing subject and objective world	no view from nowhere no objective truths

A BRIEF HISTORY OF FOUCAULT'S COUNTER-HISTORY

Ideas don't simply develop out of thin air, of course. They come about by reflecting and acting upon what is, and has been, available. Foucault's ideas are no exception. He was enormously influenced by Nietzsche. But he also picked up ideas from Heidegger, Hegel, and Sartre. Readers who have read philosophy will know that all these thinkers challenged the ideas of the time. Had Foucault lived in an earlier period, he may never have matured intellectually in the way that he did. Interesting enough, as was characteristic of him, Foucault didn't take others' ideas at face value. He responded and reacted to them. In short, he challenged the responses of others to ideas that had challenged them. You won't find any trace of established thinking and traditional ways of doing things in his work. If you are familiar with philosophising through the ages, it won't stretch your imagination to know that he was hugely critical of Aristotle for his essentialism, Descartes for his Cogito, Kant for his humanism, Hegel for his notion of progress and totality, and Habermas for his utopianism.

So, what is it that is so different about Foucault's thinking? For all its air of anti-tradition and anti-establishment, Foucault's thinking actually has made major contributions to social theory. Accounts of his work generally concede that his contributions included: (i) power/knowledge analyses, (ii) an analysis of the self and its emergence through disciplinary technologies, and (iii) an analysis of governmentality. These analyses evolved over a period of time and involved distinct stages of his work. They included three key concepts: discourse, power, and knowledge and it is the definition given to these concepts that are generally considered far-reaching. It is these aspects that open up a space for education to come to grips from a new perspective with all aspects of the discipline, including curriculum, pedagogy, and teacher education, and make it possible to track historical events as a way of understanding the present.

Foucault's large programme of study is impressive. It crosses diverse disciplines such as literary theory, history, sociology and philosophy. His interests have included the development of psychology and of clinical medicine, the birth of the asylum and the modern penal system, and back and beyond to Ancient Greek and Roman morality. It wasn't just history that Foucault was interested in: he has also written extensively on modern literature and has produced an analysis of the development of Western thought since the Renaissance. Keeping close tabs on some of his work shows that he was both a philosophical historian, and historicist philosopher. One of the effects of that double talent was that his interrogations paid attention to details that others had overlooked. His particular approach was consistent with his focus on forms of regulation, discipline, and governance associated with disciplines. No-one had approached the issue of institutions, for example, in quite the same way as he did—nor as comprehensively.

Even allowing for his vast work, in each of his projects there is a general interest in understanding the present—to investigate an 'ontology of the present'. As an 'historian of the present', what he is seeking to achieve is an understanding of present contemporary social circumstance. As it turns out, his driving wish was to "create a history of the different modes by which, in our culture, human beings are made into subjects" (Dreyfus & Rabinow, 1982, p. 208). Consider how he achieves this: there's no trace of a single methodological approach. Instead, he provides us with a range of models for examining practices and processes. Put sinccintly, his methodological approach varies from one concern to another and the specific approach is chosen because it happens to respond to the demands of the particular subject matter under interrogation. As we saw above, he picks on a particular concept and from that derives a theory that will answer the questions initially posed. As a case in point, in his early work during the course of studying how the concept of mental illness had changed over time, he constructed a theory that responded to the particular questions about mental illness he had asked.

When applied to education, his method allows us to interrogate usually unrelated aspects and allows us to see how they are connected. To that end, if our interest chanced to be in curriculum, we might apply his method to inform our exploration of conflicts that arise in the development of curricula, amongst parents, employers, educators, and so forth. As another example, if understanding current teacher education practices happened to be our main focus, we might want to turn to history and trace the particular factors and forces that brought us to our current way of doing things in initial teacher education. The theories we develop for these interrogations are like "temporary scaffoldings, erected for a specific purpose" (Gutting, 1994, p. 16).

One can be forgiven for saying that Foucault's work looks rather inconsistent, what with its diverse methodology and changing purposes. After all, he never develops a theory or a method that is permanent or 'set in concrete.' Even allowing for this, there is a sense of continuity throughout his work. Although we can detect differences in his general direction, it is quite clear that his entire programme of study set about breaking with convention and given structures of thought. But he did more than oppose tradition: he wanted to make it possible for alternatives and other ways of thinking and being. So despite the divergence in his approaches, Foucault was consistent in the respect of wanting to open up a space for us to think differently. He wanted his ideas to be put to use—used like "little tool boxes. If people want to open them, or to use this sentence or that idea as a screwdriver or spanner...so much the better" (Foucault, cited in Meaghan & Patton, 1979, p. 115). Foucault's hope, then, is that we might begin to search for different thinking, or for the 'other of reason.' In his view, the greatest problem we have to deal with is our own inability to think differently.

The sheer scope and complexity of Foucault's work has captured the popular imagination. But one thing you should know, too, is that his work has often led to varying degrees of acceptance. Some commentators and scholars consider him to be a brilliant thinker, an intellectual artisan, someone who over the years has constructed a variety of artefacts. Never mind that there are those who are dismissive of his work: historians who reject it as being too philosophical, philosophers who denounce it for its lack of formal rigour and sociologists who minimise it for its literary or poetic quality. But that's the thing about novel thinking—it represents a challenge to convention. The reality is that Foucault has made a major contribution to social theory. You might be surprised to learn that Foucault, himself, was his own harshest critic. As it turns out, it was his own self-criticism that pushed his thinking further in original and challenging new directions.

It's time for us to look closely at Foucault's work, and the theoretical apparatus it provides, and see how it presents a different perspective on things.

EARLY WORK

Foucault's early work focused on health and human sciences. His work interrogated the means by which knowledge of well-being and mental illness is constructed and disseminated throughout Western culture. *Madness and Civilisation* (1961) draws on his doctoral dissertation and presents the reader with a history of madness from the Renaissance to the late nineteenth century. What is unique about his treatment of the topic is his demonstration of a rupture in thinking about 'unreason'. This he shows us occurred between 1780 and early 1800s and led to a new approach in treating the insane. *Mental Illness and Psychology* (1962), on the other hand, is a study of madness in relation to psychological and existential dimensions of the individual experience. But it is *Madness and Civilisation* that gives direction to his entire subsequent project of a 'history of the present.' In this work, too, Foucault's 'power/knowledge' couplet first makes its tentative debut. Its use in this work prefigures some of his general concerns over power which will become more explicit in his subsequent work.

Let me repeat that Foucault's theory of power is tentative in this early stage of his writing. Even to the untrained eye, his treatment of power is underdeveloped and this presents certain major restrictions on the way he understood subjectivity. It wasn't from lack of interest in the concept. The problem was that the model of power he offered in the early stages was essentially negative. Between his bleak assessment of power and his expression of it solely in terms of exclusion, Foucault's view of the way power relations operate within the social realm, is extremely constraining. His neglect of the positive aspects does not allow any space in which to theorise alternative or oppositional subject positions. Things took a turn for the better in his later work.

Even if his ideas about power would not develop fully until later, what his early observations did was provide a new view of social thought and practice. Being more specific, they present an attack on the notion of 'the one true self.' You will be familiar with this construct—it's one that the media and certain other cultural institutions readily embrace. The problem was that no-one had bothered to explain how the idea had emerged. Through his writing Foucault was able to show how the 'truth' of oneself is merely a construction. His demonstration was consistent with his development of 'normalisation' and 'an ethics of the self.' It is this line of attack—the impossibility of being one's own subject or origin—that Foucault develops to a more sophisticated level in his later works.

FROM ARCHAEOLOGY TO GENEALOGY TO ETHICS

Like many other approaches to Foucauldian ideas we shall classify the work according to three main methodological stages: archaeology, genealogy, and ethics. Each time Foucault shifted ground methodologically, it was in response to enriching his main interests. Urged on by his interests, his methods changed. *Archaeology* started with a general interest in knowledge, and a particular interest in describing how systems of thought are developed in relation to historical presuppositions. *Genealogy* also started with a general interest in knowledge and moved to an interest in exploring the connection between knowledge and power. The purpose was to trace how thinking emerges and is transformed. Let's not forget the third change in his methods. *Ethics* started with a general interest in knowledge and power and a particular interest in the self. Things turned towards people themselves—not the person in isolation, but the relation that the self has with knowledge and power. We shall look at what he says about that relation. But first, let's consider the other two main stages of his work.

Archaeological phase

Foucault's method of archaeology represents an attempt to move beyond his earliest work and provide a richer analysis of his historical material. His aim is for explanation, and in particular, for an explanation that searches for rules that go deeper than those offered by science. Archaeology takes discourses as its object of study, investigating the way discourses are ordered. As a methodological approach, archaeology offers a means of analysing 'truth games' by looking at history and uncovering the rules of construction of social facts and discourses, or the rules of discursive systems. One of the effects of using history and theoretical knowledge as a resource in archaeology is that it allows us to make links between various domains of our lives that would not otherwise necessarily render themselves connected. It allows us to entertain connections between, for instance, curriculum policy and identity in education that would ordinarily be excluded from our analyses.

Foucault's archaeological method rejects the phenomenological idea that social facts are constructed primarily in consciousness. In other words, Foucault moves philosophy away from the hope of locating foundations or origins, as in earlier work, to the development of a method that is able to explain the central role that history plays in any given system of thought. The kind of question asked is: "how is it that one particular statement appeared rather than another?" (Foucault, 1972, p. 27). The thing about answering that sort of question, was that Foucault was able to reveal how the relevance of statements and, indeed, entire systems of thought, such as economics, grammar, and natural history, are constructed historically in specific discourses within particular circumstances. For example, he was able to show how the criteria of rationality was mandated by various systems of thought and he revealed the ways in which these systems of thought produced truth. And, more than that—he was able to show how these rules varied from one episteme (or period of thought) to another with little or no overlap. You will appreciate from this that an episteme is *not* a foundation that 'goes all the way down'. It is a *practice* that is time bound and has global application within a given culture. It sets out the conditions of possibility of knowledge for that culture. Foucault himself tells us that an episteme specifically refers to:

> ...the total set of relations that unite, at a given period, the discursive practices....The episteme is not a form of knowledge...or type of rationality which, crossing the boundaries of the most varied sciences, manifests the sovereign unity of a subject, a spirit, or a period; it is the totality of relations that can be discovered for a given period, between the sciences when one analyses them at the level of discursive regularities.
>
> (Foucault, 1972, p. 191)

Foucault develops his archaeological method explicitly in *The Order of Things* (1970) and in *The Archaeology of Knowledge* (1972). In both these works he presents a history of order and identity that are imposed on things—a history of the 'same'. *The Order of Things* is concerned with the question of how language has varied over time; the answer is provided by describing the diverse ways that language has both existed in and referred to the world. In *The Archaeology of Knowledge,* written shortly afterwards, languages are seen to be historical in the sense that the structure of thought of different periods arises from different systems of linguistics. In both works Foucault focuses on how disciplinary knowledges are made to function. He shows that the historicity of the concepts and objects which have to do with thought, knowledge and power, is at one and the same time unique, specific and general. In other words he shows that all systems of knowledge are in fact statements or discursive events.

This is just as true of the discipline of education as it is true of any other body of knowledge. Take the example of mathematics. Way back in the fourth century Plato came up with the statement that mathematics had an existence of its own. He believed that mathematics was beyond or external to the mind. Naturally enough, a proposal like this, elevated the position of mathematics considerably. Plato's student, Aristotle, took the view that understanding mathematical relationships involved experimentation and observation and explained through a process of deduction. His 'statement' of mathematics set the scene for the development of logical processes that researchers draw on to substantiate scientific claims.

Other statements about mathematics followed. For example, Francis Bacon in the early 1500s, wrote about pure mathematics and mixed mathematics and Descartes in the 17th century took thinking about mathematics back to the idea of deduction. As if these shifts weren't enough, in the mid 1800s non-Euclidean geometry brought in a new truth about mathematics, one that allowed new mathematical structures to be developed without the constraints of an eternal world. Further shifts occurred in the 19th and early 20th centuries and contributed to the rise of three new schools of thought established around logicism, intuitionism and formalism. A more recent 'statement' is based around the idea of mathematics as a human activity. The idea is that mathematics arises from complex interactions between factors in the cognitive and social domains.

If we were to use an archaeological approach to explain what we know about the changing nature of mathematics, we would focus on conceptual issues, rather than utilise methods within the history of ideas. For one thing, we would not represent the passage of time, during which ideas about mathematics changed, as a logical flow of causally connected events, each with its discrete significance and each forming part of an overall pattern or meaning to the history of mathematics. For another, we would not explain the changes in relation to a universal schema. Such an explanation would deprive the various conceptions about mathematics of their own impact and their uniqueness. By working with a lack of interest in both universals and progressive growth, our archaeological method would characterise the historical events as having no essence, or, more correctly, as fabricated in a haphazard fashion.

But it's not just universals and progress that are put under scrutiny in archaeology. There is one more thing–the stable subject position. In conventional historical analyses, history reveals and affirms elements of essential human characteristics. One's present sense of identity is always reconfirmed and this has the effect of preventing any awareness of 'otherness'. You may already be well aware that the stable subject position is exactly what anchors conventional historical accounts. It was this tradition of taking for granted the stability of individuals that Foucault began to question and rethink.

Let me be more specific here. Foucault took exemption to how the subject had been formulated historically. The sheer improbability of having a fixed identity, the unlikelihood of a subject existing prior to language, and the impossibility of being the origin of meaning, were arguments that Foucault put forward, and all were advanced in opposition to the stability of the subject. He attempted to explain them and came up with the idea that the subject is a *fiction*. By this he didn't mean that the subject was a figment of the imagination. What he meant, precisely, was that the subject is generated by the structural discursive rules that govern all thought and speech. Language plays a key role here in his formulation. But that's the thing about Foucault's archaeological work—language does play a major role.

We will pause for a moment to think about what this means for subjects within education. We are talking about, for example, teachers, learners, curriculum planners, researchers, and so forth. For all their apparent hard and fast stable appearance, they are all merely productions of practices through which they are subjected. But more than this—teachers and other professionals are not the ones accredited with producing knowledge about education. Knowledge about education is an *effect* of a primarily linguistic discursive formation. It is an effect of a set of fundamental rules that define the discursive space in which education exists. There are particular rules of formation in education, just as there are in all the human sciences, that, unknown to the actors involved, regulate, and determine the spectrum of speech acts, and actions, that can be taken seriously at any given historical moment. It is these deep-seated rules that circumscribe the possibility of thought concerning what exactly education is. If that's not enough—they also set boundaries on what is taken as true.

Before we move onto Foucault's next methodological stage, it's a good time to pause and think seriously about traditional ideas about history and how the method of archaeology contrasts with those traditions. We will highlight the differences between archaeology and the history of ideas in Table 3.

Table 3. Differences between the method of archaeology and history of ideas

Archaeology	**History of ideas**
Concerned with discourse and how discourse regulates conditions of possibility.	Concerned with documents, thoughts, representations, themes.
Search for the historical constitution of knowledge.	Search for origins and foundations of knowledge.
Uncovers rules and their status that underwrite the ways of viewing the world.	Treats documentary and archival material as transparent and reflecting the view of the world.
Examines rules regulating what constitutes truth, relevance and legitimation.	Acceptance of authoritative pronouncements on truth, relevance and legitimation.
Deals with specificity and difference.	Deals with universals, continuities and closure.
Subject position generated by structural rules that govern thought and speech, taken in specific circumstances by any number of individuals.	Subject position taken as prior to language, author of own articulation, and origin of meaning.
Associated statements coexist with other statements.	Associated statements are the context for articulation.

Genealogical phase

Genealogy builds on and extends the rich insights offered by the archaeological method. It wasn't so much that archaeology's emphasis on discourse was a problem, but that there were other elements that needed to be accounted for. To put it bluntly, there were non-discursive aspects that could not be ignored. So from observing practices from 'afar', Foucault now also viewed events from 'the inside'. He also attempted to explain how discourses emerge and how they are transformed. It will come as no surprise that once he was able to do that, the scope of analysis was considerably broadened. But Foucault did more than this—methodologically, this is where the concept of power comes into its own, interacting with knowledge and the body. It is the means by which Foucault is able to trace the making of identities, selves, social norms and institutions.

This shift to genealogy focused Foucault's attention during the years following 1968 when it first emerged as a concept in his essay "Nietzsche, Genealogy, History". The method has aroused much critical attention in that it questions the necessity of dominant categories and procedures. But this is not to suggest that the method itself is merely a play on rhetorical possibilities. Foucault insists that the genealogical method (sometimes known as the philosophy of the event) is *not* an intellectual game. He argues that his method is a serious attempt to explain how the "knowledge which is ours today" (Foucault, 1991, p. 70), and especially how knowledge of man, could come to exist.

Genealogical analyses that explore the interaction of power and knowledge within the practices and social structures of education are able to highlight the profound influence of discourse on shaping everyday life in education. One very good example of a genealogical analysis is to be found in the work of Tansy Hardy (2004). Tansy uses the approach to describe the teaching approach currently legitimated in mathematics classrooms in England. Power is pivotal to her analysis. She investigates technologies of power, showing how power operates through discourse. In that investigation she is able to reveal the way in which the rules of formation of this mandated pedagogy profoundly influence the way mathematical knowledge is constructed. Crucially, such interactions make particular identities, and not others, available and realisable for students. The significance of this idea is that such interactions situate students within their power structures, normalising—hence both constraining and enabling—the ways in which students are constructed as learners in the present.

Understanding the present through the past was what Foucault was doing in all his writing. In genealogy his primary motivation in the past was not its reconstruction, nor its origins, nor essential truth. Rather, his focus was on locating traces of the present. In this he was hugely influenced by Nietzsche. You may be aware that Nietzsche had earlier taken issue with traditional historical analyses and, contrary to what other philosophers of the time were doing, had abandoned the search for an exact essence of things. That is to say, he had abandoned the search for the origin of the founding moment that will explain everything. In exposing the 'will-to-truth' that lay behind talk of 'reason' and 'truth' and 'essence', Nietzsche had argued that truth is a purely rhetorical construct. This, you will understand, was a revolutionary idea but it was one that had a lot of appeal to Foucault.

The upshot was that Foucault captured Nietzsche's stand against the search for underlying laws and finalities. To that end he claimed that "truth is a thing of this world" (Foucault, 1984, p. 72). As he saw it, questions of history—in fact questions of all knowledge—are about authorised discourse, and have nothing to do with the search for truth. What he means by this is that history and knowledge are the result of struggles over practices and methods, all attempting to authorise what discourses will come to count and to determine who will speak with authority. Clearly, if struggles are involved, then power is involved too. And the way Foucault worked out how power was involved was an accomplishment so original that it provided a unique approach to history.

Foucault argues that a history of the present cannot be systematised and interpreted in terms of the meanings it reveals, but must be understood as a conflict between different power blocks. It is the task of the genealogist to shed light on associations that have not been readily apparent and discover how discourses of truth operate in relation to the dominant power structures of a given society. Foucault would begin the task by asking: What are the institutions and systems of knowledge that can readily be identified? What are the relationships between them within particular groupings which characterise our present era?

Let's be more specific. Foucault's genealogical method looks at relationships. It outlines a series of external social forces through which he traces the uneven and haphazard processes of dispersion, accumulation and overlap that govern the limits of discourse. What he is trying to do is expose the strategic nature of those groupings of knowledge usually considered to be either relatively independent of power or linked only in a vague or inadequate way to institutional politics. To that end, he tries to make visible the unexpected and the superficial, to group together phenomena that are usually kept separate, and to differentiate phenomena that are usually grouped together.

It was a thoroughly innovative idea. It counterbalanced his thinking about the autonomy of discourse, as proposed in his archaeological method. For all his forward thinking, it wasn't until Foucault shifted his archaeological understanding of discourse that he was able to catch the imagination of many other people. That isn't to deny that his earlier idea of discourse didn't have a novel air, but to make the point that it was his genealogical understanding of discourse as determined by and also constitutive of the power relations that permeate the social realm, that set the conditions of possibility for discourse. By any measure, the reformulated 'discourse' was a great advance. It allowed Foucault to suggest that, far from being teleologically governed, the historical processes that spark the emergence of events or discourse, are in fact discontinuous, divergent and governed by chance. This is a monumental claim in the sense that he is saying that historical development cannot be self-evident. One of the effects of this claim is that it brackets the whole question of validity and truth. As Foucault puts it:

The problem does not consist in drawing the line between that in a discourse which falls under the category of scientificity or truth, and that which comes under some other category, but in seeing historically how effects of truth are produced within discourses which in themselves are neither true nor false.

(Foucault, 1980, p.118)

Turn to ethics

In his later works Foucault conceded that the emphasis he placed on the effects of power in his archaeological and genealogical work carried certain limitations. Power in his earlier formulations tended to overstate the efficacy of disciplinary power, and this had the effect of precluding the possibility of one's resistance to forms of disciplinary domination. When these shortcomings became apparent he initiated a change in focus—a shift in emphasis from the body to the self. This shift is most obvious in his two volumes of *The History of Sexuality* published just before his death in 1984, that is, in the two works *The Use of Pleasure* and in *The Care of the Self.* The important thing about this shift is that Foucault was now able to acknowledge the potential of creativity and agency within social constraints. The approach he took was through a process which involved the adoption of an attitude of self-critique and the exploration of new modes of subjectivity.

Foucault maintains that his *ethics of the self* is more politically optimistic and emancipatory than conventional proposals of ethics in that it aims to "promote new forms of subjectivity through the refusal of [a] kind of individuality which has been imposed on us for several centuries" (Foucault, in Dreyfus & Rabinow, 1982, p. 217). His argument is that a progressive politics might best be served not through strictly imposed moral obligations, but rather through an ethic of who we are to be, and what, therefore, it is possible for us to become. In academic jargon, he means that progress is made through the formation of a critical ontology of the self. Here he understands 'critical', not in the sense of the Enlightenment meaning of *critique* in relation to *regulative truth,* but in the sense of *critique as its enabling condition.* Interestingly, 'critique' is a term borrowed from Enlightenment thought. It is interesting because Foucault is usually understood to be an '*anti*-Enlightenment' thinker. Urged on by a need to justify his stand, he outlined his reasons in his essay *What is Enlightenment?,* written towards the end of his life and published in *The Foucault Reader* (1984).

'Autonomy' is another Enlightenment concept that Foucault reformulates for his own ends. In its redefinition autonomy is linked to the idea of political resistance or opposition—a questioning of what appears as natural and inevitable about one's identity. By making this connection Foucault proposes that autonomy is coextensive with the development of a theory of resistance—an 'ethics of the self'—or what he calls a 'modern ethics'. In this proposal we can see how autonomy becomes necessary to freedom, where freedom is a state in which the individual exercises critical judgment of dominant beliefs. One important consequence of this proposal is that it makes it possible to analyse together an individual's socio-cultural situation and her capacity for self-governance. In other words, it becomes possible to investigate technologies (or practices) of the self—those rules of conduct that she sets herself intentionally and voluntarily, given her particular socio-cultural conditions.

In his ethics of the modern self Foucault also names these practices of the self as an 'aesthetics of existence', and this term draws our attention to the fact that the self is never pre-given. Foucault would like us to think of the self as a 'work of art', continually in process. In fact, he insists that we are obliged to continually 'remake' ourselves, ever mindful of our limits: "modern man...is not the man who goes off to discover himself...; he is the man who tries to invent himself. Thus modernity ... compels him to face the task of producing himself" (Foucault, 1984, p. 42). What the idea of 'limit attitude' entails for us is an appreciation of what we are or what we cannot surrender if we are to constitute ourselves as autonomous subjects. As Foucault sees it, what we might become stands as the political, ethical, social, and philosophical problem of today. The harsh reality is that if we shun the responsibility of authentic self-creation we come to be entirely fabricated by others. Fashioning an entirely new self is not possible, of course, but we can use aesthetic strategies to reformulate available resources.

Happily for education, Foucault's ethics of the self has large-scale application. His non-essentialist conception of identity as well as his redefined concept of autonomy, offers current work in the field the opportunity of thinking through some of the discipline's most pressing issues. One of these is the issue of diversity. Diversity is part of our way of life today and is an important phenomenon within our primary [elementary], secondary and tertiary classrooms. Yet, how does one constitute one's identity, amongst a diversity of others, within contemporary regulated forms of subjection? How can the growth of capabilities be disconnected from the intensification of power relations? We could fathom that out by interrogating how diverse groups of people, engaged in classrooms, come to an understanding of the potential of their own individual freedom and how they constantly explore the limits of their own subjectivity.

As another example, we might ask how can a teacher create an inquiry classroom when both the systems and the personnel of the school tend to operate against this kind of pedagogical approach? Foucault would propose that a teacher can do this, in the first instance, by questioning (explicitly or otherwise) the boundaries of the school's understanding of quality pedagogy, and showing how those understandings are necessarily contingent and historically specific. At this point the possibility of transgressing the so-called limits is made available to the teacher and this, too, is the point where the potential for new forms of subjective experience is established.

It is important to note that Foucault makes a distinction between socially imposed 'ethics' and self-constructed 'morals'. On the one hand, the wider social level incorporates imposed 'prescriptions' of moral codes that determine which acts are permitted or forbidden, which acts are validated, and which are not, in a whole range of possible behaviours. On the other hand, at the level of the individual, he refers to the ways and means by which we constitute ourselves as moral subjects of our own actions. For Foucault, a critical ethos relevant for contemporary life involves those latter actions situated at the level of an individual's daily practices. An examination of these will reveal the different ways in which the self is formed as an ethical subject. Foucault (1988) argues that we should consider all of the practices as a whole that "constitute, define, organise, instrumentalise the strategies which individuals in their liberty can have in regard to each other" (p. 19). What he is interested in are those games of truth and error which are played in the constitution of ethical subjectivity:

> ...the games of truth and error through which being is historically constituted as experience; that is, as something that can and must be thought. What are the games of truth by which man proposes to think his own nature when he perceives himself to be mad; when he considers himself to be ill; when he conceives of himself as a living, speaking, labouring being.
>
> (Foucault, 1984, pp. 6-7)

KEY CONCEPTS

The subject

Among the many ideas that Foucault worked with, none was more at odds with phenomenology than his concept of subjective experience. Foucault's particular approach refused to attribute individuals with certain capacities. He denied that individuals were their own source of meaning, knowledge, and action. To be frank—and this might seem surprising—he doesn't have a theory of the subject at all. He preferred to side with the 'death of the subject', rather than getting into the philosophical/ontological/epistemological debate about how the subject is actually formed. But that's not to say that he avoids the question altogether; rather, he turns it into something empirical, asking about the ways in which the individual has become a problem for knowledge in our culture, and asking how individuals are made subjects in our culture.

For him, subjective experience is created by constantly changing social and cultural conditions and circumstances. Even humanity, for all intents and purposes, is socially constructed. And because of that, he claimed that humanity could only be studied by tracking the history of how it developed. And that is exactly what he did. He tracked that history in *The Order of Things*, maintaining that all modern-day knowledge is based on a particular conception of human reality.

So, we have it from Foucault that there is something amiss with the modern conception of the subject. That's because it does not take into account the subject's situation, its location, its function, its perceptive capacities. He claims that the subject is in fact determined by regularities that are way and beyond the reach of consciousness. Interesting, and giving us pause for thought, it is the modern conception of the subject that has traditionally been privileged within the discourses of education. It relies on assumptions and beliefs drawn from liberal humanist thinking. Let me elaborate: Liberal humanist thinking is drawn from two world-views: humanism and liberalism. Humanism is characterised by the belief in an essential human nature and in the power of reason to bring about human progress. Liberalism is characterised by a belief in the inalienable right of the individual to realise herself to the full. Pulling the two together, liberal humanist thinking has generated a powerful theory but it's a theory in which the subject's experience is neither sought nor even valued. It is neither sought nor valued simply because liberal humanist thinking relies on a view of the world in which subjectivity is the source rather than the effect of language. What's more, it also relies on an absolute division between the individual as speaking subject and the external reality of the world.

In contrast to this line of thinking, Foucault's starting point was that subjectivities are produced within discourse. We learn from him that the meanings that people produce are the result of political struggles and these struggles involve personal, psychic and emotional investments. These meanings have the capacity to both reproduce subjectivities and to modify them. What we don't hear him say is that essential, core individuals are located at the deepest interiority. You take my point, of course, after all if he acknowledged the subject-as-the-prediscursive-origin-of-knowledge, he would be contradicting his own ideas. In his archaeological phase, more than any other, he was at pains to eradicate this essentialising tendency. To put it simply, he believed that the truth about oneself is not something given, not something in our nature, and not something we have to discover for ourselves. It is something we need to *create* for ourselves. Did he mean to signify that there are no subjects—that the subject can be wiped out from philosophical thinking? Quite the contrary: he argued that subject is a transient fold in the order of discourse.

Having let it be known that the idea of an autonomous and sovereign subject was a bone of contention, he turned his energies to finding out what kind of historical conditions make various types of quite specific and differentiated subjects *possible* in the first place. His interrogation centred on how particular kinds of subjects are *produced* as effects of discursive relations. Among the many interesting interrogations he undertook, is his analysis of how processes of subject-production, or subjection, are affected by modern scientific forms of knowledge. This helped him show that 'man' cannot be his own Origin—that there is no essential core of hidden truth. He took the view that if you believed experience has an essential core of hidden truth, then you lay yourself open to oppressive systems of thought and behaviour.

> If there is one approach that I do reject...it is that...which gives absolute priority to the observing subject, which attributes a constituent role to an act, which places its own point of view at the origin of all historicity—which, in short, leads to a transcendental consciousness. It seems to me that the historical analysis of scientific discourse should, in the last resort, be subject, not to a theory of the knowing subject, but rather to a theory of discursive practice.
>
> (Foucault, 1970, p. xiv)

Discourse

Discourse is a confusing concept for the simple reason that there are many conflicting and overlapping definitions. The way that Foucault uses 'discourse' is quite different from normal usage. Generally, in everyday speech, when we say 'discourse' we mean 'talk'. The same is true in education. Of the many articles and reports that focus on discourse, most will be referring to communication and speech. At another level, if you happen to be a scholar in formal linguistics, your work with discourse will involve finding general underlying rules to explain the linguistic or communicative function that works through texts. The point is that in nearly every setting in which we use the term 'discourse', what we are really implying is human conversation.

Human conversation is too narrow to describe Foucault's concept of discourse. He wanted something more encompassing than a linguistic technicality, or spoken words that highlight interactions between people. As he saw it, these concepts limited how knowledge could be conceived. In his creative way, he uses discourse to mean taken-for-granted 'rules' that specify what is possible to speak, do, and even think, at a particular time. Put another way, discourses for him refers to different ways of structuring areas of knowledge and social practice. They are immensely powerful. The reason is that they produce truths.

An interesting background point about Foucault's concept of discourse is that it helps us understand poststructuralism better. As we saw earlier, poststructuralism is a theoretical position that moves away from structuralism. By all accounts, structuralism had its beginnings in the work of de Saussure (1958) as an approach to language. Gamely, de Saussure came up with the novel claim that language is a system of signs whose meaning and order do not originate from social life or the creative intentions of individual speakers. What he proposed instead was that the meaning and the order of language come about from the relations of signs to other elements in the system. Each system, he believed, is marked by an inherent logic which relates the elements to one another. And it was the task of structural linguistics to fathom out this logic. By fashioning signs as a separation rather than a dependence, it became possible to imagine signs differently. The meaning of a sign could then be determined not merely by its correspondence to a real thing, but as constituted through its *difference* from other signs and other meanings.

Foucault believed that things were not quite right with de Saussure's system of signs. What was not being accounted for was the historical and contingent nature of all linguistic expression. At the height of his critique Foucault was able to propose the concept of discourse in a way that dealt with history and contingency. For Foucault the term discourse quite clearly refers not simply to language as a system of signs but to relatively well-bounded areas of social knowledge. Discourses are more than ways of giving meaning to the world; they imply forms of social organisation and social practices, at different historical times, which structure institutions and constitute individuals as thinking, feeling and acting subjects.

Discourses do not merely *reflect* or represent social entities and relations; they actively construct or *constitute* them. Discourses surrounding, for example, the category, 'effective teacher', provide teachers with the identities through which they will be recognised by others. Perhaps more crucially for those working in education, these identities are how teachers come to recognise themselves. Because power is constituted in discourses, then the meaning we have of effective teachers, and so forth, depends on the social, historical and political conditions under which they are categorised. The ways in which we understand an effective teacher today might be quite different from an earlier period. And it may well be different again in years to come. By thinking of discourse in this way it makes it possible to consider the historically specific relationship between bodies of knowledge and forms of social control and agency.

The important thing for Foucault was not where discourses come from, nor whose interests they serve. He explored why we are compelled to use them and what effects of power and knowledge arise from our use of them. And he tried to determine what makes discourses possible in the first place. He asked: 'what is able to be said?' and 'what is able to be thought?' Foucault took the investigation to its obvious conclusion by looking at the forms of 'governance' that circumscribe these discourses, or units of knowledge. That led him to explore 'rules' and 'processes' with a view to working out how, within relations of power, people become knowing, knowable and self-knowing subjects. Putting it another way, he explored the rules that decide what is possible to know—those rules which constrain and enable, specifically, being, writing, speaking and thinking, within given historical limits. He was interested in the set of rules that enabled certain understandings to be entertained at one time and constrained at another time.

Power

This is a good place to take a look at Foucault's theorising of power. The thing that stands out more than anything is its striking originality. In fact, this is the concept that is generally considered to be the most radical dimension of his intellectual work. Not only is it radical, it has had a direct bearing on the way people think of power in the world today. It was a concept with which he was preoccupied throughout his history of the present. His analyses are so closely bound to power that they cannot be separated from it. That is because, for him, power is a pervasive factor of human social life, under any condition.

Power, for Foucault is constituted through discourses. It is a positive, enabling, constitutive and productive force. To explain, he tells us:

> What makes power hold good, what makes it accepted, is simply the fact that it doesn't only weigh on us as a force that says no, but that it traverses and produces things. It needs to be considered as a productive network which runs through the whole social body, much more than as a negative instance whose function is repression.
>
> (Foucault, 1980, p. 119)

To say that Foucault's positive understanding of power was innovative is certainly an understatement. His was nothing like traditional understandings. In analyses that preceded his, the approach was to equate power with the law and conceive its existence in the juridical terms of constitution and sovereignty. In this conceptualisation both the 'sovereign' who wields power and the 'subject' upon whom the power acts are conceptually prior to the exercise of power in this relationship. To this end, power is *consequential* of, rather than instigative in, their existence in this relationship. The same is true of Marxist versions of political power. It is negative and repressive, acting on something already constituted.

In the course of Foucault's work, power came to be considered as something quite different from coercion, prohibition, or domination over others by an individual or a group. He took issue with analyses that express power merely in centralised and institutionalised forms in which an individual or group deliberately imposes its will on others. He explicitly opposes and denies that power is possessed, proposing as alternatives, 'exercise' and 'practice' in place of 'possession'. You might have guessed by now that the significance of this strategy was that it allowed him to avoid saying what power essentially is. No matter, because he criticised psychologistic attempts to 'explain' power. He suggested that analyses should avoid explaining power in terms of intentions, motives, aims, interests or obsessions. More than anything else his consuming interest rested in the *effects* of power's exercise. As he sees it then, analyses should be focused on looking at the effects of power rather than the *explanations* for its exercise.

As it turns out, Foucault maintained that power underlies all social relations from the institutional to the intersubjective. You can imagine the reaction that this claim received. He went on to explain that there are three modes through which power operates: 'dividing practices', 'scientific classification', and 'subjectification.' When he talks about dividing practices he means practices, involving power relations, that distinguish and separate people. Think about the sorts of practices that divide the 'slow learner', and the 'gifted and talented student'. As if to make his point drive home, he showed how scientific classification categorises the human and social sciences. For example, in his early work he showed how the human sciences emerged in the 19th century. It wasn't until that time that the body became an analysable, treatable, and curable object. As for the third mode of operation, he talked about subjectification, by which he means the processes by which people actively constitute themselves.

As a complement to the three modes by operation, Foucault explains that power circulates in practices in the sense that it is employed and exercised through a web-like structure in which individuals are its vehicles. Power is 'capillary' in its operation. It works through the lowest extremities of the social body in everyday social practices. In order to understand the operation of power, we need to understand the particular points through which it passes. It is local, continuous and present in the most apparently trivial details and relations of everyday life. The upshot is that analyses should focus on the local and regional points of the destination and on the diverse and specific manifestations of power. Foucault claims that one needs to investigate the historical 'conditions' of the mechanics of power in ascending order of social levels. That means that for us in education, we need to look to the fringes or to the micro-level of society, for example, to the practices and methods of power's exercise in the classroom, and so on, to investigate how mechanisms of power have been "invested, colonised utilised, involuted, transformed, displaced, extended" (Foucault, 1980, p. 99) by more general forms of power, leading to those types of social domination that are readily identifiable.

It is in *Discipline and Punish* that Foucault traces the transformation from a system of justice expressed through violent spectacle to one that rationalises punishment with the modern power techniques of imprisonment and surveillance. He maintains that the operations of modern disciplinary power that developed gradually in the late eighteenth century mark a shift from sovereign power which is overt and visible, to 'disciplinary' power which is exercised through its invisibility via normalising strategies. In our present era 'disciplinary power' constitutes a new form of pastoral power. It is also totalising in that it is constitutive of all social interaction. It is effective as a normalising force because it is relatively invisible in its operations. That is, individuals are regulated not only through overt repression but also through a set of standards and value systems associated with normality which are created and maintained in subtle and diffuse ways. As the most well-known of these practices, 'the gaze' represents a technique of the power/knowledge couplet which enables those in control to regulate the behaviour of those in their care.

> Traditionally, power was what was seen, what was shown and what was manifested...Disciplinary power, on the other hand, is exercised through its invisibility; at the same time it imposes on those whom it subjects a principle of compulsory visibility. In discipline it is the subjects who have to be seen. Their visibility assures the hold of power that is exercised over them. It is the fact of being constantly seen, of being always able to be seen, that maintains the disciplined individual in his subjection.
>
> (Foucault, 1977, p. 187)

Power-knowledge

It is very difficult in Foucault's work to separate power from knowledge. Some go so far as saying that his *power-knowledge* formulation is his signature statement. Let's explain what his formulation means. He says that power and knowledge directly imply one another—that there can be no power relation without a field of knowledge being constituted, nor any knowledge that does not, simultaneously, presuppose and constitute power relations. It is impossible to grasp the sense of what this means without appreciating that in putting the two concepts together, as he does, he is redefining power as coextensive with knowledge. On the one hand, he says that all knowledge is the effect of a specific regime of power, and on the other hand, he says that forms of knowledge constitute the social reality that they describe and analyse. It's because he maintains that they are different categories, that he conceptualises every relation between forces as a power relation, where force is never singular but exists in relation with other forces. Having come up with this revolutionary idea, he then attempts to uncover the political and strategic nature of clusters of knowledge that are ordinarily considered to be either relatively independent of power or linked only in a vague or inadequate way to institutional power.

Power-knowledge-truth

At the point where power and knowledge are inseparable, what Foucault does is connect them in a circular relation with 'truth'. He links truth with *systems* of power that produce and sustain it, and to *effects* of power which it induces and which extends it. By all accounts he wants us to think of power and knowledge as mutually supporting and inevitable elements in games of truth. This is a curious contention. Did he mean to signify that power, knowledge and truth, when taken together, have specific applications in certain circumstances? No, what he intended was that power, knowledge and truth underwrite *all* human relationships. In making this sweeping claim, he is questioning—even discrediting—contemporary ideological systems of thought. The exact reason for Foucault's disinterest in systems of 'ideology' remains speculative. What we do know, however, is that his real interest was in the *effects* of the power-knowledge nexus, and this he was able to do by exploring how effects are made manifest through different discourses or discursive formations.

Regime-of-truth

At the heart of power-knowledge effects, through discourse, is Foucault's notion of *regime of truth*. Foucault, like a number of other social theorists, argued that every society produces its own regime of truth. What is more, he suggested that what is taken as 'true' in social interaction is not to be considered as universal nor indeed even necessary. In present-day Western society the regime of truth includes discourses of the human sciences which include the discourses of education, psychology, medicine and law. The interesting thing is that he showed that acceptable discourses become intelligible through their reliance on certain practices. They are not necessarily the same discourses as were acceptable a few years ago. For example, where several decades ago or so, people accepted that girls did not have the biological make-up to succeed in mathematics, today the truthfulness of this belief would be severely criticised. People in that earlier time willingly accepted the truth about girls' inferior intelligence because the statement was made to function as true. It would help your understanding of how a statement could function as true if you thought about it in the following way: the proposition that girls cannot achieve well in mathematics drew its authority from those with appropriate status who were assigned the task of producing (academics), regulating (professionals) or distributing (media, politicians, educators) the knowledge, via methods and norms of practice that were sanctioned at that time.

> Each society has its regime of truth, its 'general politics' of truth: that is, the types of discourse which it accepts and makes function as true; the mechanisms and instances which enable one to distinguish true and false statements, the means by which each is sanctioned; the techniques and procedures accorded value in the acquisition of truth; the status of those who are charged with saying what counts as true.
>
> (Foucault, 1984, p. 73)

Governmentality

In his earlier analyses of disciplinary practices Foucault's reconstructions of phenomena were based on official discourses. As a consequence he tended to overstate the efficacy of disciplinary power because 'other' conflicting knowledges and discourses were excluded. As we noted earlier, when these shortcomings became apparent he developed a more productive understanding of power. In any case, it is through his notion of *governmentality* that Foucault advances our understanding and offers a more fluid approach to the interpretation of individual experiences. What is of interest is that the new formulation continued to preserve the idea that individual subjects are constituted by power. That isn't to say that in his new proposal power operated narrowly and uni-directionally. But it is to make the point that its role became more open and diffuse. Power was no longer confined to external and impersonal mechanisms and institutions. Instead, domination and resistance were conceived of opposing effects of the same power relations. In particular, power became both an objectivising and a subjectivising force through the process of differentiating between violence, domination, and give-and-take within everyday relations.

The notion of governmentality didn't involve an especially major shift in subject matter, but it did signal a ground-breaking shift in Foucault's thinking *about* the subject matter. By any measure, it was a remarkable achievement because what Foucault was suggesting was that individuals are active agents with the capacity to fashion their own existences. But, as it happens, governmentality is double-edged. It both targets the individual as the means with which to maintain social control, and, at the same time, it provides the individual with the very techniques with which to resist this government of individualisation. To help in this process, Foucault introduces the category of the 'self'. But of course the *self* is nothing like the 'docile body' in his earlier work. It is the *self* that opens up new possibilities for education because it offers a more complex and layered notion of identity. It suggests an understanding of identity as an active and never-completed process of enculturation. To this end, the self suggests a notion of the individual in education as enculturated across a vast number of subject positions, some of which apply to a much greater degree than others, but over all of which the individual may exert some degree of autonomy.

Technologies of the self

Technologies of the self are descriptors for the particular practices and techniques through which the subject fashions her own identity actively. The concept is particularly useful because its points to the ways in which the subject relates to herself. Technologies of the self influence the ways in which subjectivity is constituted and the ways in which experiences are shaped. The subject's thoughts and actions are also governed by them. It is these technologies of the self, these fashionings, that were not able to be given expression in Foucault's earlier notion of disciplinary practices. Though technologies of the self are unquestionably influential for experience and subjectivity, their primary application is not causation. There is no direct connection between individual action and social structure that holds true for *all* individuals in any system of governing. Let me explain. The patterns found in a culture which are proposed, suggested and imposed on an individual by her culture, her society, and her social group have to be viewed at the level of the individual's daily practices. Each type of authority derives from its own specific set of social forces and power relations in the way it produces, regulates, surveys and labels its activities, according to its own ensemble of rules. Let's take the example of the pedagogical relation. The pedagogical relation has its own background of specific historical practices. It also has its own logic, even though it might be located within wider sources of domination, such as curricular reform movements, official mandates, and school policies. In this relation, teacher authority, to which the student is complicit, is subsumed by more global structures *but is never reduced to them.*

CONCLUSION

Now that you have some new understanding about Foucault's work and been introduced to the kind of thinking that made a large contribution to social theory, it's time to take stock of what you have learned. As we noted in this chapter, Foucault's ideas mark a radical change from contemporary thought, and because of that, they are not all that easy to grasp. You can develop a better understanding by taking the time now to reflect on his thinking. Try to summarise the work's central organisers (themes and stages); try to pose a few critical questions about what the key ideas mean; and try to think about how the concepts present a challenge to concepts in other work with which you are familiar. Once you have done that, you will be ready to apply his ideas and see how they work in practice. The following activity takes you through these suggestions, step by step.

ACTIVITY

1. Name the three main stages of Foucault's work. Compare and contrast the approach taken in the first two main stages.
2. Note down at least six of Foucault's key concepts or terms.
3. Clarify how Foucault's conceptualisation of power is at odds with conventional understanding.
4. Write down your understanding of what Foucault means by 'discourse'.
5. Choose an area of education that is of interest to you. Discuss how you could use one of Foucault's analytical methods to critically interrogate an aspect within your chosen area.

CHAPTER 2

AN ARCHAEOLOGY OF LEARNING

IN THIS CHAPTER

- Behaviourism
- Cognitivism
- Constructivism
- Sociocultural formulations
- Activity/Situativity/Social Practice theory

DISCUSSION QUESTIONS

1. Identify the learning theory with which you feel comfortable. Describe the key ideas of this theory.
2. If you have changed your theoretical position over time, why did you change?

Now that we are getting a grip of Foucault, we will put some of his ideas to good use as we explore the way in which the concept of learning has taken shape. Our approach will be through an archaeology. An archaeology traces events differently. It is a different kind of analysis, not only in the understanding it provides, but also in its insistence to figure out how people work those understandings out. People have argued long and hard over how learning happens. The consensus within the discipline seems to be heading for a proposal that gives us insights about the student-acting-in-community. We will get to that in due course. For the moment it is enough to know that proposals about learning have been shaped with different emphases and have begun with different starting points. And typically, competing stories about classroom learning reflect different versions of social life within different social conditions.

How do people work out how students learn? How can they know what actually happens when students 'take up' new ideas? How can they be sure about what goes on inside students' minds? The question we might want to pursue, above all, is how can so many different things that are said about learning seem so convincing? By charting the development of how we understand learning our analysis will demonstrate how particular 'rules' or discourses, at particular times, make it possible for certain understandings about learning to be entertained and legitimated in classrooms. Our focus will not be on discovering the *true* learning theory, simply because, to be absolutely frank, none exists. We will reflect on the concept of learning, in its shifting and mobile space, and will demonstrate how claims to truth about how people learn are provisional and open-ended.

BEHAVIOURISM

Behaviourism is a traditional perspective proposed by the discipline of psychology. It became highly influential and dominated many aspects of public life, during a specific era when leadership and economic security were top priorities. The theory rested on the assumption that changed behaviour is related almost entirely to external events. In more detail, the idea is that behaviours can be observed and shaped through successive reinforcement. This kind of thinking built on ideas already well established among behavioural psychologists. Scientists like Watson and Skinner had claimed that the limits of learning are biologically determined but, even so, within those biological limits, development is driven by connections between stimuli, responses, and reinforcement.

When these ideas were applied to learning in educational institutions they were taken on board and flourished. This was during the 1950s and 1960s, in part, because the specific social circumstances of those post-World War II years made alternative thinking about progress and learning both necessary and possible. During this time, education, and particularly science and mathematics, came to be seen as a 'political panacea', a major instrument for achieving national objectives. Education was seen as a means to full employment and the source of new ideas for technological growth. During this era stability and order became imperative. So did predictability. It is no surprise to learn that learning became equated to external observable variables. The focus was on behavioural change, as observed through the acquisition of skills, rules, and algorithms.

Gagné is one name we associate with behaviourism. Like other behavourists, Gagné, was able to explain how certain behaviours could be modified or even eliminated by the classroom environment. Learning, for him, didn't mean simply observable changes in performance; it also involved hierarchical order. What interested him was how learning is built up. In *The Conditions of Learning* (1965) he offered a three-phase performance model to describe incremental steps or stages through which learning and high performance takes place. But what he failed to do was describe exactly how learning takes place.

What is important from a pedagogical point of view, is that his 'building blocks' placed an emphasis on making skills automatic through practice—and still more practice. It is readily apparent that Gagné considered drill and practice routines as crucial for the acquisition of knowledge and the development of more complex systems or higher order concepts. In many of the research studies that these ideas initiated, achievement was measured according to right or wrong answers on standardised tests and classroom management principles were not determined by the needs of the students but revolved around the status of the teacher as expert, together with the knowledge to be learned.

This way of proceeding has important consequences for classroom practice and organisation. Ability groupings, tracking, and capacities and learning and teaching styles became key signifiers. The view of classroom life that emerged was determined by considering the relation between the teacher and the learner as linear. Teaching in the behaviourist frame came to mean the transmission of instructional strategies which produces new learning. The teacher transfers by direct instruction his of her knowledge into the minds of learners. *Transfer* here means a relation which yields results which are universally true for all learners—a relation which is uncontaminated, and independent of contingency and history of learners. The pedagogical model consistent with these understandings is sometimes named the technico-rational conception of teaching and learning. Learners are said to *acquire* new knowledge and skills not only by observing and imitating the teacher, but also by absorbing ideas, and making sense of those ideas from the teacher's explanatory statements. In the behaviourist equation practice and praise are the independent variables, and performance indicators and test scores are the dependent variables. This is a one-way process of active teacher and passive, yet receptive, learner.

Because behaviourism engages with external concrete and measurable forms and events, there is no possibility of entertaining the 'mind'. Even though new facts about the learner could demonstrate outcomes–achievement, performance, progress–the passive treatment of the learner could only serve to confirm the learner's marginal status. With no effective theory of agency for the individual learner, the model did not allow for a critical grasp of how actual learning took place. It is no surprise that what amounted to a naïve endorsement of behaviourism, in time, led to a critique of it. New perspectives emerged, each critically and sensitively overturning the dominant way of thinking about learning.

COGNITIVISM

The challenges to behaviourism around the 1980s came from several directions, including cognitive science and information-processing theories. Despite their differences, this diverse field of cognitive positions shifts from an interest in external behavioural change to focus on the 'mind'. Cognitivists argue that learning can be systematised and interpreted as intra-psychic cognition, specifically through stimuli and responses. They view the learner as an information processor and knowledge as that produced by the learner's usage of cognitive processes. The interest is in describing the internal information processing which connects the outer stimulus with the learner's response. As far as learning goes, it occurs through experience of a stable and objective world.

Most of what we know, or believe we know about cognitivism, is thanks to Piaget. Piaget's ideas developed around the 1920s and 1930s and became a foundation for cognitivist thinking. Whereas the behaviourists had been drawn to psychometric models of learning through a concern with progress and achievement, Piaget's attention was focused elsewhere. By doing a lot of research and watching a lot of children engaged in thinking and reasoning activities, he was drawn to the idea of universal cognitive growth. His work became extremely influential in education during the 1950s and 1960s when they were translated into English. Even before Piaget's studies (e.g., 1959), John Dewey (1916) had been advocating for the individual as the unit of analysis in discussions about learning. And at the same time as Piaget's studies were being undertaken, Brownell had also taken up the learner's cause. Brownell (1928) and Dewey, along with Piaget, all insisted that learning comes from experience and active involvement. These were revolutionary ideas at their time and they changed the character of learning.

Piaget was suspicious of behaviourist accumulation of knowledge theories. He came up with the idea that learning occurs within evolutionary stages. And he used his theory of maturation stages to account for the differences and changes in human learning and also to describe the viability and coherence of children's thinking. His claim was that a child's learning proceeds from the concrete to the abstract through four stages of development, leading, finally, to mature cognitive functioning. He defined the four stages as: sensory-motor, preoperational, concrete operational, and formal operational. These stages map out development through a hierarchy in which each level is dependent on the child actively exploring the environment. In the description, specific attributes are assigned higher status: the analytic is privileged over the synthetic, the verbal/symbolic takes precedence over the visual, and the logical/deductive is primary to the analogical/contextual.

Having figured out his developmental stages, Piaget then set about sketching an answer to the question of how learning actually takes place. As he saw it, the learner seeks to maintain equilibrium or balance as the result of interactions with, and reflections, upon the environment. In his terms, learning is precipitated by disequilibrium or cognitive perturbation. Exposure to confusion, ambiguity, challenge and refutation prompts an equilibration process that involves a reconstruction of knowledge. Piaget explains the resulting equalising adjustment process by proposing that new information is *assimilated* into the schema, and information which builds upon what is already known is *accommodated.*

Right at the core of Piaget's work is the assumption that it is possible to structure cognition. And what he proposed would structure and integrate cognition are what we know as 'schemata'. His 'schemas' represent the mind's knowledge structures (Skemp, 1976) since they are believed to be a measure of the individual's information processing capacity. Schemas describe changing and expanding mental pathways which represent and organise every experience the individual has had and learned. Construction of schema comes about from active speculation. It is through schema that new skills and new understandings develop. The process doesn't stop there because the new knowledge brings with it enhanced ability and a movement through the stages, to process in the mind the complex information coming from the outside world. Insightful though his genetic evolutionary theory was, what it could not account for were differential meanings constructed at different ages within the same environment.

CONSTRUCTIVISM

The influences of Piaget are far-reaching within education. Post-Piagetian formulations of knowledge, such as constructivism, however, have tended to place more emphasis on the learner's active construction of knowledge. Constructivism, during the 1980s and 1990s, became a key term in the vocabularies of some education commentators and a backdrop for classroom teaching practice and management, teacher education, and research. Von Glasersfeld's (1996) radical constructivist position is one in which the behavourists' proposal of passive reception of knowledge is no longer credible. In place of passive reception, von Glasersfeld wants us to consider the active cognising subject. He maintains that the subject's knowledge of the world is in a constant process of construction, individually localised and situated.

Many education authorities have followed post-Piagetian tendencies. They hold to the idea that knowledge is constructed by learners as they make connections between new and existing experiences. Those experiences take place as learners interact with the social and physical environment As a consequence their mental activities are extended and reorganised. Learners actively seek out and make mental connections that link aspects of their physical and social environment with certain numerical, spatial and logical concepts. Like Piaget, many neo-Piagetians take the general sequence of levels through which students progress, as well as the general categories of intellectual structure that students construct, as being relatively fixed and universal. Failure to learn is considered the responsibility of either the individual teacher in not providing the requisite skills, or the individual student's incapacity to grasp conceptual knowledge.

What is useful about the constructivist description of knowing is that it offers an explanation of the nature of knowledge and provides insights into learning. But first and foremost an epistemological position rather than a theory of learning, it describes how cognitive processes might be acquired and developed. This is an individualist approach to learning in which the external context is linked *yet peripheral to* self-organising individuals. Learning is organised around the metaphor of transference of a conceptual idea from one physical locale to another. Drawing on humanist sensibilities about the individual, learning necessarily relies on the autonomous learner, who is understood to be a stable, core, knowing agent. It would seem that for the constructivist, it is the nature of the student's *developing internal representation* that remains of primary interest. In short, the individual mind is privileged, while history, circumstances and social conditions are, for all intents and purposes, understood through the mind of the individual.

On the surface this may not seem like a major issue but it turns out to be the theory's stumbling block. The problem is that radical constructivism does not offer an explanation of how we make sense of ideas, given our history, and positioned as we are within our cultural and social environments. For a large number of people in education, a learning theory that is strangely silent on social processes, has obvious flaws since it can't provide an explanation of, for example, intersubjectivity. To make certain that all aspects are dealt with, many argue that learning can only be understood in terms of the social and cultural context in which it is embedded. Put bluntly, for many people in education, a theory of learning requires attention to the social and cultural resources made available during the learning encounter.

SOCIOCULTURAL FORMULATIONS

In contemporary discussions of learning there can be few terms more widely encompassing than 'sociocultural'. The term is big enough for us to derive some general principles of learning, and yet small enough to allow for variations in activating those principles. If you were to lay all the sociocultural theories side by side and run your eye over them, you would inevitably find that, in relation to cognitivist formulations, the ideas tend to be more outward looking. What is striking about sociocultural formulations of learning is their unavoidable commitment to the social—but it is a commitment which is revealed in varying degrees. No matter the level of integration with the social, you have probably already deduced that socioculturalists question those aspects of learning which cognitive psychology holds as 'mentally acquired'. By way of compensation, sociocultural theorists suggest that learning, in fact, is 'social' or 'cultural', constructed by people in engagement and discussion with others. In our discussion we will be considering the way in which a number of different sociocultural positions make this point explicit.

Socioculturual positions took seed in an era of broad social change in Western countries. It was an era that witnessed emergent political groups with increasingly divergent ideas and demands concerning justice, equality and social legislation. The effects of these new sensibilities on scholarly thinking were far-reaching. Questions about the individual learner were raised as a result of intersectional, multicultural and postcolonial identity claims. New theories were put forward to take into account differences in settings and circumstances. Vygotsky, for example, proposed that the origins of thought are *entirely social.* He insisted that there is not a lot to be gained from radical constructivism in its insistence that knowledge is independent of the situations in which it is acquired. As if to underscore the point, he said that conceptual ideas develop from the 'outward' to the 'inward', or, putting it another way, from the intersubjective to the intrasubjective. So strongly did Vygotsky feel about the social aspect of learning that he said: "learning awakens a variety of developmental processes that are able to interact only when the child is interacting with people in his environment and in collaboration with his peers" (Vygotsky, 1978, p. 90). These ideas are the inspiration of many sociocultural theories of learning.

Simply telling us that learning is social doesn't actually give us a description of how learning takes place. It transpires that Vygotsky's semiotic mediation theory takes care of the internal controls in the learning process. Briefly, then, in Vygotsky's theory, it is the zone of proximal development (zpd) where changes in the child's control and responsibility take place. These changes are made in response to social negotiations about meanings. You get the distinct impression, then, that Vygotsky believes that shared consciousness, or intersubjectivity, is absolutely fundamental to learning. As far as classroom learning goes, learners mobilise cultural and social resources to develop, appropriate, and exchange mathematical understanding. In the broader interpretation, cultural resources might be people, artefacts, technologies, symbol systems, environmental designs, rituals, and ways-with-words.

Social constructivist positions on learning ascribe a greater weight to the role of social processes and language in the construction of knowledge than do constructivist formulations of a more radical persuasion. In social constructivist interpretations of classroom life, special emphasis is placed on the cultural and social processes through which knowledge is formulated. Outwardly, social constructivism seems to address the problems that come with radical constructivism. The reality is, however, that the construction of knowledge never strays too far away from the individual mind. The social functions as a *shaper* rather than a *constitutor* of learning. The result is that the social constructivist position on learning as *influenced* by the social does not effectively change classic definitions of the cognitive agent–the learner. Despite the fact that the importance is paid to social interaction, traditional assumptions about individualism tend to linger.

By the late 1980s and the 1990s, researchers were beginning to grasp the potential of sociocultural ideas for the learner's equitable learning experience. The **interactionist** or **participatory** (see, for example, Bauersfeld, Krummheuer, & Voigt, 1988) approach develops the idea of learning as participation in social practices. In this approach two central lines of interest are apparent. To begin, a number of participationists base their work around a microsociological perspective that has particular influences from symbolic interactionism (e.g., Blumer, 1968) and ethnomethodology (Garfinkel, 1967; Mehan, 1979). Their work involves understanding the ways and means by which meanings are negotiated and become validated within the local events of classroom life. A second interest is in analysing the ways in which the learner makes sense of new ideas as he or she interacts within a sociocultural relationship with others. Whatever the preoccupation, interactionists develop their thinking around an understanding of the learner as the stable, core knowing agent, cast within the dynamics and the regularities of the microculture in the mathematics classroom. Learning takes place as the individual negotiates meaning within social interaction.

Each of these perspectives provides an account of the social basis of individual learning experience. Taking their starting point from a number of different quarters, they have all incorporated an interpretation of the social origins of thought. In their separate ways they have merged the social with the individual, providing complementary accounts of individuals-in-community.

ACTIVITY

Choose one theory of learning discussed so far.

1. What assumptions, commitments and values underlie the theory?
2. What kind of subject position is made explicit for the learner?
3. What are the practices that are legitimised in this theory?
4. Describe the social conditions around the time of the theory's development.
5. Identify the key figures instrumental in the development of the theory.

ACTIVITY/SITUATIVITY/SOCIAL PRACTICE THEORY

Situated theories of learning, social practice theory, and activity theory, some people believe, amount to much the same thing. It is impossible to ignore this influential body of work even though it developed in response to concerns about the reproduction of social inequalities in schools, rather than through an interest in learning *per se*. If you look carefully at the content and focus within the theories you'd be hard pressed not to notice that their conceptual grounding stems from the work of post-Vygotskian activity theorists, such as Davydov & Radzikhovskii (1985), Engestrom (1987) and Vygotsky's collaborator Leont'ev (1978). Overlaid with insights from anthropology and critical theory, activity theory provides the inspiration for many current proposals about how we learn.

Scholarly application of activity theory has spread far and wide throughout education. So what is new about this theory? To begin with, activity theory explains that learning is not merely brought about through the mechanism of social practice but is actually inherent in ongoing participation within a community. Putting it another way, we can only know the world through the meaning systems established through the communities of practice in which we engage. This may not sound radically different from other formulations of knowledge but what it is suggesting is that thinking, meaning and reasoning are constituted socially in a mutually relational manner. This is a subtle shift from saying that learning is 'influenced' by the social. The important thing is that by emphasising the mutual relational effects of the social and individual, activity or situativity theories reconfigure the way we think about learning and knowledge production.

Let's discuss these ideas more fully. To say that theories of situativity merge the social and the individual is certainly an understatement. In fact, in their merging, they privilege neither the individual nor forms of social practice. What they do instead, is make interconnections between learning, language, perceptions, and the social world, by talking about learning as full participation in the practices of a community. In making no distinction between learning and social participation, activity theories signal something quite different from the idea of social and cultural forces as *shaping* a learner. Conditions are created for learner participation and it is the various activities in which learners engage, and with which they interact, which will co-produce their knowledge. The significance is that the learner is inextricably *connected to* a dynamic social context. Learning, or cognition, occurs collaboratively in the context of shared events and interests. It becomes tangled up with the participation and activity of others.

A grasp of these ideas leads us to think about the individual and the context as mutually co-constitutive. By all accounts, too, participation is not restricted to face-to-face interactions with others. Instead all individuals are viewed as elements or aspects of an encompassing system of social practices and individuals are viewed as participating in social practices even if they act in physical isolation from others. One good example of an application of the theory is demonstrated in the work of Nunes, Schliemann and Carreher (1993) which revealed how students who traditionally fail in school mathematics could be successful in street situations involving mathematics. Another good example of how co-constitutivity plays out can be found in the work of Walkerdine (1988) which locates mathematical meanings *in* practices and not independent of them. In claiming that knowledge might be *produced* rather than found, these theorists have provided a counterbalance to conventional notions of learning. Their untraditional approaches remind us that learning might not simply be a matter of memorisation or putting something into practice; anything we learn cannot escape entanglement in social practices.

Enactivist and **complexity** theories of learning add a new twist to the influences of the social. Enactivists highlight the dynamic and interactive adaptations of the learner, and address questions of 'being' rather than 'knowing'. Their accounts are nothing like cognitive approaches to learning because they draw on ideas from biological systems. When biology is the foundation, then it is no surprise to learn that enactivism focuses on *interconnections*, rather than separations. A good application of enactivism for education can be observed in the work of Davis and Simmt (2003). In that work learning is understood as a complex learning system that allows ongoing and recursive adaptations. The interest is not in how the individual construes the world, as it is in the radical constructivist position. Neither is the focus on some collective interest through participation. Rather, the individual and collective are investigated *in their complexity* within nested learning systems. Individual and collective knowledge are not uncovered, nor are they invented; rather they emerge and evolve within the dynamics of the spaces students share and within which they participate. The learner is intricately caught up with knowledge precisely because learning occurs as part of a layering of complex systems of relationships within constantly changing learning circumstances and conditions.

A similar biological metaphor is used by Lakoff and Núñez (2000) in their **embodied** theory. Ideas are "not held by institutions or individuals but are embodied by human beings with normal human cognitive capacities living in a culture" (p. 359), situated in and productive of larger, social, cultural and historical thinking. The conceptualisations of one person are not assessed as a measure of 'fit' or 'match'; rather they are said to be viable (or otherwise) in relation to another's conceptualisations.

Lave's work might well be called the paradigmatic example of co-constitutivity. In her series of classic studies (1988, 1996; Lave & Wenger, 1991) she never lets us forget that learning is about increasing participation in particular social practices. Her observations and analyses of learning in action within routine activities of tailors' apprentices, supermarket shoppers, Weight Watchers, and so on, together put up a thoroughly persuasive case that learning is an integral part of the specific activity, context and culture in which it is located. People, their activities, their interests, their goals, and the ways in which all these interrelate, are what produce learning. When Lave talks about 'apprenticeship' she is referring to initiation into and increasing participation within a social tradition. She uses the term 'legitimate peripheral participation' (LPP) as a conceptual tool to bridge and identify, at any one time, both the knowledge of the learner and the community of practice. And she explains the process of becoming knowledgeable through trajectories of participation within communities of practice. The key point in the theory is that becoming a learner in any community, then, is a process of participation in the practices within that community of practice.

The strengths and limitations of activity theory for education are beginning to be explored. Some have celebrated the notion of participation and engagement among people, activities and settings. They believe that recognising the critical part the social plays with the individual is a way forward. Others have strong reservations. They say that the individual-acting-within-settings undermines the cognising individual. There are other objections too. A number of researchers have pointed out that learning through participation in communities of practice is a useful way to explain the practice of learning to *teach,* but it doesn't say much about how students learn in the classroom. Lave claims there is no need for a learning mechanism because mechanisms 'disappear into practice; mainly people are becoming kinds of persons" (1996, p. 157).

Other kinds of tension are apparent too, and one of these concerns the notion of 'shared meaning' that is implicit in social practice theory. As Foucault's theories have made us well aware, shared meaning is, quite simply, beyond our grasp. How can we know for sure that meaning is made in the same way amongst all members of the classroom community? Trouble is, it's simply not possible for this to happen. The learners in the classroom who we observe 'sharing meaning' are simply our own constructions of learners. And our constructions are always made with a view from our own history, our own experiences and our own expectations. Thinking about learning in the way that activity theorists do, does not allow us to come to grips with the whole story. There are more things happening during learning that have yet to be explained.

CONCLUSION

Theories of learning help us understand how people come to understand ideas, events and situations. Without theories, there would be no way to organise our thinking about how students latch onto the big ideas in classrooms. Alternative conceptions of learning lead to different views about what learners ought to do and the sort of thinkers they might become. But one thing the theories we have examined all have in common is that, to a greater or lesser degree, they have something to say about the social/individual relation. What they cannot agree on is where the emphasis should lie. If you classified yourself as a cognitivist, for example, you would offer a robust conception of 'the mind' or interiorisation. But you would tend to draw the line on social and cultural processes. If you supported activity theory, you would criticise the central processor model of mind. But, then again, your conception of individual learning differences would tend to be undeveloped.

What is different about our interrogation from traditional historiography is that it leads us, much as we might want to resist doing so, to think about knowledge about learning as a discursive event. Like all Foucauldian histories, our account of learning is back-dropped by specific social and intellectual events that helped the ideas to develop. The development of the theories appears haphazard, governed by chance and random events and through particular 'authorities'. We might even go so far as suggesting that what we currently know about learning in classrooms has taken seed within different power blocks.

An archaeological analysis, like the one we have just studied, provides a refreshingly new way to think about concepts. Now it's time for you to try your hand at the method of archaeology as a conceptual interrogation. The activity that follows will allow you to do that.

ACTIVITY

Current education initiatives in many countries put literacy at the forefront and mark it up as a key competency for everyday life.

1. Find out when literacy became a central concept in policy formulations within your country of residence.
2. What factors and conditions led to the emergence of literacy as a category of specific interest?
3. What elements (if any) within education had to change to make literacy legitimated as a category?
4. What specific assumptions of the learner underlie the literacy learner?

CHAPTER 3

DISCOURSE ANALYSIS

IN THIS CHAPTER

- Discourse
- Discourse analysis
- Subject positions and texts
- The policy text in context

Every theory has its pluses. Policy makers, at any given time, latch onto the attributes of a theory that appear to explain educational processes and events in a sensible and coherent way for the particular people they target. We can think about the choices policy makers make by using an analogy. If an optometrist has a wide selection of lenses in stock, we would expect to find a suitable lens that provides us with the vision to correct a specific visual defect. The same is true for educational theories. If a number of different theories explaining the same issue are in circulation, one of those theories will provide the policy maker with the insight that is conducive to his or her particular view of the world. Just as failing eyesight over the years requires a change of optical lens, so too will a change in the policy maker's social, economic and political world view prompt a review of thinking about education. It will do more than that, as it turns out. A change in thinking about a process brings with it a change in thinking about the persons directly implicated. For example, a change in thinking about learning will initiate a change in thinking about the learner.

A resource we can use to explain the learner in a helpful way is Foucault's concept of discourse. It will help us explain how individuals come to behave, speak, and even think in a way that seems 'normal' to them. To put the concept to its best use, and to make sure that the material we are going to be dealing with never strays too far from our main objective, our approach will be through discourse analysis. Discourse analysis will guide us when we interrogate part of a written text taken from a curriculum document mandated for schools. The idea is to see if it might be possible to understand and explain the effect that policy texts have on learners. Not just on learners themselves, though, because part of what we are looking at is how policy texts influence social structures.

DISCUSSION QUESTIONS

1. What educational policy documents in current use are you aware of?
2. How does the curriculum document, used in schools within your country today, compare with the curriculum document it replaced?
3. What kind of learner is made explicit within the most recent curriculum document?

DISCOURSE

In exploring how subject positions and experiences are made available to people and groups, Foucault focused on discourses. For him, discourse was a methodological tool to develop a theory of the relation between knowledge and forms of social control. Those who had the enviable privilege of attending his inaugural lecture at the Collège de France, back in 1970, would have heard a lot about discourses since his lecture was titled "The Order of Discourse." Interesting enough it was during the previous year in 1969 when *The Archaeology of Knowledge* was first published in French, that he had described in detail how discourses—and indeed knowledge itself—are formed through rules and categories. Some commentators are of the opinion that *The Archaeology of Knowledge* provides a methodological backdrop to *The Order of Things*.

Discourse is not to be confused with statements and speech acts. What distinguishes Foucault's understanding of discourse from language is context. In fact, discourses only make sense within contexts. For another thing, the concept of discourse is not quite the same as ideology. This is because discourses do not merely reflect or represent social entities and relations. Instead, they actively constitute them. Perhaps a better way to think of discourses is that they perform the role of conceptual schemes, or relatively well-bounded areas of social knowledge. They function like sets of rules, providing us with the knowledge about what is possible to speak and do at a given moment. And they do that by systematically constituting specific versions of the social and natural worlds for us, all the while obscuring other possibilities from our vision. So the concept of discursivity connects thought, speech, and action. But the thinking, acting and speaking that discourses map out for us do not remain static. Those practices change over time, or in Foucault-speak, they are historically variable.

Discourses are historically variable ways of specifying knowledge and truth. We can't speak of them as existing in one era or another. And because discourses are always located in complex relationships one with another, we can't say that they change in a linear fashion. Instead we tend to use the word 'episteme' to try to capture that complexity existing between and within discourses. Discourses give 'truth' or meaning to the world by tracing out forms of social organisation. Take the example we looked at in the last chapter. There we found that learning was constituted in different ways by different discourses, in different periods of time. For the behaviourists, learning is procedural, students are, in the main, silent, and teaching is transmissive and authoritative. For the enactivist, learning is configured within a classroom network of systems, in which the teacher and learners all contribute to the knowledge production of those within the classroom community.

The crucial point about discourses, for the work we are going to do in this chapter, is that they do more than give 'truth' or meaning to the world. They produce particular kinds of subjects as effects of discursive relations. Putting it another way, they position people in different ways as social subjects. So discursivity is not simply a way of organising *what* people say and do; it is also a way of *organising actual people and their systems.* It hardly seems possible, but there you are. They operate right across society, in all society's processes, not simply in its educational, economic, and political processes. Run your eye over any spoken, written or electronic texts, and, all going well after completing this chapter, you will be able to see that there are discourses running through all those texts. Those discourses are connected to a wider network of power relations which make possible (as well as regulate) particular understandings of, for example, learners in the classroom. If learners are understood as 'capable' or 'struggling', for example, it is simply because a set of critical links has been forged between a number of elements to make that understanding possible. One of those elements might concern the status of education; another might have to do with the status of learning; and yet another element might involve the institutional sites from which these elements originate.

If all this sounds rather perplexing, just keep in mind at this stage that discourses position people differently. Take the example of the terms used for learners—gifted and talented, academically challenged, kinaesthetic, and visual learners—these are just a few in circulation. These are not merely words or terms for the learners involved—they carry a much greater significance. These learners actually experience learning in the way that the discourses permit them to. They organise their meanings with regard to these discourses. In the classroom they come to know what is considered 'normal' and 'natural' and how to recognise different categories of learners. All that is because the discourses relating to, say, academically challenged students, tend to make the academically challenged learner think, feel and act like what others expect of an academically challenged student. We can go as far as saying that discourses shape the experience of being academically challenged.

Broadly speaking, discourses sketch out ways of being in the world. Foucault speaks of the discursive construction of subjectivity to get the point across that discourses define the possibilities, as well as the limits, of meaningful existence. This happens not simply for classroom learners, but for all of us. In our work in education, as well as within the family and in the other social fields in which we lead our lives, discourses construct the understandings we construct of ourselves. They tell us what it means to be, for example, a researcher, a teacher, a partner, a parent, and, like we saw earlier, what it means to be academically challenged, or gifted. The bad news is that discourses have the *effect* of producing truth. They are the means by which *reality* can be read. And so they are powerful. There are practices of disciplining and regulation going on that produce us as specific entities. The fact of the matter is that discourses transmit and produce power without us even being aware of it. We wouldn't be wrong in saying that they operate duplicitously. They mask their effects to such an extent that to the people concerned, their practices appear to be common sense.

We cannot entirely construct a set of meanings about ourselves without falling back on the meanings provided by other people and other texts. For our academically challenged learner, just like all other learners, this power may be exercised by classroom teachers, by school principals, by the education system, by future employers, even by officials such as those within the health sector. Subjectivity, for the academically challenged learner, becomes a site of control. Those who are labeled as particular learners are caught up, without their knowing, in issues of power and regulation. At the point when the learner chooses to identify with the subject position offered, the regulation is complete. Stop and think for a moment of the consequences (both positive and negative) of that thought for our academically challenged learner.

This is how Foucault himself describes discourses. He says that discourses are:

> practices that systematically form the objects of which they speak…Discourses are not about objects; they do not identity objects, they constitute them and in the practice of doing so conceal their own invention.
>
> (Foucault, 1981, p. 49)

This might seem wholly pessimistic for our academically challenged learner, but take heart. At any given time, the meaning we give to our learner will vary. The good news, is that because discourses are historically specific, we can't think of them as lasting. Neither can we think of them as absolutely true or absolutely false. Here's another way to think about it: the way we understand academically challenged learners will depend on the discourse taken up by the particular institutional practice we are engaged within at the time. The possibilities for meaning and understanding are set by that specific practice. For example, the academically challenged learner will mean something quite different within a student cohort of high achievers, than within a teaching community whose objective is to empower disenfranchised learners. The truth is that there are always a range of meanings, linked to specific practices, floating around at any one time. All of these offer the academically challenged student a specific subject position, as well as particular rights and responsibilities attached to that position. For the learner, it's not an issue of accepted or unaccepted discourse, just as it is not an issue of dominant or dominated discourse. Things are not so cut and dry. Many discourses exist at any one time. They originate from different sources, and as you might have guessed, they embody different interests. But the point is that they all work to shape our thinking, our viewpoints, our beliefs, and practices. In short, they offer us preferred forms of subjectivity.

In and between different discourses, we get a sense of our own distinct subjectivity. The sense we have of ourselves comes about from the flux of meanings provided by a whole constellation of discourses that, at one time or another, compete for our attention. What is extraordinary from our point of view is that this multiplicity of discursive practices, in the long run, offers us great potential. There is always another meaning possible. We are certainly not trapped within one discourse or another. There are always different meanings available to us and these come about as other factors and influences are brought to bear. There is room for manoeuvre—room to undermine the power that either acts upon, or is enacted by, a specific subject positioning. As far as our academically challenged learner is concerned, there is always a space for negotiating through the various subject positions offered in the differing discourses. We can never be fully reduced to the subject positions on offer. There is always space for agency.

> We must make allowance for the complex and unstable powers whereby discourses can be both an instrument and an effect of power, but also a hindrance, a stumbling block, a point of resistance and a starting point for an opposing strategy.
>
> (Foucault, 1980, p. 101)

ACTIVITY

In this activity the gifted and talented learner will be our focus.

1. What subject position, rights, and responsibilities (if any) are provided for our gifted and talented learner within the discourses relating to the following entities or institutional practices:
   - (i) National official school performance data sets.
   - (ii) Schools which group classes according to achievement.
   - (iii) Schools which group classes according to heterogeneity.
   - (iv) Students who are designated 'average' students.
   - (v) Parents of gifted and talented students.
2. From your responses, identify any competing discourses that exist for defining the gifted and talented learner.

DISCOURSE ANALYSIS

The idea that discourses make specific subject positions available to people and shape the experience of being is an enormously powerful one. Foucauldians would explain this idea as the discursive construction of subjectivity. If that wasn't enough to comprehend, they would say that people, such as school learners, can only be interrogated through the notion of discourse. Learners *are* the production of the discursive practices through which they become subjected.

One of the easiest ways to track how this happens is through the method of discourse analysis. This is the method we will use to explore the discursive practices which constitute classroom learners. The method will provide us with a way of understanding how conventional meanings of learners are established. By paying close attention to language we will investigate how language functions, in a very strategic manner, to fashion subjectivity. If we didn't look carefully at language and the processes by which meanings and categories are constituted, we could only impose an oversimplified model of what it means to be a learner. With our method we will be able to see how meanings, generated through discourses, are produced as a social fact by subtle yet pervasive exercises of power relations.

Our particular version of discourse analysis is known as *critical discourse analysis*. It will be helpful in our exploration of the discursive construction of subjectivity. Most of what we know about critical discourse analysis owes a large debt to Fairclough (1992, 1995). In Fairclough's critical discourse analysis, the starting point is in Foucault's theory of language and social power. What the method does is put the spotlight on *linguistically*-oriented analysis but not in the conventional sense. It examines features of texts as distinctive *social* actions, and because of that it is able to pay detailed attention to the very real effects that discourse has on individuals or groups of people. Once we have figured out those effects we will be able to put forward an argument about the regulation and control of people. The 'critical' aspect of the method comes from the part it plays in showing how people, despite the fact that they are caught up in power contestations, still have a space for agency.

The method of discourse analysis is particularly appealing because of its practicality. It is practical in the sense that it deals with naturally occurring talk and written text and provides a readily usable categorical system for us to analyse. It examines the details of the texts as found, and tries to link analytic claims closely to those details. Some further explanation will be helpful here. When we explore how particular learners are positioned by discourse, we are looking at how discourse maps out a specific version of the social and natural worlds. We try to figure out how historically variable 'discursive formations', or systems of rules, make it possible for certain statements and understandings, but not others, about learners, to occur at a particular time. So you can see from this that discourse analysis goes further than offering 'transparent' speech acts. It engages with issues of power by exploring in what specific contexts, among which specific communities of people, and by what textual and social processes, particular subject positions are crafted and made available.

The real advantage of using this method is that it is able to reveal how discursive practice constitutes relations of power. If this seems a complex idea, then look at it this way: the method helps us see how different discourses attempt to position, locate, define, and regulate people, in different ways. In other words, discourse analysis has the capacity to trace the way in which different discourses create different effects with regard to the way in which people's subjectivities are made up. The fascinating point to make about discourse analysis is that it is able to capture a sense of the unspoken underlying what is said or written. What's more, it is theoretically powerful, in that it constantly engages theory and practice in a continuous process of inquiry.

Identifying subject positions boils down to identifying relationships between individuals, social structures, and institutions. That's not as easy as it may sound. To carry out the investigation, we will be guided by the process outlined by MacNaughton (1998):

- Identifying how people are categorised, as formed and expressed in language.
- Identifying the social practices through which meanings are given to the categories.
- Identifying the patterns of emotional meanings and investments in particular categories.
- Naming the discourses that are formed by the categories, practices and emotional investments.
- Identifying the institutional basis of discourses that construct and are constructed in texts.
- Identifying the social power relations and effects of the different discourses that construct and are constructed in texts.

Foucault has another way of putting it:

> The problem is at once to distinguish among events, to differentiate the networks and levels to which they belong, and to reconstitute the lines along which they are connected and engender one another.
>
> (Foucault, 1984, p. 56)

SUBJECT POSITIONS AND TEXTS

Policy texts are sites where subject positions are created and where meaningful experience is constituted. For all their formality, it happens that policy documents are one of the easiest ways to track how subjectivity is produced. The reason is simply this: policy is one of the central means by which behaviours are regulated and made productive within the population.

In the following sections we will explore how the various discursive resources, made available in a national policy text, are organised and articulated. We will do that systematically, interrogating the subject position of the school learner. What we are interested in, particularly, is in unpacking how the text designates learners in particular ways and in how it names categories of difference as a linguistic and discursive artefact. In other words, we want to see in what ways the text constructs subjectivities and social relations.

As we work through the analysis what we will find is that the text operates with particular political interests. Consider the fact that the text constructs and cultivates some, but not other, subject positions for learners within schooling. It soon becomes clear that specific decisions have been made regarding precisely what subject position will be available to the learner. Decision making, such as this, by policy makers, alerts us to the fact that subjectivities are strategically fashioned through relations of domination and power. And the method of discourse analysis allows us to see this for ourselves. We will find that the policy text not only positions, locates, defines, and enables learners, it also regulates them.

As you will be well aware, the curriculum policy text is not the only site where discourses generate subject positions for learners. Many other discourses, including those constructed by the family, popular culture, the economy, and religion, all vie for the student's attention. As it turns out, though, national educational policy, because of the services that ensure its implementation, is a particularly powerful text. It clarifies social issues, problems, as well as future interests. And it identifies all these as in need of addressing. Generally speaking, policy texts are considered utopian and visionary. Through their official statements, agendas are set, priorities are enforced, some topics of knowledge are prioritised whereas others are minimised or disregarded. Some subject positions are elevated and some are not. In this sense, then, a policy text functions as a cultural institution, endorsing particular subject positions for learners.

The policy text excerpts that we will be interrogating are taken from *Mathematics in the New Zealand Curriculum* (1992). It is the current official and authoritative document for mathematics in New Zealand classrooms. In the next section we will go behind the scenes briefly to find out how *Mathematics in the New Zealand Curriculum* came about and whose political investments and interests came to 'count' in the text. From that short discussion we will develop an appreciation of how statements made with authority in policy texts are premised on a set of claims to truth which are historically specific and which are not the only or necessary way to understand school knowledge.

THE POLICY TEXT IN CONTEXT

In developing curricula documents, educators discuss, debate, and defend particular narratives of the subject (the learner, the teacher) and the institution (the school, the classroom), some of which will come to figure in the final document. To put you in the picture, when *Mathematics in the New Zealand Curriculum* was introduced to primary and secondary schools in 1993, it was set within a new era for education in New Zealand. It was focused on developing ways to improve the 'quality of education', in order, in part, to arrest public disillusionment with the state. For nearly ten years prior to its introduction, the country had felt the full effects of government policies, whose underlying principles were those of corporate managerialism, increased centralism, and instrumentalist and technicist approaches focused on efficiency and effectiveness. The effects of those principles played out in practices of deregulation, performance contracts, 'user pays' which increasingly permeated everyday experience.

Under the umbrella of the *New Zealand Curriculum Framework*, *Mathematics in the New Zealand Curriculum* is part of the most extensive restructuring and policy reformulation in education over the last century. *The New Zealand Curriculum Framework* was launched after extensive community consultation and took the form of a 28-page document for teaching, learning, and assessment in New Zealand schools. Mathematics is one of the seven essential learning areas of *The New Zealand Curriculum Framework.* It draws on the National Research Council's 1989 publication in the United States *Everybody Counts - A report to the Nation on the Future of Mathematics.* But its translation into government policy was not as straightforward as it might seem. Its development was caught up in conflict and opposition stemming from a number of personalities competing for voice. The final form of the text has to be seen as reflecting the negotiation and compromise that took place during its development. Most of these struggles took place behind closed doors but a glimpse of the dynamics of the conflict is possible within the policy statement. Essentially, it represents a two-pronged response to, first, the calls from the mathematics education community for improved student *understanding* and, second, a state imperative for improved student *achievement.*

The policy text creates particular subject positions through words, conventional illustrations, linguistic and discursive signs (for example, headings, subheadings, précis, summary points, key concepts, tables, charts, boxes, asterisks and highlights). These are contained within an inter-textual discourse: the achievement objectives, suggested learning experiences, sample assessment activities and sample development band activities through the six main achievement aims - the 'strands'. These six crucial areas of school mathematics knowledge are categorised as 'number', 'measurement', 'geometry', 'patterns and algebra', 'statistics', and 'mathematical processes'. Together they mark out a field of knowledge that constitute school mathematics. Both the object-level content and pedagogic forms of the school text are expanded upon by textual metanarratives that embody and legitimate representations of the 'real', namely, mathematics, the learner, development, cognition, pedagogy, skills and the teacher. The various sections are clearly attributable to one discourse type or another.

Looking at key terms

So that we can explore the way in which the policy text produces and constructs its objects of study, we will systematically itemise the discourses which appear in the text and draw out the categories relating to people. By drawing out the terms which put these objects to work we will be able to specify the particular *logic* and kinds of *practices* and *orientations* which work to construct a version of the student as a learner. This will enable us to piece together any relationships that have been constructed for the learner with others. It will clarify how the document, by producing the terms of school mathematics, and the parameters of school mathematical practice, provides the learner with access to its field. Put simply, we will be able to see how it creates what it means to be a subject within these practices.

We begin by looking at the key terms which appear in the whole text of the 'Introduction' of the document. You will find the line numbering down the left hand side helpful for later reference.

> Mathematics is a coherent, consistent, and growing body of concepts which makes use of specific language and skills to model, analyse, and interpret the world. Mathematics provides a means of communication which is powerful, concise, and unambiguous.
>
> As a human endeavour, mathematics involves creativity and imagination in the discovery of patterns of shape and number, the perceiving of relationships, the making of models, the interpretation of data, and the communication of emerging ideas and concepts.
>
> The "New Zealand Curriculum Framework" includes mathematics as one of the seven essential areas of learning. Mathematical understanding and skills contribute to people's sense of self-worth and ability to control aspects of their lives. Everyone needs to develop mathematical concepts and skills to help them understand and play a responsible role in our democratic society. Mathematics education aims to provide students with those skills and understandings.
>
> The "New Zealand Curriculum Framework" also asserts the importance of eight essential sets of skills: communication skills; numeracy skills; information skills; problem-solving skills; self-management, competitive skills; social, co-operative skills; physical skills; work and study skills.
>
> The need for people to be numerate, that is, to be able to calculate, estimate, and use measuring instruments, has always been identified as a key outcome for education. Mathematics education aims to contribute to the development of the broad range of *numeracy* skills.
>
> In an increasingly technological age, the need for innovation, and problem solving and decision-making skills has been stressed in many reports on the necessary outcomes for education in New Zealand. Mathematics education provides the opportunity for students to develop these skills, and encourages them to become innovative and flexible problem solvers.
>
> The ability to communicate findings and explanations, and the ability to work satisfactorily in team projects, have also been highlighted as important outcomes for education. Mathematics education provides many opportunities for students to develop *communication* skills and to

> participate in collaborative problem-solving situations, thereby contributing to the development of many *social and co-operative* skills.
>
> Increasingly, information is communicated through the use of data graphics. The communication of information through graphics is particularly common in the mass media. It is important that people can draw sensible conclusions from charts, tables, and graphs of various kinds. At the same time, increasing numbers of occupations demand the ability to collect data, to understand and use information technology for the organisation and interpretation of data, and to present reports and summaries. Mathematics education gives young people the opportunity to develop information skills through learning and practising data handling and data interpretation (p. 7).

The system of knowledge classified as school mathematics possesses its own inner logic. Discourse markers such as 'coherent', 'consistent' (Line 1), 'specific language', 'skills', 'model', 'analyse', 'interpret' (Line 2), 'concise', 'unambiguous' (Line 4), 'creativity', 'imagination' (Line 5), 'discovery' (Line 6), 'control' (Line 11), 'calculation', 'estimation' (Line 20) 'measurement' (Line 21), 'problem-solving' (Line 24-25), 'decision-making' (Line 25), 'communication' (Line 29), 'collaboration' (Line 33),'data handling' (Line 41), and 'interpretation' (Line 42), all operate on school mathematics in such a way as to determine what is possible to think, say, and experience.

The logic of reason

The key terms point, first and foremost, to the logic of *reason* as defining the criteria for thought, speech and action within and about school mathematics, and a model of *development* which takes the child as central, creative, and discovering. This comes as little surprise because for many people school mathematics *is* student-centred. Likewise, for many people, mathematics *is* reasoning. Foucault, himself, elaborates on mathematics:

> In France at least, the history of science and thought gives pride of place to mathematics, cosmology, and physics - noble sciences, rigorous sciences, sciences of the necessary, all close to philosophy: one can observe in their history the almost uninterrupted emergence of truth and pure reason.
>
> (Foucault, 1970, p. ix)

The status of rationality then becomes a very important issue in the understanding the subject position made available within the policy text to learners. To help us understand the implications of this status, it is useful to think about mathematics as very much a major aspect of our society. We tend to ground our knowledge claims in reason. In all aspects of life, reason not only represents truth it also embodies it. Most people assume from this that, generally speaking, reason operates identically for everyone.

The policy text identifies specific categories for the learner. Drawing those categories out, and observing the kinds of language that is used to organise them, helps us identify the particular discourses which construct a specific version of the learner and what it means to know. Referring back to the 'Introduction' quoted above, lines 14, 27 and 32 construct a version of learners in universal terms, as 'students'. Line 42 extends the notion of 'students' wider to embrace 'young people'. Students and young people are disembodied and universalised, constituted as belonging to the wider world of 'everyone' (line 12) and 'people' (lines 20, 37) and in this sense are obligated to become mathematically proficient for democratic citizenry.

The learner in the passage above rests on a belief in the existence of a universal, homogeneous and 'essential' human nature, an essence which lies at the heart of the individual which is unique, fixed and coherent and which makes him what he is. The pronoun 'he' has been purposefully used here because, though it is not so obvious from the passage above, it becomes clear, later, that the reasoning student in this text is also male. It follows that if the rational autonomous individual learner is male, then the female learner is centrally and strategically implicated in that discourse, as 'the other'. It follows that the learner, as the very rationale for the curriculum statement, is an object premised on certain sanctioned categorical descriptions.

The reasoning individual has been central to Western political thought, politics and social organising from the mid-seventeenth century. Working with Foucault alerts us to the fact that reason, as it is grasped today in western society, is the effect of a specific regime of power, and is not necessarily the only way of thinking. Foucault claims that what is accepted as rational is derived from power-knowledge formations and our understanding of reason is merely an effect of discourse. There are no *a priori* categories or concepts that shape what we know. We can take from that proposal that the idea that rationality 'goes all the way down' is questionable. Rationality can never provide the means to absolute truth. But the crucial point for us is that reason's importance is able to be sustained by processes of normalisation and naturalisation. Processes, such as those, always involve the exclusion and silencing of those who do not exhibit the category descriptor in question, in our case, reason.

Once we become aware that there are processes in operation that work to sustain the elevation of reason, we can begin to see how it is intimately tied to the social organisation of power. Those particular thought structures that are either derogated or excluded are those that represent 'the other of reason'. These include 'irrationality' or 'emotion'. It becomes important to look at those who represent reason and those who do not. We will return to this issue later in the chapter. But, before that, we will investigate the sort of relations with others in mathematics that the learner is made available.

Pedagogical relations

The way we think about learning has important implications for the way in which we conceptualise how learners will relate to others in the classroom. Investigating those aspects, both implicit and explicit within our policy text, allows us to define the discursive space established for pedagogical relations in school mathematics. In the following passage the text sets out certain fundamental ideas about the activity of learning.

> This scheme explicitly recognises that each learner is an individual whose learning development and rate of progress is different from others. Different students will be ready for particular mathematical content and experiences at different times (p. 17).
>
> As new experiences cause students to refine their existing knowledge and ideas, so they construct new knowledge. The extent to which teachers are able to facilitate this process significantly affects how well students learn. It is important that students are given explicit opportunities to relate their new learning to knowledge and skills which they have developed in the past (p. 12).
>
> A balanced mathematical programme includes concept learning, developing and maintaining skills, and learning to tackle applications. These should be taught in such a way that students develop the ability to think mathematically.
>
> Students learn mathematical thinking most effectively through applying concepts and skills in interesting and realistic contexts which are personally meaningful to them. Thus, mathematics is best taught by helping students to solve problems drawn for their own experience (p.11).
>
> Teachers can create opportunities for students to develop these characteristics by encouraging them to practise and learn such simple strategies as guessing and checking, drawing a diagram, making lists, looking for patterns, classifying, substituting, re-arranging, putting observations into words, making predictions, and developing proofs (p.11).
>
> The importance of the use of apparatus to help students form mathematical concepts is well established. Using apparatus provides a foundation of practical experience on which students can build abstract ideas. It encourages them to be inventive, helps to develop their confidence, and encourages independence (p. 13).

Like other official curriculum texts in education *Mathematics in the New Zealand Curriculum* endorses a particular theory of learning. It offers, what we name here as, a meta-textual commentary. Because it comes with such authority, it's certainly a commentary worth getting to know more about. The first point to make is that it presents a justification for a pedagogy that aims to reform mathematics teaching, thereby creating new modes of activity, new ways of being and new interpersonal relationships. The second point underwrites the first in that its particular regimes of truth make possible both what can be said and what can be done. A closer look shows how the commentary shapes difference by encouraging and sanctioning particular pedagogical relations and practice. We will take a closer look. We will look at the argument that is being presented and the particular educational voice and ethos from which it speaks. In turn, this will provide insight into the types of practices legitimated and the subject positions constructed for learners. Our focus will be on the way in which the text actualises some pedagogical practices at the exclusion of others.

There can be no statement that in one way or another does not re-actualise others.

(Foucault, 1972, p. 98)

Analysing aspects of sentence structure, we begin by looking at verbs, as they relate to the teacher. In the second passage taken from the section headed 'Catering for Individual Needs', the text explicitly expresses its demands on the teacher in the pedagogical relation with reference to two actions: 'facilitate' (Line 7), 'are given explicit opportunities' (Line 9). The third passage drawn from 'Approaches to Teaching and Learning in Mathematics' asks that teachers teach by 'helping' (Line 18) students. In the same section teachers are required to 'create opportunities' (Line 20), and that teaching is in part to do with 'encouraging' (Line 21) students.

These *verbs* reveal to us that, in relation to the learner, the role of the teacher is to facilitate, help, encourage, and create a mathematical learning situation. These practices hint at the responsibilities of the teacher, positioned as facilitator, identifying and focusing on problems and issues. The practices can also tell us about the assumptions of the learning process which are at work. Below listed are the *nouns* found in the passages above (and, in brackets, the contextual sense which can be made of them). The nouns provide us with a more expansive way to explore the differential rights and responsibilities of the teacher and the learner. It throws up, too, the network of pedagogical relationships in which the teacher and the learner have both been constituted.

'individual' (unique, to be singled out)
'development' (idiosyncratic to the learner)
'progress' (made at different rates)
'content' (body of mathematical knowledge)
'experiences' (mathematical teaching and learning opportunities that present)
'times' (marker of temporal stages for learning)
'knowledge' (personalised understandings of mathematics)
'ideas' (personalised conceptualisations of mathematics)
'opportunities' (classroom practice as deemed relevant to each student)
'skills' (conventionalised techniques)

'programme' (identifiable boundaried content and methods for teaching and learning)
'concept learning' (as in abstract notions)
'applications' (as in contextualised activity)
'ability' (marker of mathematical development)
'thinking' (the correct way to 'do' mathematics)
'concepts' (abstractions)
'contexts' (the real world situations)
'problems' (the best way to approach mathematics)
'characteristics' (that which is required of the modal student)
'strategies' (ways of going about mathematics)
'diagram' (representation of a mathematical situation)
'lists' (itemised recordings)
'patterns' (similarities according to some given criteria)
'observations' (what is seen as relevant to the problem)
'words' (linguistic communication, as opposed to symbols)
'predictions' (what might happen in the future as deduced from a problem solution)
'proofs' (processes, conventional or otherwise, to establish meaning)
'apparatus' (equipment, either everyday or specially devised for modelling a situation)
'foundation' (base of resources)
'confidence' (seen as crucial, and supposedly not often usually apparent)
'independence' (able to work by oneself)

Key words are repeated ('experiences', 'knowledge', 'skills', 'concepts', 'opportunities', 'apparatus') and these, taken together with the other nouns marked out, construct a version of the teaching/learning process. Another way to think of these words is that they naturalise or normalise the 'space' and 'scope' in which pedagogy is to take place. The passage controls this space by fixing limits around what can take place. In relation to both the well-being of the individual and society at large, the teacher must carry out these obligations and "relate...new learning to knowledge and skills...developed in the past" (Lines 9-11). Looking at how these words are set within the text we get a sense that the social and educational experiences identified will enable individual progressive growth and collective social transformation. The experiences, as set down in writing in the text, form the learning reality for the student. They construct pedagogical practice in which the learner is deeply implicated.

Lines 5 to 6 reveal that it is the learner who constructs a world ('As new experiences cause students to refine their existing knowledge and ideas, so they construct new knowledge'). Cognition is thus understood to be a process of 'meaning making' in which the individual makes sense of prior, socially-developed knowledge ('individual', 'ideas', 'skills', 'concept learning', 'contexts', 'thinking'). In other words, learning is a matter of constructing personal, as well as socially viable understandings, about the world ('patterns', 'observations'). In that sense, then, mathematics is a both an individual and a socially produced phenomenon ('opportunities').

It will be helpful to name the positions created for the learner. The text draws its ideas about the learner from constructivism. Constructivist learners freely and rationally construct their own meanings. Much of the structure about the individual's knowledge may be hidden or may compete with that of the teacher, but given the proper facilitating hermeneutic conditions, the true description of mathematics will, it is implicitly claimed, ultimately emerge. This is a very compelling idea. It implies that the learner is powerfully positioned as the source of meaning in mathematics. Within the pedagogical relation, the teacher is 'on the same side' as, or deferring to, the student. The teacher's task is to search for a 'deeper' interpretation of mathematics drawn from the individual's experiences. And as teachers and students engage in a mathematical discussion about the world, they will uncover together the same mathematical reality. From the vantage point of discourse analysis, however, the imperative toward individual competence is constrained by the implicit and explicit capability of teachers. In this sense the text that sets itself up to be liberating, is nonetheless linked to teacher effectiveness and power.

Never mind that the theory of learning advocated is not named, what separately emerges is that by describing learning and, as it turns out, by shaping the conduct of the pedagogical relation, the text provides first-hand evidence of particular powerful disciplining practices at work. The process by which it does this is as follows: it starts by taking the plight of the individual student seriously. It then assembles a relationship between the teacher and the student—a relationship whose field of practice revolves around a deep truth which is both known and hidden. The pedagogical relation marks out a logic for finding that truth: the compliant teacher will, through idiosyncratic 'readings' and interpretations of students' practice, forge this mathematical 'truth' about 'knowing'.

When we look at what the text has to say about 'knowing', from the perspective of Foucault's work, we begin to see it as an apparatus of social regulation. That is because it defines what will be taught and thereby determines what will count as knowledge. The position on knowledge, taken within the text, has significant political and ethical consequences for how teachers treat students, and in particular, the sorts of technologies and practices through which learners can be managed in the knowledge process. These contain and put boundaries around the learner's reality and thinking in mathematics. Foregrounding norms and ethics like this for learners is a form of regulatory power.

Many of us have always been of the opinion that the mathematical truths uncovered in the classroom lie outside the sphere of power. Discourse analysis provides us with a methodological tool to unmask power relations. It allows us to interrogate critically the exclusions through which subject positions are established.

Valorising difference

Earlier we made the claim that the learner in our policy text, just like the learner in traditional educational discourse, is distinctly male. We noted that, if that is the case, then the female learner is directly implicated in that discourse, as 'the other'. It follows that the learner, as the very rationale for the curriculum statement, is an object of attention, premised on lacking certain sanctioned categorical descriptions, and for whom an agenda for change is required.

This is clearly noticeable in the discursive positioning of the female learner, who is constituted with a specific subject position and with a set of textual and social relations. In the instance of discourse-at-work through the 'Introduction' in the text the learner's position, as essentially male, sits alongside a commentary based on the presumed deficiencies of others. This section to the text is titled 'Catering for Individual Needs'. Configured around a discourse of 'difference,' this section of the text draws on notions of ability, background, gender and ethnicity. This discourse constitutes the 'different' learner as a pathological, cultural and gendered subject through the constructs 'lower ability', 'exceptional ability', 'Maori students' and the category 'girls'. In our investigation we shall concentrate on how the identity of the 'girl' is made possible.

> The suggested learning experiences in this document include strategies that utilise the strengths and interests that girls bring to mathematics. Techniques that help to involve girls actively in the subject include setting mathematics in relevant social contexts, assigning co-operative learning tasks, and providing opportunities for extended investigations (p. 12).
>
> *And later:*
>
> Girls early success in routine mathematical operations needs to be accompanied by experiences which will help them develop confidence in the skills that are essential in other areas of mathematics. Girls need to be encouraged to participate in mathematical activities involving, for example, estimation, construction, and problems where there are any number of methods and where there is no obvious 'right answer' (p 12).

One of the advantages of putting Foucault to use is that it doesn't take too long to appreciate that the female learner enters into a discourse that becomes a site for her differential engagement with mathematics. The long and the short of it is that she enters a politics of discourse. She enters that discourse from a different location than does the male learner. Not only that, she has a different motivation. She learns of the grids which have been formulated to determine what counts as mathematics in secondary school (*not* routine mathematical operations; *not* single-method and single-solutioned problems). But more importantly, she learns that school mathematics is gendered (boys have confidence in multifaceted approaches and solutions, girls do not). It is notions like these, through the support and authentication they receive from institutional practices, like that of the classroom and the school, that fashion the 'reality' of the schoolgirl in mathematics. Those discourses offer her appropriate ways of being and behaving within the classroom.

The curriculum statement organises difference by casting girls in school mathematics as pathological. The girl, both as an object of mathematics education and as one engaged in school mathematics, presents an issue and a *problem* for understanding her subjectivity in the mathematics classroom. Because girls lack autonomy over their own schooling they are in need of liberation from oppression ('needs to be accompanied', lines 6; 'will help them', line 7; 'need to be encouraged', line 8). What this suggests is that the policy text implicitly assumes deficiencies within girls and presents prescriptive remedies and packaged answers to alleviate these deficiencies. The text, by fixing its subjects within its classificatory grid, regulates them and exercises power over them, by labelling 'girls' as lacking in confidence, and naturally drawn to 'cooperative learning tasks'. Power/knowledge is integral to the text and it is through these formations that the 'girl' is produced and is subjected to systems of regulation aimed at governance.

It is not just within educational policy texts that we catch a glimpse of girls' presumed deficiencies. The idea of the deficient girl circulates much more widely through all forms of social life. Of course, the idea lays itself wide open to debate and popular slogans such as 'girls can do anything' are typical responses. But back to our deficient girl in mathematics. She is a phenomenon with quite a history. The phenomenon is nowhere more evident than in the regimes of truth constructed in the early gender research through researchers' attempts to explain the subordination and exclusion of girls in mathematics.

Girls' reasoning capacities, of course, are not 'naturally' deficient. Our policy text proposes new norms of social relations that will promote equitable practices in mathematics. It presents a proposal for more equitable practices through a curriculum aimed at critiquing and transforming existing educational organisation. The desire for equitable practice is persuasive because it promises the antithesis of all that is undesirable for girls in current educational relations in school mathematics. It is also compelling in that it offers the potential for imagining and building more productive pedagogical relationships. Motivated towards this vision the curriculum document reveals a resolution to emancipate girls, by shaping, and controlling educational experiences in order that they might achieve at the same levels as males.

However, in another sense, the deficit logic, and the intervention it engenders, are themselves regimes of truth in that they *regulate* gender identity, whilst simultaneously claiming emancipation. For our purposes this suggests that the practices that the official document proposes, in fact, institute social processes of regulation and control. Through the curriculum statement, categories of difference and gendered self-other identifications are named and established. Viewed from the vantage point of critical discourse analysis, the policy document provides evidence of particular disciplining practices that shape notions of difference through the way it makes distinctions. It anticipates and encourages the proliferation of the notion of girls' general mathematical inability, by *presuming* girls' inferiority, despite evidence from numerous researchers that girls' achievements now appear to either equal or surpass those of boys.

An interventional strategy for gender and race

> In many cases in the past, students have failed to reach their potential because they have not seen the applicability of mathematics to their lives and because they were not encouraged to connect new mathematical concepts and skills to experiences, knowledge, and skills which they already had. This has been particularly true for many girls, and for many Maori students, for whom the contexts in which mathematics was presented were irrelevant and inappropriate. These students have developed deeply entrenched negative attitudes towards mathematics as a result.
>
> An awareness of these issues has led to improved access for girls to mathematics, but the participation rate of female students in mathematics continues to be lower than that of male students at senior school level and beyond. This limits later opportunities for girls and women (p.12).

The text argues for a pedagogical strategy that will assist in teaching girls and Maori students school mathematics. The strategy is to begin with distinctly female or Maori 'interests' or 'strengths', principally because these students' interests have been subordinated, separated or devalued. The text establishes a benchmark for what will count as 'doing mathematics' for girls and Maori students. It will require that the teacher reads reflexively from the student's world to mathematics, grounding mathematical understanding in its unique application. In essence, students' ways of being in the world are connected in classroom practice with mathematical knowledge. The power/knowledge relationship authorised here is not just between the student and the institution of school mathematics; it is also between the parties within the pedagogical relation—the teacher and the learner.

These efforts parallel wider attempts to 'find a voice' for particular students in school mathematics. In these efforts, reconstructing relations is understood as providing both a place and power to speak. This is because a speaking position for the learner could be seen as a way of creating and fashioning meaning, asserting standpoints, negotiating with others, and establishing convictions and solving problems in everyday life. However the issue of speaking on behalf of particular students is not a simple matter. Highlighting the experience of particular groups has the effect of failing to recognise contradictory realities in everyday school life. The fact is that each student's knowledge is constantly negotiated through interactions with others. Girls' experiences of mathematics are never universal. Neither are the experiences of Maori students. Describing their experiences as singular does not give grounds for making claims about the production of knowledge. But if those experiences are to be taken as singular, the power of significant others within the classroom to legitimate and sustain those experiences becomes central to an understanding of the knowledges of the minds of girls and Maori students.

The issue of development

For the learner, a grid of performance marks out the activities that will constitute mathematics. In this our final section of our analysis the focus will be on 'number' for 'level 2'. We could have taken any level and any particular aspect of mathematics specified in the text. All would have conveyed the same messages. In our chosen level, five achievement objectives are identified and these require the student to enact a particular activity (e.g., 'read', 'explain', 'order', 'write', and 'solve'). Modal auxiliaries are offered as 'suggested learning experiences', 'sample assessment activities' and a 'sample development band', and these all acknowledge localised teacher decision making for particular student cohorts. There is an implicit belief that effective learning of number is conditional on and "depends on a prior understanding of other ideas" (p. 16).

Number Level 2 (p. 36-37)

Achievement Objectives:

Exploring number
Within a range of meaningful contexts, students should be able to:
- read any 3-digit whole number;
- explain the meaning of the digits in 2- or 3-digit whole numbers;
- order any set of three or more whole numbers (up to 99);
- write and solve comparison problems;
- write and solve story problems which involve halves, quarters, thirds, and fifths.

Suggested Learning Experiences

Exploring number
Students should be:
- developing a number sense by exploring number in the context of their everyday experiences and the world around them;
- counting, recording, ordering, and comparing numbers;
- investigating number patterns with and without the aid of a calculator;
- exploring the number system from 0 to 1000 and beyond, using a calculator, structured materials, money, and measurement;

* exploring place value by using grouped discrete objects, structured materials, measurement, money, and a calculator, and by counting in Maori;
* exploring the place of number within their own cultures;
* investigating odd and even numbers;
* investigating ways (including using a calculator) to rename numbers. For example:

10 = 6 + 4	53 = 50 + 3	167 = 100 + 67
= 2 + 2 + 2 + 2 + 2	= 40 + 13	= 100 + 60 + 7
= 1 + 2 + 3 + 4, etc	= 33 + 15 + 5, etc	= 150 + 17, etc

This set of achievement objectives is listed as the requisite competence for learners at level 2, one of eight loosely-defined stages, outlined within a system that sets up a loose correspondence between years of schooling and mathematical content and experiences. This text lists discrete sub-skills, which, reassembled, are understood as knowledge that carries specific educational value, and by implication, it is knowledge that is beneficial both to the individual and to society at large. A chart on page 17 clarifies that the mathematical content, above, is designated for New Zealand learners who will represent for the most part an age cohort of 8-9 years.

The question relevant to this information is: Can age levels be equated to levels of mathematical experience? Psychology sought to pin down a solution in the form of a scientifically validated enterprise. Let me explain: developmental psychology made use of a model of nature derived from evolutionary biology. It incorporated into this model certain aspects of early educational work to construct and legitimise a disciplinary regime of truth about natural stage-wise progression of knowing. And this is exactly what the text does. It harnesses age to knowing, based upon some truth. By explicitly setting out categories of stages to describe, with particular accuracy, how things happen, the text implicitly endorses the view that development means natural stage-wise progression. But the notion tends to lose its persuasiveness when we realise that the notion is argued by a circular logic of a presumed sequence of development.

Hierarchical notions like development have come under attack from a number of quarters. Valerie Walkerdine is one critic who has written extensively on the issue. After a lot of research and careful thinking she argued that 'development' would be better read as the *effect* of policies and regulations, rather than a *justification* and a *validation* for them. The problem for learners, from this interpretation, is that if it is true that development is an effect of policy, then relations that link knowledge with power are part and parcel of its practices. The hard reality is that it is through these power-knowledge relations that the learner becomes a 'subject'. It seems widely controversial to say it, but once we view development in this way, then we have to admit to the fact that the mathematical development of the learner is not 'natural.' The learner's development is merely a *production* which has to be understood in relation to its historical formation and the effects it achieves. This is a different kind of thinking and probably not the way you have thought about the concept of development in the past. It certainly gives us food for thought.

From what we have discussed so far, it follows that development, as classified in the text, produces a set of empirically verifiable facts of progress in school mathematics. Those activities, behaviours, and actions which comply with the text's categories for the learner, are read as normal development, and hence are sanctioned. Those activities, behaviours, and actions that lie outside the practices are obviously not. They are denigrated. The important thing is that any cognitive development that a learner experiences will take on a meaning only when it is related to the categories that the text has highlighted. Once a student's 'natural' ability is calibrated in small bites, according to the categories of the text, then this paves the way for a student to become classified as, for example, a fast, average, or slow learner. From what appear to us as impartial criteria, the learner comes to understand the truth of her or his 'natural' mathematical ability. The fact that the truth of mathematical ability happens to be an apparatus of observation, surveillance, and regulation is totally obscured.

You may well have guessed from all this that working with Foucault leads us to understand cognition as an effect of a specific regime of truth. This is important because once we think about cognition in this vein, then we can no longer think of the learner as the origin of all meaning. In Foucault's terms, the learner is a *fiction,* generated by the structural rules that govern discursive formation, regulating all thought and speech. It makes little sense, then, to speak of the search for a 'deeper' understanding of mathematics, as if we could strip away layers and draw out 'true' knowledge and understanding. And that's because certain regulatory social practices are central to the very formation of the learner's subjectivity. The practices of our policy text are no exemption.

In the following transcript taken from a secondary school student's interview, we can get a sense of what is meant by 'the learner is a fiction'. Amanda, our senior secondary school learner, is created by rules, constraining what is possible to do, think and act in the classroom.

> During the lesson I usually listen and when [the teacher] is finished, I write everything down that she's done. Otherwise I'm writing and listening at the same time and it's sort of..., it's not really..., I don't really understand it totally.
>
> [I] just watch. Like, if she's writing while she's explaining, I watch what she's doing. I write it down.
>
> And when you're by yourself, just go through it again. Don't just copy it straight down; just take your time writing it. Sometimes it might mean that you're behind someone else who has been busy writing it down as the teacher has been talking. But that doesn't matter.

From the perspective of discourse analysis, Amanda provides a commentary on a common event in the secondary school mathematics classroom. She tells us how mathematics is done. She orchestrates a relationship between mathematics and the student in which the learner is to 'watch', then 'write it down' and later 'go through it again'. Lines 1-7 set out that logic. In this logic, the learner moves reflexively from the teacher's talk to the writing and back to the remembered talk, and interpretation is grounded through the process of writing. In this way, teacher talk, the learner, and mathematical knowledge are linked. But Amanda's account is not simply about her own practice: it also anticipates and responds to a hypothetical contrary argument made explicit in Line 9: 'Sometimes it might mean that you're behind someone else...' The payoff for Amanda comes from her statement 'But that doesn't matter'.

Developing this analysis further, in Line 1 Amanda outlines the subject position taken by introducing the first person pronoun 'I'. A shift occurs in Lines 5-7 from 'I' to 'you', and in doing this she transfers from a personalised account to her construction of a more general learning position. The implied imperative 'you' in 'don't just copy it straight down; just take your time writing it' positions her with a sense of authority, identifying, focusing on, and providing answers to the question of learning. These shifts mark out and position the implied 'other students', in cahoots with her personal 'watch then act' approach. It's plain to see that within Amanda's talk is an implicit understanding of how to conduct pedagogical relations. In effect, her narrative is constructing an identity and a set of institutional and social relations for the learner in her classroom. She establishes benchmarks for what counts as 'doing mathematics' and 'being a learner' from a particular vantage point. Drawing on Foucault's thought, 'doing mathematics' is constrained and enabled by the conceptual and material limits of possible learner subject positions and textual practices available within this particular classroom community.

CONCLUSION

Discourse analysis is a powerful bottom-up approach for getting to the heart of what texts—both spoken and written—produce for the people they target. It's a way of demonstrating how curriculum texts create knowledge about schooling and create knowledge about forms of social organisation. When we stop to think of policy texts in this way, it becomes easy to see that it teaches us powerful lessons about what comes to count as curriculum. It also becomes easy to see how specific categories and versions of the student are developed and established so that students learn how to recognise, represent, and 'be' a learner in the classroom. For specific moments of time, it helps us identify and understand the underlying values that shape what appear to be commonsense understandings of the learner. Of course, let's not forget that these positions change over time. As new policies replace old ones, new versions of the learner and curriculum become available.

This kind of interrogation is useful in that it demonstrates the historical contingency of learners in school subject areas. And it also demonstrates the enormous authority and control wielded by policy documents, in the way that they order, measure, categorise, normalise, and regulate people, processes, and knowledge. The place of the power of official policy documents then becomes very important to our understanding of learners' subjectivity. Happily, for us, if analysing discourse reveals power, it also reveals potential. It happens that discourse analysis is an important tool for initiating change. That is because it opens our eyes to other possibilities so that we can create more equitable forms of organisation, and more expansive ways of thinking and acting.

ACTIVITY

For the following two texts:

1. Identify the general concepts that organise the specific positions taken within the text.
2. Explain what terms are used to expand on these concepts.
3. Describe the pedagogical practices that are legitimised in this discourse.
4. Explain the subject position(s) made available to learners in the text. Pay attention to:
   (a) Any patterns of difference constructed for the subject position.
   (b) Any emotional meanings that those differences might convey for the learner.
5. Consider the possible effects on who can speak and be listened to within the text by identifying any power relations that are established between different discourses.
6. Consider what investments policy makers might have in differentiating learners.

- Practitioners must ensure that the individual needs of all children are met, including additional or different provision required to meet particular individual needs.
- Parents, carers and families are central to the well-being of the child. Practitioners must therefore build positive relationships with parents or carers in order to work effectively with them and their children. Young children are vulnerable and learn to be independent by having someone they can depend upon. Providers must ensure that each child has a key person within the setting.
- No child should be excluded or disadvantaged because of ethnicity, culture or religion, home language, family background, SEN, disability, gender or ability. Providers must actively plan to meet their needs, and to promote equality of opportunity and anti-discriminatory practice.
- Schedules, routines and activities must flow with the child's needs, with practitioners planning for individual children using sensitive observational assessment. There must be no tests for children at any stage within the EYFS.
- Children learn by doing, rather than by being told. Learning is a shared process and children learn best when, with the support of a knowledgeable and trusted adult, they are actively involved and interested. Practitioners must therefore ensure a balance of adult-led and freely chosen or child-initiated activities, to be delivered through indoor and outdoor play. In order to deliver the maximum impact on children's development, high-quality care, development and learning must work together.
- Providers must be proactive in developing effective partnerships not only with parents, but with other carers, settings and practitioners important to the child. The experience of the child must be coherent and coordinated. This is particularly important for children who attend more than one setting.
- Practitioners must plan activities on the basis of children's developmental progress and interests so that they work towards the Early Learning Goals. In the final year of the EYFS, practitioners must record progress towards the goals and complete the Foundation Stage Profile.
- Practitioners must report children's achievements at the end of the stage to their parents or carers.

Early Learning Goals and National Curriculum levels at Key Stages 1 & 2. Primary National Strategy, Department for Education and Employment (DfEE). England.

All students, regardless of their personal characteristics, backgrounds, or physical challenges, must have opportunities to study and support to learn mathematics. This does not mean that every student should be treated the same. But all students need access each year they are in school to a coherent, challenging mathematics curriculum that is taught by competent and well-supported mathematics teachers.

Too many students—especially students who are poor, not native speakers of English, disabled, female, or members of minority groups – are victims of low expectations in mathematics. For example, tracking has consistently consigned disadvantaged groups of students to mathematics classes that concentrate on remediation or do not offer significant mathematical substance. The Equity Principle demands that high expectations for mathematics learning be communicated in words and deeds to all students.

Some students may need more than an ambitious curriculum and excellent teaching to meet high expectations. Students who are having difficulty may benefit from such resources as after-school programs, peer mentoring, or cross-age tutoring. Students with special learning needs in mathematics should be supported by both their classroom teachers and special education staff.

Likewise, students with special interests or exceptional talent in mathematics may need enrichment programs or additional resources to keep them challenged and engaged. The talent and interest of these students must be nurtured so that they have the opportunity and guidance to excel in mathematics.

Principles and Standards for School Mathematics, 2000.
National Council of Teachers of Mathematics (NCTM)

CHAPTER 4

THE SUBJECTIVITY OF THE LEARNER

IN THIS CHAPTER

- Subjectivity as constituted in discourses
- Power
- Knowledge
- Donna's performance

All of us have been school learners at some stage of our lives. Some of us have even appeared in classrooms as teachers. It wouldn't take much for us to come up with examples of classroom experiences where students think and act differently from teachers. Why do they? Is it because teachers are more intelligent than students? Is it because students take on a subordinate role and teachers hold an authoritative position in the classroom? What is it that makes people behave in the way that they do? It would be helpful if we could discover what makes people tick. It would be helpful if we could learn about subjectivity.

We already know something about subjectivity. We found out from the preceding chapter that subject positions are set out for learners and teachers within curriculum policy texts. We can learn a lot from analysing such texts. We all know, however, that, despite their authoritative lines, curriculum policy texts tend to be adapted and transformed by those for whom they are written. Why does that happen? It happens because policy texts are simply one of many discourses that attempt to define learners. Policy texts cannot determine, in any final sense, how curriculum statements will enter into the lives of particular learners. Defining actual learners is an adventure into subjectivity that takes us into the realm of everyday life in the classroom. It is an exploration of the discourses that make themselves available to learners.

DISCUSSION QUESTIONS

1. Download three articles published by three different education journals during the past year. The articles should investigate classroom life.
2. Identify the methodological tools that the authors of each article employ to investigate classroom life.
3. What additional data, if any, would you expect you would need to gather, in order to analyse classroom life in each article using Foucault's concept of discourse?

SUBJECTIVITY AS CONSTITUTED IN DISCOURSES

Students are caught up within discursive practices within the classroom, just as much as they are in their everyday activities. The thing about discursive practices is that they envelop us in every aspect of our life. From the way we decorate our homes to the way we dress and walk down the street, we are operating according to 'rules' that 'speak' to us about specific ways of doing things. We wouldn't necessarily dress the same this year as we did twenty years ago. Nor would we necessarily appear the same today as we did yesterday or tomorrow. It's not so much 'feelings' that make us appear different, as the discourses that are at play that made us feel differently at different times. But then that's the thing about discourses—they act upon us differently from one time to the next. In Foucauldian language discourses operate in a way that reveals the historical contingency of the subject positions made available to us.

The subject positions that discourses make available to students in the classroom are no exemption. Like all other practices, classroom practices operate with methods that govern, regulate and discipline people according to a set of unwritten and often unarticulated rules. These unvoiced rules descend from groups of statements, such as we noted in the policy text. We noted how some statements differed slightly in substance. There even seemed be one or two contradictory claims. But even so, the curriculum policy text, as far as its position on the learner went, had a certain sense of coherence about it. And it carried a certain authority. We might imagine that because of its authority the policy text represents the one true statement about learners. This is a necessary deceit to get us to think in these terms. In reality, there are other discursive formations which take noticeably different 'perspectives' from the policy text. To be sure, some of these will have some crossovers with the policy text. Yet others will have a completely different 'take'.

The reason that it is important to extend our investigation into the learner beyond the subject position established in a policy text is that a wide range of discursive formations have something important to say about the learner. These discourses are mostly unofficial. Whatever their stand, they all compete for the learner's attention in a way that we can't fully imagine. That leads us to think of the learner as a product of discursive practice. This idea is tremendously important because it signals a fluid, rather than fixed, subjectivity, as a result of the operation of strands of power. It's a way of conceptualising people that is quite different from functionalist accounts that would have us think of people as adapting to social norms. One of the effects of paying attention to the idea of learners as intimately connected to discursive practice, is that it leads is to think of power. But unlike traditional thinking of power in the classroom as simply that between teacher and student, in putting Foucault to use, we will be thinking of power involving everyone from all sides.

Just as our exploration into the policy text examined truth through discursive practices, so too will we do so here. But the difference is that this time, in turning our gaze on the classroom, we will be accounting for power struggles between discursive formations. Taking power into account means that we will need to look carefully at power and its relationship to knowledge, and putting Foucault to use allows us to focus on the *effects* of power. The second point to remember is that everyone in the classroom participates in a social web of power that allows him or her to develop as a learner (or a teacher). Let's imagine then, power knitting the social fabric of classroom learning together and regulating its practices. With that image, we are in a position to explore how learners negotiate contestation and conflict in their self- and world-concepts and how they attempt to solve these dilemmas through language. This kind of analysis will help us understand the defining effects of classroom life. Before we undertake such an analysis it will be wise to revisit the concept of power.

POWER

Foucault, you will recall, is more indelibly remembered for his analysis of power. His abiding conviction was that power and knowledge are intimately connected. It was a brave idea and what made it all the more striking was that it completely put paid to conventional ideas. This was the first time that someone had come up with a formulation that did not have anything in common with typically mechanistic understandings that have been handed down to us since the 17th and 18th centuries. Once you understand Foucault's philosophy of power you quickly get an appreciation of how it breaks with, for example, the Marxist version that conceived of power as existing in macro-structures such as the state, and working through institutions like the legal system and education. In the Marxist version, power is top-down, and its specific purpose is to control populations of people.

As far as Foucault is concerned, this view of power is inherently flawed. His alternative view brings to the fore the everyday minute operations of power. It also highlights power's diffusiveness. These two aspects, of course, make us aware of other tendencies within his approach such as the fact that this bottom-up analysis stretches from the micro-levels of social life to the widespread global nature of power and domination. Whereas convention would have us think that by challenging power at its highest levels we could wipe it out, Foucault maintained that power is exercised within the social body, not from above it. He believes that changing any aspect of the field of power doesn't make the slightest difference to its existence. And the reason is simply because power operates through networks and alliances in a pervasive, ever-mobile manner.

What it comes down to, is that power relations are an integral part of our personal and public lives. Always in tension, they are exactly the stuff that knits us all together. Let's not get ourselves bogged down in philosophical discussion. Instead, imagine for the purposes of edification, that in the classroom, power operates like the light on the classroom ceiling, shining on all the classroom participants and their daily practices. Even in a classroom environment that provides equitable and inclusive pedagogical arrangements, surprisingly, power shines through the classroom social structure. It operates not only at the macro-level of the school but also within lower levels of practice such as within teacher/student relations and school/teacher relations. In fact power invades cultures and all social structures. It "reaches into the very grain of individuals" (Foucault, 1980, p. 39).

Power is everywhere, through and through. In the whole of the history of educational research, very few studies have assumed that power operates in anything more than in the conventional 'political' sense. Most analyses with a political bent track power operating in macro structures. They conceive of power as an entity being used for political purposes, such as in curriculum development, or in the construction of mathematics textbooks. With Foucault's theories it became possible to construct plausible explanations for how power operates even at the mundane and routine levels of everyday life. Yet observations aren't likely to show up power operating through single one-dimensional arrangements. Instead, it would show power in networks that shift continually in a very unstable fashion, changing as alliances are formed and reformed. Here's what Foucault had to say about all this. He says that power appears in:

> the multiplicity of force relations immanent in the sphere in which they operate and which constitute their own organisation; as the process which, through ceaseless struggles and confrontations, transforms, strengthens or reverses them; as the support which these force relations find in one another, thus forming a chain or a system, or on the contrary, the disjunctions and contradictions which isolate them one from another; and lastly, as the strategies in which they take effect, whose general design or institutional crystallisation is embodied in the state apparatus, in the formulation of the law, in the various social hegemonies.
>
> (Foucault, 1984, p. 92)

The point that Foucault is trying to get across is that, if we had a mind to do it, we could observe power operating throughout society, not upon actual things from the outside, but within chains or systems, that are linked in one way or another. So we can't say that power is found in this discourse, but not in that. It is everywhere, running along the same, similar, or different tracks. If we paid serious attention to the way power operated, we would notice that the links connecting the chains together tighten or loosen their hold over time. Rather like the tide that ebbs and flows, so, too, does power change its grip on the system within which it operates.

The idea that power invades all societal processes is, incidentally, almost always presented in contemporary discussions, such as within the media, as a very recent one, but in fact it owes a large debt to Foucault. The only recent thing about it is the attention that people are beginning to pay to it. The reason that it is so appealing is that, rather than highlighting the negative aspects of power, the idea brings huge potential for people within society. Let me explain. In our sea analogy, the turn of tide allows us to drift into shore on an incoming tide. Swimmers and surfers, for example, invariably take advantage of its shift. In much the same way we can take advantage of power. We can take advantage of the points of resistance that open up, as a result of changes in the grip within the system. So let's not forget the positive potential of power.

ACTIVITY

Write short notes on the following key points about power.

- Power operates within the social realm, not from above it.
- Power works bottom-up throughout the social body in every practice.
- Power is integral to our personal and public lives.
- Power is productive and not simply repressive.
- Power is local in application but more widespread in effect.
- Power relations are not binary but multiple in form.
- Power does not create a division between dominator and dominated.
- Power circulates through networks and alliances.
- Power operates in a mobile fashion.
- Power opens up points of resistances.

KNOWLEDGE

If you had to select one aspect of power's potential, you could scarcely go beyond the fact that power is tied up with knowledge. In fact the link between the two is so strong that power and knowledge are inseparable. Foucault's explanation of the power-knowledge relation is so insightful, yet so unexpected, that a lot of people find it difficult to figure out what is the more startling—the explanation or the sheer thinking that went on to dream it up. Never mind all that, the fact is that we would be in good company if we agreed that the power-knowledge relation is Foucault's greatest contribution to human knowledge.

What is so incredible about the power-knowledge relation is that it goes against the grain of normal thinking of power. We tend to think that power corrupts truth and that if only we could eliminate the influence of power we could get to the bottom of truth. We could 'know' the truth. And what we conjure up when we speak of knowledge or truth, are facts or figures. These are important of course, and Foucault doesn't deny their existence; nor does he deny that power can be repressive. But his focus was on the productive aspects of power and his scope was broader and included everyday knowledge. In the normal course of events, we don't think of power as implicated within day to day practices. We don't think of power as regulating what appears obvious. We don't think of power as providing us with knowledge about ourselves, about others, or about social practices. But that's precisely the mind-shift we need to make in order to comprehend the power-knowledge relation.

Try thinking about the relation as a pair of Siamese twins. Such is their dependency on each other, that it isn't possible, in the final analysis, to separate one from the other. To talk about power is to talk about knowledge, and to talk about knowledge is to talk about power. You can't have one without the other. So we can't underestimate the way power is implicated in everything we understand to be true. Interestingly, this takes us back to discursive practices because discursive practices are what set limits on what we can possibly know. Now that we have come full circle, we can begin to appreciate that when we know, understand, or make sense of something, we cannot think of our knowledge as god-given. We have to think of our knowledge as constrained by discourses that govern our sense making. And the knowledge includes the knowledge we have of ourselves.

If what we know turns out to be a function of power, then it would be helpful to understand its modes of operation. In the classroom, just as in any other social institution, power is diffuse and dynamic, constantly changing in relation to the people located within its walls. Everyone in the classroom participates in a social web of power. Put bluntly, power is the essence of classroom life. Power knits the social fabric of the classroom and structures its pedagogical practices. The discourses relating to a specific classroom take into account the classroom's routines, its material and technological forms, its pedagogical practices, as well as its discourses relating to individual differences with respect to class, gender, competency, and a range of other social determinations. The influence of these discourses is felt on everyone in the classroom. They contribute to the development of school knowledge in unique ways.

We are going to attempt to understand power's operation in the classroom by examining negotiations that take place amongst classroom participants. Put another way, our focus will be on intersubjective relations and the discourses that make them possible. Our observations will be widely cast and will include the personal, psychic, and emotional investments that learners have in particular discursive practices. We won't overlook struggles between competing discourses. All these create spaces for a range of responses, reactions, and possible creative inventions from the learner. But the exercise of power makes certain responses more likely. From our investigation we will be able to draw some conclusions about the subjectivity of learners and their multiple layers of engagement in classroom settings.

Just to remind you, in Foucauldian research, learners are the product of the discourses and practices through which they become subjected. What it comes down to is that subjectivity is produced and reproduced from the practices and discourses that have competed for learners either in the past or currently. As a consequence the truth about learners is intimately connected to discursive practice and the political struggles involving the personal, psychic, and emotional investments that the learner has in these practices. Agency for learners is not about their forceful posturing in the classroom but rather about an awareness of the discursive restrictions and enablements made on them about what it means to be a learner.

DONNA'S MATHEMATICAL PERFORMANCE

In this section, we are going to describe and analyse particular classroom practices in which mathematics enters as a relational practice for one girl whom we shall name as Donna. In the process we will take care not to elevate or devalue her experience. Instead, what we will do is try to understand her mathematical experience as positioned within relations of power. Once we think of experience in those terms, it will be possible to observe the classroom discourses and practices that attempt to claim her attention. What will become clear is the way she is caught up within those discourses and practices and how she endeavours to resist them, positioned as she is as, at one time powerful and at one time subordinate in the classroom.

Along with her classmates, Donna is studying calculus for the first time in her coeducational Year 12 class. For the duration of my time in this classroom, I made continuous audiotape recordings of the teacher's talk to the whole class and Donna's talk—her clearly audible, public conversations with the teacher; her barely audible, private exchanges with a classmate who will be known to us as Brett (who always sat next to her in class); and her whispers and mumblings to herself. In analysing the transcripts, I tried to trace how Donna is constituted within discursive practices and to track the constant refashioning of her identity and investments in mathematics, as she lived and rearranged them in her talk.

"If You Minus in the Negatives You'll Get Further Back"

In the classroom, mathematics is a social performance in which what comes to count as mathematics is the school's and the teacher's interpretation of the official curriculum. How one does mathematics—in this case 'differentiation' in the calculus class—is related in some important ways to the more general regulatory systems of curriculum control. In this relationship, the authority of the teacher and the subordination of the students both tie into wider hierarchical systems. The following excerpt exemplifies how what counts as differentiation is constructed by the teacher with definitive moves, actions, and statements. She is differentiating $y = 2/\sqrt{x}$

> Teacher: We'll do y is equal to one over square root of x. I mean, two over the square root of x. That's the same as two over x to the half. You did this earlier in the year in exponents work and we write that as two x to the negative half. It must be on the top line before we can start differentiating. Now we apply the rule so all we've done is to get it into a form in which we can differentiate. Get it into what we call a power form. Two times negative a half is negative one and this is x to the power negative three over two. Negative one and a half. Negative three over two. Right-oh. So we've got here minus x to the negative three over two. Or we can write that as being minus one over x to the power three over two in the bottom. And if we put it back into surd form, that's negative one over the square root of x all cubed, x cubed. That's another way of writing it.

Differentiating rational functions containing surds (that is, containing irrational roots) requires that students first apply the rules of exponents. These rules exclude the possibility of leaving the variable in the denominator; the variable must be brought up to the numerator before the process of polynomial differentiation can begin. After the rules of differentiation have been applied, the function is returned to its original form, using the rules of exponents. The mathematical logic assembled within the teacher's discursive strategies reads as follows: Rational functions with surds → exponents → polynomial differentiation rule → exponents. This chain presents a set of claims about how differentiation should be carried out. For this class, a set of specific and ordered mathematical practices constitutes the very subjectivity of the student in this classroom. That is to say that the subject position of differentiating rational functions is made available to the student through the teacher's specific discursive practice. The student's subjective experience is located within that particular discourse.

The classroom is a relatively autonomous unit that has its own logic and specific history. Yet, at the same time, it has been "invested and annexed" by more "global [mechanisms of] domination" (Foucault, 1980, p. 99). Classroom practice is simultaneously autonomous and regulated. To understand what that might mean for students' mathematical practices, it is helpful to think of the students' take up of how to do mathematics, as offered through the teacher's discursive strategy, as relational. It is natural to think that the way in which students do mathematics is always determined, situated, and constrained. But we need to keep in mind, too, that students are not passive entities within an externally imposed system. Although a dependency is established between structure and agency, this relationship is dynamic in the sense that both teacher and students can attempt to modify and change it.

Students make sense of what mathematics is made explicit to them by attending to a range of signifiers. Classroom convention, language, rhetoric, power, and history all work through students' interpretations of mathematics in ways that neither the curriculum writers, nor the teacher, nor even the students themselves, can fully control. Donna's classroom was maintained with care and pride, organised in the manner of tradition in mathematics classrooms, with pairs of desks in rows. Mathematics posters, daily notices of the school, and a small number of large travel postcards adorned its walls. These features in the room were part of a much larger ensemble of apparatuses regulating not only ways of behaving, but also ways of thinking. Foucault (1977) wrote of the way in which the emergence of "disciplinary power" haunts the school. He says:

> A certain significant generality moved between the least irregularity and the greatest crime: It was no longer the offence, the attack on the common interest, it was the departure from the norm, the anomaly; it was this that haunted the school.
>
> (Foucault, 1977, p. 299).

When I entered the classroom for the first time as a researcher, I was taken by surprise at the sense of being immediately transported back into the student life-world in the classroom. What I felt then was precisely what I had felt from so many years of multiple layers of knowing: the classroom size, its high windows, its whiteboard (once a chalkboard) and teacher's desk up the front, the rows of desks, the smells, the cupboards and bookcases. These were brought out of storage in the unconsciousness mind to point to a familiar pattern of classroom cultural logic, routine and action. What was more obvious to me now, however, and what, as a student, I had never been able to articulate, was the pervasiveness of power: the way in which it "reaches into the very grain of individuals, touches their bodies and inserts itself into their action and attitudes, their discourse, learning processes and everyday [classroom] lives" (Foucault, 1980, p. 39).

The effects of power within the classroom on Donna are more subtle so that she takes for granted the rows of desks, the mathematics exercise work book in which she, like all the students, draws a red line down the middle before she proceeds with her work down one column, then the other. She fails to notice, as anything but usual for this classroom, the 20 or so minute teacher exposition at the whiteboard, in which students write frantically before she wipes her work off, and which is followed by a much longer interval during which students work at set examples. Nevertheless, certain issues of power and regulation confront Donna.

> Slow down! [laughs] Yea. Sort of rush, rush, rush, really. Sort of, you write down whatever's on the board but taking it in is a different story. You've really got to go home and do some exercises at home and work through it yourself. For me, anyway, to actually understand it, because this, you don't have time to do the exercises before she's rushing you onto something else. And if she's like, well, I've got a short attention span and it makes it even harder.

Donna's subjectivity is not constituted solely as the object of regulatory practice. Her subjectivity, like that of others, is created in a number of practices, and these are often competing, offering different opportunities and possibilities. The following four passages give us some indication of the varying discourses, social relations, practices, and student subjectivities that are possible within the genre of the mathematics class. The first is a discussion between Donna and her classmate Brett on the derivative of $y = 1/x^3$. After a brief exclamation at Brett's audacity in trying to copy, the discussion revolves around finding the solution to the mathematical problem.

Brett: Can you move your book so I can copy?
Donna: *[Laughs in disbelief]* AH, EXCUSE ME! You shouldn't be copying!
Brett: *[Checking answers]* Negative four over three?
Donna: Yep!
Brett: How?
Donna: Because that's a three, that's also negative three, which is three over three. So just imagine that as negative one over three and minus three over three, which equals four over three.
Brett: One minus three is only two.
Donna: OK. Do it on the calculator, It's NEGATIVE, because, OK, a third negative minus three over three equals one and a third, which is four over three.
Brett: Why?
Donna: Because it's, it's, think of a, um, a time line. You are already in the negatives, and if you MINUS in the NEGATIVES, you'll get further back.

In the second excerpt, the teacher has been differentiating $y = \sqrt{x^5}$ for the class at the whiteboard:

Brett: How does she get to go from five over two to three over two?
Donna: Because you've minused ONE WHOLE, which is TWO OVER TWO. So in other words, you go five over two, minus two over two, equals three over two.

These two passages demonstrate Donna in the role of *subteacher.* She again takes up this position in the following:

Donna: Four minus three's one. And it's the change between the 'x'. That's cool.
[to Brett] You're doing it right.

These excerpts show us that there is a space for student agency. They also speak to us about the position of girls within the mathematics classroom. Walkerdine (1990) has noted that in her research with girls of all ages, *nice, kind,* and *helpful* were the three most common terms used by teachers to describe girls' work within the classroom. Helpfulness, as it relates to Donna's talk above, is linked closely with assisting Brett in carrying out the differentiation process as established by the teacher.

In the following lesson, Donna and Brett are finding the instantaneous rate of change at various points.

Donna: Two point zero one squared. OH! Yeah, minus four. Yeah, that's just the 'y'. Why, yes, you ARE right!
Brett: Of course I'm right. Was there any doubt?
Donna: *[Giggles]* YES! I told...I MADE YOU DOUBT! That is so funny! *[laughs]*

One view of the position of girls taken from the classic studies is that they receive less teacher attention than boys in the classroom. Research carried out in the 1980s reported that girls ask fewer questions than boys, receive less praise, are not called on as frequently, and have their work monitored less frequently by their teachers, and are generally placed through subtle means in a lower hierarchical position than boys. As Walkerdine (1989) has noted, teachers often considered boys as having "potential," whereas girls' achievements are based on "hard work and rule-following" (p. 268). The discourses that have traditionally shaped girls' classroom interactions with their peers have sustained the idea of her as the passive and dependent product of a large-scale patriarchal system. While such accounts have been important for the development of feminist interventionist practices, they do not adequately deal with subjectivity in which relations of power are continually changing.

As we have seen earlier, Foucault (1980) takes issue with the view of power as a possession. If power is not something that is acquired, seized, or shared, then the ways in which power has been construed by existing studies of girls and boys in mathematics classrooms becomes problematic. The power relations that constitute girls as mathematics learners are not simply microcosmic reflections of a more widespread, authoritarian pattern of governance. Rather, every positioning is determined by its own specific set of social forces and power relations. In Foucault's understanding, the girl is able to become both powerful and powerless, depending on the terms in which her subjectivity is constituted. Contrary to claims from traditional research, she has a degree of autonomy and independence in the way she acts, especially in the ordering of her day-to-day classroom existence.

The excerpts taken from Donna's classroom experiences stand in opposition to the idea of one-way subjection. From the excerpts, we can begin to see that while Donna's practices are defined by the classroom and wider social context, by no means is she completely reducible to them. This argues for a more robust understanding of her subjectivity as constituted through practices of subjection and, in a more autonomous way, through practices of liberation. In the above examples, it would have been easy to explain Donna's agency and self-determination in terms of *freedom,* in the form of a recovery of her authentic *natural* self, as some would want us to do. Foucault argues that this essentialist view is too simplistic because it fails to take into account how people actively and continually fashion their existence through the adoption of various and sometimes contradictory practices. A more useful approach is to look at the discourses in action.

Let's briefly examine those discourses in action more closely. In the dialogues above, focusing our attention on turn-taking rights, both Donna and Brett assume equal shares, but it is Donna who controls the direction and duration of the discussion. Clearly, Donna's control has much to do with her access to knowledge of mathematical processes and meanings that are currently denied to Brett. In that respect, her position as a girl in school mathematics has already been redefined for her and allows her to avoid participating in any contestation over power. The discourse within which both Brett and Donna are operating is not about stereotypical arguments of dependent and oppressed girls but rather about mathematical knowledge as a powerful educational and social performance. What is important here, is that the category *female* is not necessarily a less powerful category in school mathematics terms than the category *male.* Its meaning is derived from within the discourse in which it is used. Of course, it will not be the only discourse competing for Donna's attention at any one time. The sort of discourse she prioritises will depend, in part, on the investments that Donna sees within it for herself.

How do we read Donna's talk in the classroom? In listening to the tapes over and over, I became more and more convinced that Donna easily *took up the tools* of the discursive practices of how to *do* mathematics, operating and legitimised within her mathematics classroom. She exercised a form of self-policing by checking her answers against the solutions given in the question-and-answer booklet. Correct answers were sanctioned from within the discourse itself. However, in every lesson, any evidence of Donna's incorrect or uncertain work resulted in her immediate switch of discourses. She took up particular discourses and practices of femininity, organised around notions of lack, inferiority, affect, and unreason. But these instances were possibly momentary slippages and might be better understood as token gestures to cultural definitions of femininity to which Donna herself may not have been fully prepared to submit.

To the public world of the classroom, Donna presented as both hard-working and capable. Her classroom recordings opened up a world that was not visible to me before. It was a world that called attention to unmarked and obscured relational practices and to competing discourses at work. Working with Foucault, it was possible to come to some understanding of how gendered relations are created and sustained within the classroom. Just as gendered subjectivity is person-specific, it is also circumscribed by place and time and the specificity of classroom life. In offering insights about subjectivity the intent has been to produce an account that did not universalise or normalise her position in mathematics. It attempted to demonstrate how Donna lived out contradictions and how they operated in the limited terrain of self-production that was open to her. Inside all of this, I have tried to place an understanding of unconscious meanings and processes and their place as a central organiser in Donna's mathematical work.

CONCLUSION

Our analysis of classroom life has taken a different turn from conventional practice. The best way to describe it is as a mode of *critical* inquiry that examines the way power infuses itself within and operates through the discourses and practices of classroom life. The inquiry allowed us to investigate the methods of regulation operating through discursive practices of the classroom and explore the role that power has in the constitution of subjective experience. We noticed instances of discursive governance taking place, and the effects of teacher, peer- and self-regulatory practices on one student, and how it impinged on her thinking and acting. It was then possible to see how mathematical thinking is produced within discourses and practices, how mathematical knowing is made 'real' to students, and how power infuses the 'reality' of classroom life.

Donna's attempt to construct and negotiate herself as a learner of mathematics within specific discourses encourages us to rethink the notion of an individual girl who has classroom experience and think instead of her in the Foucauldian sense, as constituted through intersubjective (and hence, social) experience. Doing mathematics is a matter of taking up sanctioned subject positions as well as exploring the possibility of other subject positions that are regularly closed to girls. It is in this slippery space, where the regulation and exploration converge, that transformation can occur.

ACTIVITY

Towards the end of the previous chapter we looked at how Amanda described how to do mathematics. We will now return to Amanda. Drawing on the following short transcript from Amanda's interview, use Foucault's understandings of discourse, power, and knowledge, to analyse critically the constitution of Amanda's subjectivity.

I really enjoyed my primary [elementary] school. It was really good. A lot of the maths we did in third form [Year 9] I'd already done in form 1 and 2 [Years 7 and 8], so I was re-doing things but I suppose that was quite good. Revising everything.

I'm a pretty organised person. If my room's messy, it's a tidy mess. I know where everything is, even if it is messy. If it's out of place, it's a tidy out of place.

CHAPTER 5

STUDENTS' IDENTITY AT THE CULTURAL CROSSROADS

IN THIS CHAPTER

- Identity
- Colliding discourses
- Mothers and daughters and low socio-economic status
- Mothers and daughters and high socio-economic status

Most of us who do research in education have an insistent urge to understand what is going on, and, above all, to understand what people are really like. We want to get to the bottom of subjectivity, particularly at the level of the school. But many of us have run up against the sheer complexity of school experiences. Explaining complexity is not that easy. How is it that we seem to know so much about many things in education yet still not be able to predict human behaviour? One moment we seem to 'know' this student or that teacher. Yet, the next moment, something the student or teacher does or says, throws the analysis right off beam. As a case in point, think about an occasion where you felt the pull of different realities and you ended up not fully understanding why you made the decisions you did and the person you became.

Subjectivity, we know, is constituted in discourses. Explaining subjectivity means exploring discursive investments. It happens that some cultural discourses exert a very powerful pull on us. Though they intersect with a whole suite of discourses at the cultural crossroads, all trying to get hold of our attention, some, more than others, bring a powerful dimension to the way we take up our identity. These cultural discourses tell us what kind of things we should do, think, and hope for as a gendered, classed, and raced individual within society. We pay attention to what these discourses tell us because we want to behave appropriately and live our lives so that we fit in with others. Yet they do more than that: without our fully realising it, cultural discourses contribute to our life chances.

ACTIVITY

List down the first thoughts that come into your head about how you 'see' yourself. Now think about yourself in two other contexts and write down what you see as your subjectivity. Compare these other thoughts about yourself with those you had earlier.

IDENTITY

Most of us have asked ourselves at some stage of our lives "Who am I?" The trouble is none of us can adequately answer this kind of question. The reason is that the person you are is constantly changing. As we noted in the previous chapter, our identity has a lot to do with the discourses and practices we find ourselves within. We are all caught up within discursive practices within every aspect of our lives and everyday activities. The identity markers we write about ourselves are influenced by the discourses that operate on us. They make us feel, act and think differently at different times. It's not surprising that the things you listed about yourself in the activity above changed as you associated yourself with specific contexts. While you might want to think of yourself as a person who has 'got it together', the reality is that identity is fragile from one time to the next. It is evanescent. We all take up multiple identities and we do this when different discursive formations are made attractive and available to us.

Of course there are some things about ourselves that we all would like to take for granted—things that we consider stable and unchanging. Take, as an example, our gender. Many believe that gender is a part of our identity that is fixed. After all, we are biologically equipped with particular gendered attributes, and there are no two ways about it. We can't change the way things happen to be. This kind of thinking is called essentialism. The consensus not so long ago was that all of us had a real and fundamental essence. What is extraordinary from Foucault's point of view is how convincing this argument once seemed. Not only that, it is extraordinary how long the argument held sway.

But perhaps we *can* change the way we seem to be. Perhaps we can change our gendered selves. We need only turn to recent medical science to observe how it is possible to change, for example, one's sex, and changing one's sex will influence the way we embody gender. And that makes it easier to understand people as the product of the discourses and practices through which they become subjected. Not so long ago we would have found the notion of a true unchanging gendered self totally convincing. However, essentialist thinking about the permanence of an identity marker like sex is not the kind of thinking that Foucault would support. In putting Foucault to use, the notion of a true self is a fiction. Rather, subjectivity is produced and reproduced from the practices and discourses that have competed for the production of subjectivity either in the past or currently.

What follows from this sort of thinking is that the categories male and female are inherently unstable. To see these categories as neither fixed nor finite is undoubtedly to occupy a very different position in thinking about experience. It would help here to think of gender and any other identity marker, for that matter, as cultural discourses that operate as a way of classifying and distinguishing between characteristics, traits, and attributes. In emphasising differences and similarities between things, an identity marker, like gender, simply provides us with meanings and reference points to understand how to perform gender—both how to think of and how to embody what it means to be female or male.

When we perform gender we are negotiating through a wide range of discursive formations that compete for our attention in a way that is often beyond our comprehension. Or putting it another way, our identity as at the cultural crossroads of discursive practice. Identity is created at the intersection of a multiplicity discourses, always crisscrossing each other. Some of those discourses support and some conflict with others. Supporting discourses lead to a sense of identity that is wholly 'together'. Colliding, contradictory discourses, on the other hand, invite struggles and produce a sense of self that is fractured.

Now, the natural question is just what do we mean by struggles? Exactly how do these discursive practices operate? How do they take hold of someone? The answer is quite simply that these practices operate in a context of power relations. The category that we label as school learner, for example, is a site of constant struggle over power. It seems strange to think of a learner in this way, but there it is. And the way it happens is like this: A range of discourses are made available to the learner. For the discourses, it's a matter of staking a claim on the subjectivity of the learner. Inevitably, it's a matter of competing with other discourses to become attached to the subjectivity of the learner. Of course the learner can respond in various ways and this is what learner agency is all about. A discourse can be resisted either outright or in part by a learner. Alternatively, a particular discourse can win over the learner's affections completely. These struggles over membership to the category learner are happening all the time which is why it is all the more remarkable that learners seem so grounded.

Struggles that vie for the learner's attention are not generally the object of attention in traditional research. Yet there isn't a great deal about learners that researchers can't find out about if they have a mind to, even if it requires using a different set of strategies. What Foucauldian researchers in education do is account for the 'truth' of the learner by looking at how he or she is constituted within practices and discourses. Based on what they know about discourses they explore how discourses systematically constitute versions of the social and natural worlds about what it means to be a classroom learner. The first point to remember is that Foucauldian researchers don't make hard and fast claims and explanations about what the learner is truly like. In fact they could never actually know the truth of the learner. What they do, instead, is show how truth about the learner is provisional, open-ended, and relational. They pay attention to the ways in which meanings that inscribe subjects are made and allowed to make sense.

In the classroom, subjectivities that traffic in conflict tend to involve tangled stories of continual self-reinvention—reinvention that comes from struggles over who one is. Foucault is well aware of the struggles over creating an identity:

> This theme of struggle only really becomes operative if one establishes concretely—in each particular case—who is engaged in struggle, what the struggle is about, and how, where, by what means and according to what rationality it evolves.
>
> (Foucault, 1980, p. 164).

In the following transcript we meet Donna again. In the last chapter we explored how Donna's subjectivity was the product of a range of discourses. Now we are going to examine the ways in which her identity is forged and contested in the classroom. In the short discussion we will observe Donna's identity as it is under construction, and its changeable and sometimes unpredictable status. It needs noting here that we will use the term subjectivity in an effort to convey the fluidity of identity construction. As you read the account, note how the analysis does not slide over the gendered and media-enculturated history she brings with her into the classroom. In your reading, look for the way in which learning emerges through her history.

COLLIDING DISCOURSES

Discourses vie for Donna's position, offering her competing ways of organising and giving meaning to her classroom work. In doing so, they offer her a wide range of subjectivity modes. Some of these discourses validate the status quo; others contest the ideas that are taken for granted and the particular interests that they represent. On some occasions, these competing discourses operate simultaneously. In the four excerpts below, it is difficult to grasp what is going on. One productive approach to explanation is to look at the competing discourses at work:

1.	Donna and Brett are working on finding the derivative of $y = 1/(2x^4)$. Donna has worked out the answer correctly as $y' = -2x^{-5}$
Brett:	How did you get that then?
Donna:	A woman's prerogative! *[giggles]*
Brett:	Seriously, how did you get it?
Donna:	Can't remember. No, I can't. *[giggles]*

2. Donna and Brett are working independently on finding the derived function of $y = 3x^3$. Donna checks the answer as $9x^2$.

Donna: Why is that squared? Oh, I know why! I'm so blonde. No, I'm not. I get it!

[to Brett] Did you get it? Did you do that? Bet you didn't!

Brett: Shouldn't that be a 'three'?

Donna: No, because, I know with those ones there, you've got to bring that down one. So it's nine *x* squared. So I've got it right, now.

3. Donna is working on differentiating $y = 3/(2x^5)$

Teacher: *[to class]* x to the power negative two is one over x squared. Are you all happy about this? If you have one over 'a' to the power negative three, it's the same as *a* cubed. If you have one over *m* to the power...

Donna: *[whispers] x,* five, that's negative, isn't it? And that's negative. Makes that a negative, so that's three over two. So that's negative four. Fifteen over two, *x,* negative four. *[checks answers]* Mmmm? What? Uh? I'm so blonde! Why this, that becomes negative, dumb, dumb, dumb, dumb, dumb, dumb.

4. Donna is working on finding the gradient of the tangent to the curve $y = l/x^3$ at the point (-1, -1).

Donna: *[To teacher close by]* I don't get number eight.

Teacher: Number eight? Right-oh. How do you differentiate that?

Donna: You bring this up to the line.

Teacher: Which of course is *x* to the negative three. So, the derivative is, negative three, *x* to the negative four. *nx* to the minus one. OK? Which is negative three over *x* to the fourth. So the gradient of the tangent, at what point? Negative one, negative one. So negative one is negative three over negative one to the fourth.

Donna: Oh! OK. *[teacher moves away]* How blonde can you get!

There are traces here of what the literature calls "bumping" discourses. They have the effect of confusing meanings and blurring male-female category memberships. What it means for Donna to be female in this classroom depends on the discourse claiming her attention at anyone moment, yet as we can readily see in the above passages those discourses overlap and bump into each other. Donna talks of a "woman's prerogative" and "blonde." These were not the only occasions during the research in which she spoke of being "blonde." We can glean from the sense in which she uses these words that she is reproducing and legitimising certain dominant cultural forms of femininity.

Right from infancy girls as well as boys are immersed in and come to learn the cultural patterns through which dominance and subordination are achieved. Popular culture plays a significant part in shaping their understanding of the world and of themselves, of gender relations and values, and of social power. To that end, cultural and media representations enable learning about gender to take place. Cultural texts operate like what Foucault labels as regimes of truth. By this he means those truths that a society produces and that are taken as "true" in social interaction. One Western cultural discourse of gender played out in the images of television, magazines, and advertising is that of the blonde, yet alluring, female-dumb. The ways in which girls negotiate and experience the messages of cultural texts is crucial to any understanding of their subjectivity.

Cultural discourses are hugely significant in the constitution of our subjectivity and those that sketch out how we might perform gender in our lives are by no means an exemption. The extent to which we enact gender in everyday situations depends to some degree on the discursive and conceptual resources made available in intersubjective encounters. In the following section we explore the part that specific cultural resources play in the technologies of gendered subjectivity. The small group under investigation consists of, first, 2 girls who attended a small low socio-economic state primary [elementary] school that attracts students from an ethnically mixed urban area. Second, under investigation are 2 girls from a small private full fee-paying primary [elementary] school for girls within the same metropolitan catchment.

In the project the girls (aged 8-9) and their parents were interviewed in relation to perspectives on the place of girls in education and in society today. Their interviews provide a glimpse of the women's and girls' self-conscious views of themselves within society. I quote at length from the interview data of the mothers particularly, and use this strategy deliberately to demonstrate how language "constructs the individual's subjectivity in ways which are socially specific" (Weedon, 1987, p. 21) and to reveal how discourses work through words to organise thinking and experience.

MOTHERS AND DAUGHTERS AND LOW SOCIOECONOMIC STATUS

> Sally lives with her mother and three siblings. At nine, she is the oldest child in the family. Her parents have recently separated. Sally was born when her mother was 17 and at that time, planning for a career in nursing. Those plans were cut short with marriage and the responsibilities of bringing up the children, the youngest of whom is now two years of age. To help the family finances Sally's mother took on a caregiving job at the local hospital. She hopes one day to fulfil her original dreams and complete a nursing course which she has just commenced. Although day-time child care for her two pre-schoolers is expensive, she believes that long-term nursing career prospects will help ease the financial burden. She describes her day as *very tiring; getting to bed quite late and up very early. It has to be quite structured and I have to have a routine to follow because once we get out of it, it's chaos.*

> Lisa's family consists of her mother, her mother's unemployed partner, and her older brother. Her father lives in another country and has formed a new relationship and family. Since the time when she had her first child at 19, Lisa's mother says that life for her has *always been about the kids, what's good for them, this, that and the other. I come last.* Now that she has taken a job as teacher aide at the local primary school she has, as she puts it, *the opportunity to do what I want.* That also means that Lisa and her brother help out more with daily household chores. They *do the dishes, hang the washing on the line and vacuum the floors*, all tasks that were familiar to Lisa's mother as a child being raised in a household of 13 children. *Mum couldn't do everything for everyone; we had to pitch in and help.*

What do girls expect of their post-school opportunities? How do mothers read their daughter's relationship with the future? Many people believe that the ultimate wish for any parent is the child's normality. For the mothers whose daughters attend low socio-economic schools, normality is intimately caught up with material and social positioning as well as the practices that work through class disadvantage. In Foucauldian thinking, it is through a range of discourses working through personal experiences and histories, that these mothers have learned what is an acceptable and appropriate career option for their daughters. Underlying these histories and experiences is a deep concern for their daughter's own well-being. Lisa's mother explains the sorts of qualities she hopes her daughter will develop:

> *Overall when she grows into an adult I would like her to be a strong willed person that knows what she wants and how she is going to get there to get it. I'd like her to be independent but also not scared to come back to me if she needs help. If she can do that I'll be happy.*

A strong will and sense of independence are precisely those aspects missing until now from the production of her own subjectivity: *it's always been about the kids...I come last.* For Foucault, her past that lacks independence would be read as closely tied to complex discourses and embodied practices that put others, rather than self, at the centre. Against this reading, is the very powerful cultural discourse that tells us that individuals are of their own making. They are deemed personally responsible for negotiating their own destiny. But for Lisa's mother others get in the way.

According to the thesis of individualisation, individuals pursue self-interests. What the thesis doesn't mention are the psychological costs for working-class women involved in such pursuits. It ignores the deep sense of guilt and inadequacy experienced by these women. And it tends to overlook the hard fact that putting one's self at the forefront has always been deemed a more appropriate pursuit for other groups. Adult life for working-class women is a continual battle to author oneself, because powerful class-based discourses work to constrain the identities that these women desire for themselves. Socio-economic status, for them, is deeply implicated in their gendered subjectivity. Sally's mother has negotiated around family commitments and put those at the forefront. She does not wish this for her daughter. She wants Sally to be *responsible*, to develop a sense of moral righteousness and responsibility, and to apply the self-technologies that regulate them both:

> *I'll support her in anything that she does but I'd like her to always be honest and up-front about things and as long as she's happy I'll always be supportive of her. But I'd like her to get a good education and get every chance she can. I always say that I don't want her ending up doing what I did because I did it the hard way. It's a lot harder doing it now with four children than what it would have been if I had stuck it at 17. So I'm quite on at her about being responsible about things and as she gets older I reinforce that more and more. I just want her to be honest and law abiding and that sort of thing and have good values about family.*

These discourses of appropriate behaviour and social practice regulate Sally's subjectivity. In the Foucauldian interpretation, these discursive practices shape her material and symbolic experience. Sally's mother's words are "shot through with a desire for…respectability" (Walkerdine et al., 2001, p. 45) for her daughter. Historically, Walkerdine et al. note, the concept of respectability, has been "both a marker and a burden of class" (p. 45). It is crucial to the narratives of working class women precisely because 'respectability' is construed around discourses and practices that lie in "the contradictory and often elusive space of 'the middle'" (Walkerdine et al., p. 45). It is within the murky middle that middle-class femininity is defined as the normative ideal and working-class femininity is pathologised. The working-class girl is situated within an uneven playing field and can never get femininity right.

Educational provision in democratic countries is founded upon a level playing field of equitable learning experiences. In these formulations of individualisation, every student has the opportunity to achieve well at school, embrace all the opportunities of modern life, excel in their chosen field, pursue their dreams and realise their full potential as individuals. The student of low socio-economic status, just like the student from a professional or executive family, "must render his or her life meaningful, as if it were the outcome of individual choices made in the furtherance of a biographical project of self-realisation" (Rose, quoted in Walkerdine, 2003, p. 240), irrespective of the constraints encountered. What does this mean for Sally, living within the constraints of working class? She tells me that she wants to be a veterinary scientist.

> *I've wanted to be a vet since I think I was six and like it's my dream job. Even though I sometimes think of other things, I think that being a vet is better. When I was six we were doing animals and once I got to know heaps about animals I kept wanting to learn heaps more. We've got a German Shepherd book because we've got a German Shepherd dog and I've got a huge big cat book that's got all types of cats in it and I can know what type of cats I've got.*

Lisa echoes Sally's ambition. She says, *I've got lots of pets. Six neons which are fish, one catfish and two dogs and one of them has got stitches.* Although neither Sally nor Lisa could offer much detail about the sorts of experiences, competencies and qualifications that would allow them to plan their veterinary vocation strategically, both appeared to believe that their chosen career was achievable and desirable. In the Foucauldian reading, a familial disposition towards animals, the school project that fuels that interest, and Sally's emotional attachments to both of these, make available certain career discourses that, in turn, occasion certain ambitions in Sally. They open spaces for specific work-place preferences. Sally's mother's understands her daughter's ambition in economic, familial and emotional terms.

> *She says that she wants to be a vet, some days, and I just say that if you've got an education you can do whatever you like later on. I tell her not to worry about anything but get an education and the world will open up to you. If you've got a bit more qualifications than someone else, well, you've got much more chance that they're going to take you than someone that hasn't. I want her to concentrate. I'm probably a bit pushy with her to do well at school because I think that it's important.*

For Sally's mother, it is education that will act as a springboard for upward social mobility. Aspirations for higher education that will lead to the professions might be read as a freeing up or an escape from hardship or misfortune. Yet the statistics are stacked against working-class students: low decile students' performance is no match for the higher attainments of all students from high decile schools. "Middle-class students are far more likely than working-class students to experience success at school. Few students from low decile secondary schools enrol in university courses. Five times as many students with higher professional origins obtain a university entrance level bursary or better, than those from low-skilled and nonemployed families" (Nash, 1999, p. 268). Categories of social class form a context for educational success.

Sally's mother makes reference to work-place hierarchies. As an unqualified, and hence low status worker, she articulates some resentment in coming to terms with systems and structures in her work-place. As she says, *people with a nursing degree come along and are higher up but they haven't done half of what we've done and they wouldn't have a clue of some of the things we know*. Education, for Sally's mother, is not a lived experience, nor is it merely a way out of routine and hard working class life. For Sally's mother, education means potential self-realisation. It offers the possibility of transcending her working-class status, as well as the possibility of real work-place power.

Lisa's mother hints at her own lost chances when she talks about Lisa's out-of-school activities. Lisa is, as her mother explains:

> *...a very sporty girl and she's academic. She loves school, and she loves her sport. I would like her to go into sports psychology or physio. She plays just as many sports as I do and she is good at them. As soon as she can take it that step further when she gets older and branch into something like that I think she could do quite well. I think girls have got the opportunities there to do it so take it.*

The processes of material and social disadvantage work in very real ways through the low decile school mothers to inform their hopes for their daughters' future. Whilst their daughters' happiness is crucial in their aspirations, there is a very real hope for a future quite different from the past: *I always say that I don't want her ending up doing what I did because I did it the hard way* (Lisa's mother). Yet the painful costs of becoming something other than working-class are not articulated nor possibly understood. Sally's mother notes: *I think to myself that she will do something really good because she's really bright and I don't want her not to use her gift because she's got the gift of it and she can pick things up really good and expresses herself really well and I think she'll go a long way.*

MOTHERS AND DAUGHTERS AND HIGH SOCIO-ECONOMIC STATUS

Carly lives with her parents and younger brother in a large house in the country. Both parents work in professional positions in a full-time capacity. Carly's mother says, *I work full time and I am a full time mum.* She notes that, compared with her own mother's experiences, she has *been able to have both pieces of the cake. It's a busy life and I'm often running from one thing to the next but that's a choice that we made and a lifestyle choice too because we work hard but we play hard as well.* It's a life that requires careful planning, considerable time and economic resources. She attributes her career advancement to her willingness to retrain which has *allowed me to make choices in different areas within my chosen career.* Sending Carly to an exclusive girls' school has not created any hardship for the family and she would be keen to do the same for their son, if such a school were available.

Jenny's family of two younger brothers and highly educated parents also lives in a large house in a rural location. When the children started to arrive, Jenny's mother made the decision that the demands of regular hours within the workplace, combined with family care and the responsibility of a disabled son, were *too hectic.* She *cast around for other ideas* and settled on a hobby. Jenny was sent to the private school after *she was failing really badly at a state school and we just looked around for alternatives and somewhere that would really help her as an individual because of the small class sizes and because of the number of specialist teachers.* For them, private schooling *comes down to money and education.* However, Jenny's mother believes that *if you desperately wanted to send your children to a private school, you would do it. You would just have to rearrange your life to somehow afford it.*

Both mothers are highly credentialed. They, first and foremost, want their daughters to enjoy the career chosen: *Basically what I want is for her to have an enjoyable career, whether that's hair dressing or rocket science, I don't care. Whatever she does it has to suit her and be fulfilling for her* [Jenny's mother]. *She has conviction and a strength of her own* [Carly's mother]. Is this career indifference merely a veneer? Does it mask a sensibility towards the part that their class status plays in educational success and career choice? The middle-class families in the study reported by Lucey et al. (2003) believed that, whatever career was embarked upon, their daughters would achieve well educationally and become like them "in the sense of having the same kind of career as them, the same levels of income, material comfort and lifestyle" (p. 295). However, "[f]or the working-class daughters of aspirational parents the message is quite different; it is clearly about *not* becoming like them" (p. 295).

Both mothers communicate a sound understanding of the transformed nature of work. In their assessment of the future, *information and technology will be changing even more rapidly than what it is now* [Carly's mother] and jobs for life will no longer be made available. As Jenny's mother sees it, *everybody will be on shorter contracts.*

> *With Jenny, I don't imagine that she'll have one job throughout her life. I'd imagine that she might have two or three or four career changes and I actually think that's quite a healthy thing because I think that helps you grow and develop and learn more and just be a better all-round person. I think that the days of leaving school and getting a job and staying in that job until you retire are gone.*

Within the changed work landscape that they envisage, their daughters will need to develop particular sorts of skills. Carly's mother explains: *I'd prioritise the ability to get along and definitely would be keen to develop skills of competition and doing your best.* Similarly Jenny's mother elaborates: *I do think you will have to be competitive. I think in a way it will be a lot tougher and people won't just automatically get employed and be allowed to cruise along.* For Jenny's mother, developing her daughter's competitive skills is an ongoing task: *Jenny is totally non-competitive so I feel that we have to encourage her to be somewhat competitive or to be competitive with herself so that she improves her performance.*

The necessity of developing skills that will contribute to survival in the workforce is not so forcefully articulated by the low decile school mothers. For both Carly's and Jenny's mother, within a highly competitive environment, it will be important to be *clear and concise and be able to present yourself and your skills well, as well as have good organisational skills. Having confidence in yourself too is quite important* [Jenny's mother]. Moreover, there is a requirement that the worker will be *conscientious and do a good job, otherwise you won't last* [Jenny's mother]. In Carly's mother's estimation, job performance should be matched with practices of self-assessment, *continually evaluating whether you can do better and how to go about doing that.*

The importance of developing skills to deal with the changing labour market is borne out in workforce statistics. Within this changing market women are participating in record numbers. As a case in point, during the past decade leading up to 2002, New Zealand women's participation in the workforce increased in proportional terms, depicting a 33 per cent rise for female employees compared with a 16 per cent increase for males. Despite the important advances women have made within the workforce, however, statistics reveal that occupational segregation between women and men factor into the gender pay gap. Some of those differentiating practices are not unrelated to women's perceived role as primary caregivers. As Jenny's mother says:

> *I think women have two jobs basically. If you've got children, that's a fairly full-time job and if you can fit something else around it that's great. But I think women have to be fairly flexible. There comes a time in your life when you have to re-evaluate and perhaps change directions. I've talked to a lot of my friends, sort of mid-thirties and we've all got young children. A lot of us have reassessed our skills and changed direction.*

In Jenny's mother's perspective, there are traces of discourses that do not sit easily together. The discourses that are claiming her attention at this moment overlap and bump into each other and these have the effect of confusing meanings over female work/home category memberships. Do these category cross-overs feature in the girls' thinking? What do the girls themselves wish to become? If Carly has a career vision, it is as a music teacher. Her mother explains that she *has learned the violin since she was three and danced since she was three.* Every week day Carly participates in at least one out-of-school activity. She practices the violin every day and attends dancing lessons three times a week. In addition, she attends swimming club and on Saturdays she plays in a T-ball team for her school in the summer and in a netball team in the winter. At nine years of age, as her mother puts it, *she has an inherent ability and desire to achieve.* Jenny, too, has a busy out of school schedule. She takes dancing lessons, attends swimming club, and plays T-ball and netball for her school. Both are involved in more formally organised pursuits than their low decile school counterparts. These purposeful activities, engaged in by girls and regulated by their mothers, might be read as a strategic development of the sort of subjectivities "associated with traditional, acceptable and respectable feminine activities" (O'Brien, 2003, p. 264).

In Jenny's world, nature figures prominently. She tells me that she *likes nature a lot—things like how the world moves around. You can't really feel it because it goes so slowly.* She would like to be *somebody who looks after nature and things like plants, trees, and helps rare birds like kakapos and kiwis.* Jenny's career choice gives expression to life experiences that are set apart from those of the low decile school girls. In her plans we find a rehearsal of a naming of categories of social conscience established in the social world. Her futures-thinking demonstrates a commitment to nature conservation but it is a commitment that, according to her mother, is based on insufficient personal knowledge about the demands of particular occupations:

> *When she was younger she wanted to be a fire fighter and she wanted to be that for a long time but then she realised that fire fighters get very dirty and she likes to be clean and pretty so she's put that by the by. Now she's said that she wants to look after endangered species, but I don't know how she'd stick it out on a deserted island in the cold and the wet and no showers or amenities, no makeup and things like that. She doesn't know the reality of what she's saying really.*

Whilst Jenny might be constantly exploring the potential for new forms of subjectivity, her mother is ever mindful of the limits of that potential. There are certain constraints to becoming the autonomous, self-realising subject. For Foucault, if there is a freedom of choice it is a freedom constrained by "a lineage of loose alliances, relations of resistance and mastery, and configurations of fluid interests…[that are] not outside the games of truth (Blake et al., 1998, p. 62).

Whatever career is imagined, all the mothers in the study are deeply committed to their daughters' academic progress. They would have happily talked about the value of education, longer than the interview time, given half a chance. What is different, however, is that mothers of daughters at private schools also have the financial resources and systems knowledge to create very real effects. In a similar vein, Reay (1998) argued in her study that for working-class mothers, "a combination of diminished resources and less social power meant that they were not able to generate cultural capital from their time and effort to anything like the extent that middle class mothers were able to" (p. 198). Educational success operates with quite different dynamics for working and middle-class parents. What seems particularly unfair is that working-class parents who 'do all the right things' cannot guarantee "the kind of educational success routinely achieved by middle-class children" (Lucey, 2001, p. 185).

What is important here in the Foucauldian sense is that particular practices of subjectification are at work to contribute towards the production of the successful or failing student. At the same time, those practices contribute to the maintenance of students' social class positioning, ensuring that for some working-class students, individual emancipation, remains elusive. As Thomson, Henderson, and Holland (2003) argue, individualisation theorists "underplay the importance of relationships and forms of reciprocity and obligation that are embedded within them for understanding the identities and practices in which individuals engage" (p. 44).

The terms that enter into the production of gendered subjectivity are, as Butler (2004) puts it, "outside oneself, beyond oneself in a sociality that has no single author" (p. 1).

REFLECTIONS ON IDENTITY

Identity is a social construct, produced at the interface of sometimes conflicting discourses. In our work in education and in our daily lives discourses command our attention, offering us ways of organising and giving meaning to what we do and think. Take a moment to think about Donna and the discourses that were operating in a competitive manner. Even for the mathematically-savvy, it was often difficult to come to any straightforward understanding of what Donna's identity looked like. Each discourse represented different interests and each offered her a wide range of subjectivity modes. She could accept, contest or transcend a particular discourse in operation, yet in doing so to construct her identity, she became entangled in their differences. The meanings of and membership within the categories of discursive practice will be a constant site of struggle as identities become posited, resisted and fought-over in attachment to the subjectivity that constructs any particular individuality.

Cultural discourses bring a powerful dimension to the way we take up our identity. This was particularly true for the girls from different socio-economic backgrounds. For them, there were issues associated with femininity, family, academic progress, and history that claimed their attention. Those particular categories were used as heuristics in the analysis to help organise their personal accounts of the possibilities that are open to young women. In using them, we were able to capture the dynamic between gendered subjectivity and life-time futures. It provided an opportunity for us to grasp an understanding of class-based practices of subjectification that contribute not only towards the production of one's life chances but also the continuation of one's social class positioning.

ACTIVITY

A student is talking about her earlier school experiences. She then tells us about her views on her current schooling.

It was an excellent school. A good basis for education and it's like, it offers a lot. It's a small community school and I just thrived there. I loved it. You know everyone. It's safe. It's all girls so you don't have the distraction of guys to learn with. But on the other hand it's a disadvantage, like, with my form two [Year 8] class, half went to [one] school, and the other half went to [another] so I was the only one from my class, my year, to come away from everyone else…

…I think it's quite good [to have classes with boys] because in the work force there are guys and girls working together and you've got to learn to have relationships, relations, on a friendship basis with guys and know how to be around them. Like some, if you're not careful you could come out of [an all-girls' secondary school] with absolutely no social skills, besides being girlie and snobby…I think it's really good having guys around. It's like, and they've also got different opinions than females.

Identify as many discourses as you can that appear to be working through this student's words. Discuss how the student negotiates her subjectivity through a range of sometimes competing discursive formations.

CHAPTER 6

LEARNING TO TEACH IN CONTEXT

IN THIS CHAPTER

- Teachers' identities explained
- Dividing practices
- Exploring context in identity construction
- Three moments of identity

We have now seen how it is possible to contemplate people as the product of the discourses and practices through which they become subjected. The question that has occurred to all of us at some point is: what kind of person would we have become if our circumstances over time had been different? What if we had been brought up within a different family? What if we went to different schools and had different teachers than the ones we did? Would our identities have developed differently? Those of us who are teachers might wonder what was it, exactly, that influenced the way we teach. These questions are all something of challenge to intuition. With the slightest change to our past experiences, our identity may have taken a markedly different form and direction.

How do structural processes and historical events contribute to the persons we become? Perhaps above all, on reflection, who are we, with respect to others, with respect to structures and with respect to history? And in relation to the focus of this chapter, what can we say about those who are starting out in the profession, with respect to the knowledge they create of themselves as teachers? These are the sorts of questions that have puzzled many of us. We wonder how teachers constitute themselves as selves with agency within structural processes that often seem so inflexible. It might not come as total surprise to learn that the individual/social relation has been a long-time dilemma for education. The idea in this chapter is to see if it isn't possible to get to the bottom of this relationship. If we can do that, then it might also be possible to identify and confront limiting and disempowering discourses that challenge the work that teachers do.

TEACHERS' IDENTITIES EXPLAINED

The intricate relationship between the individual and the social is not normally used to explore teachers' identity. Usually, researchers prefer other objects of attention. Some look at teachers' beliefs and some investigate teachers' knowledge.

And they might use these constructs to map out what teachers believe and know, often before and after a process of professional development or curriculum change. Others choose to focus their attention on teacher reflection, exploring principled thinking, reasoning and critical judgment. Still others like to work in long-term arrangements with individuals or groups of teachers with a view towards enhancing effective teaching. Each of these familiar approaches is committed to teacher empowerment and each has achieved something to marvel at—each has collapsed the personal and the public in imaginative ways. In giving teachers a personal voice, they make it possible for teachers to confront, analyse, and develop their public pedagogical practice.

Learning to teach is often described as a personal journey. The journey may not be the smoothest but, for many, it does have the compensatory virtue of being immensely fulfilling. Take the time to read such descriptions and you will find that they give you an insistence urge to know more. The most puzzling phenomenon is why a teacher takes a particular route and not another. Are there factors at play that make it easier to choose one pathway in preference to one other? Could there be some 'political tactics' within the contexts within which pre-service teachers find themselves? Keep in mind that teachers who are in-training, experience their training in different settings. They attend a university course and they practise teaching with the assistance of number of different teachers in a number of different schools and classrooms during the course of their training. They encounter and are caught up in a range of discourses and practices within those different institutional structures. Because of that, they experience varying kinds of material relations that result from their membership within those different structures. What they believe and what they do and think could be different from one context to another.

ACTIVITY

The following quotes have been taken from a transcript of a teacher's interview recorded at a number of moments throughout one year. They have not been placed in any particular order.

1. Photocopy the following quotes and cut around each separate quote.
2. Order the quotes to trace the teacher's story of herself as a teacher, from the beginning of the year through to the end of the year.
3. Compare and contrast your 'pathway' of teacher-identity-in-development with someone else's. Check with the actual progression at the end of the chapter.
4. Write a short note about what you have learned from this activity in relation to the constitution of teacher's identity.

(i) *You're in a system now where you've got so many hours to teach a subject so you're finding it's like, 'well, I've got to finish this by next week, so Pythagoras theorem, there it is, use it.' And I hate doing that, but at the same time, that's the restraints you're working with. So you kind of find the balance between being able to let them understand the maths and encourage them to understand the maths and giving them the knowledge they need to pass the exam ... I just find I've not got time to do what I want to do and I think that the general cry of all teachers really. And in a way, this Maths in Context stuff's nice, because the time restriction, it's no longer there and it doesn't matter if you're not getting through what you should do. But at the same time I've sat there thinking, I haven't got to chapter three and x's group are two sets below mine and they're on chapter four!' so I'm putting a time constraint on myself because I'm trying to keep it in balance with what everyone else is doing, but at the same time, its doesn't really matter the same as it does when you're working with national curriculum and you've got six hours to do shape, space, measure and that kind of thing.*

(ii) *I think in retrospect what they should have done, is have more time to work with that, that's what I should have done, I didn't do the next two contexts, I moved to something else, I was concerned about time, and I moved to the line graphs straight away, and I think I should've spent more time on the next context...in other lessons it's been, do fifteen thousand questions and at the end tick tick tick, it's that mad rush and that's not what Maths in Context is about.*

(iii) *I am planning it with the book and I'm sticking to it because I'm not worrying too much about - that kid hasn't got it – I'm just more doing what they were telling us to do, following the routine and it does seem to be working better.*

(iv) *You sit back at the end of the lesson and you think right ok I spent too long on that, what am I going to do next time and the next time you spend too long on it, and you think oh what am I going to do next time, and then next time you still spend too long on it. ... Because at the moment. I'm kind of going with the flow. And the flow is too slow sometimes, maybe for my group because I think they are bright enough to cope with a bit of a quicker pace.*

Transcripts used with kind permission from Una Hanley,
Manchester Metropolitan University, England

Pre-service teachers create their identities as teachers through a complex array of discursive practices. Their conscious and unconscious thoughts and emotions and their sense of self come about through the discourses and practices they inhabit. Strange though it may seem, one is never 'born a teacher'. Identity is never naturally given so there seems to be no point trying to uncover a pre-service teacher's true identity. Because of the complexity of discourses that demand their attention, pre-service teachers' ways of understanding themselves as teachers in relation to the world will always be in constant process. As they move from one context to another during training, the meanings they give to their membership within the category of teacher will be influenced by the discursive practices in operation. To confuse matters, practices within and between contexts are in a constant site of struggle over power. The teaching identity teachers might construct of themselves within the university course may well be fought over and resisted within the context of the school. During the course of their training as contexts change, they flip back and forth in their sense of self as teacher. The same is true of accredited teachers and that is why it is difficult to fix identity. And that is why it was so difficult to express a single unified locus for the identity of the teacher in our activity above.

In a way that we can't adequately imagine, the school, the classroom, the associate/supervising teacher, the teacher education course, previous classroom experiences, personal biography, and so forth, all have their place in constituting the pre-service teacher as 'teacher'. For the moment it is enough to know that they all bring with them, to the construction of teacher, particular modes of operating, particular knowledges, and particular positionings. If each has its own set of constructs that seeks to attach itself to the teacher, then inevitably some strategising will enter in. Constructing a sense of self as a teacher presupposes and constitutes a power relation. Don't think of this with necessarily negative connotations, but more in the sense of enabling. The practices that compete for the making of the teacher are generally productive and empowering.

According to Foucault, *systems* of power both produce and sustain the meanings that people make of themselves. Quite frankly, this is a remarkable idea because it suggests that identities and subjectivities are strategically fashioned and contested through systems of power in the dynamics of everyday life. This puts paid to the kind of thinking that asserts that identities are fixed and absolute. As a counterpoint to this traditional thinking, Foucault maintains that underpinning the construction of identity construction, is an *a priori* set of rules of formation governing beliefs and practices in such a way as to produce a certain network of material and embodied relations. This network doesn't merely reflect or represent social entities and relations; it actively constitutes them. For the pre-service teacher this means that he or she *is* the production of the practices through which he or she becomes subjected.

In Foucauldian talk, the discursive constitution of pedagogical subjectivity is important. It is important for us because it suggests that pre-service teachers need interaction with others and with structures, and they need exposure to discursive practices in order to form a self-concept. Indeed, the very possibility of forming and articulating concepts of one's self (e.g., as a teacher in the classroom) is ultimately dependent on the meanings of other people and systems. Identities are always relational: we can only be teachers in relation to the meanings of others. The reason for this is that other people, as well as systems in place, define what is normal. And what is not normal generates the need for normalisation, through procedures that are made both explicit and implicit. Institutionalised practices exercise control over the meaning of teaching by normalising and providing surveillance practices to keep such meanings in check.

Let's imagine that our pre-service teacher engages fully in the institutionalised practices of the school and associate's classroom within which she is working. The first thing you would notice is that she has learned to perform and enact the genres that constitute the knowledges, modes of operating and theories and practices of the classroom. You would also quickly realise that she operationalises the particular positionings and embodied practices that construct teaching in the associate's classroom. We could call her engagement complete, in the sense that she reproduces the particular identity constructed for her by the associate. The other thing you would notice is that the pre-service teacher's engagement has become self-actualised and does not appear to require monitoring and regulation. But the interesting thing is that there is no reason to assume that what it means to be a teacher in this classroom will remain stable. In fact, there is every reason to believe that meanings will shift. Based on what we already know about the construction of meaning, power will intrude when attempts are made to fix or change current representations of teaching.

DIVIDING PRACTICES

Teachers, just like all of us, take up identities through processes of classification and division. Practices that Foucault calls 'dividing practices' are fundamental to the way in which we differentiate teaching from other workplace practices. In all societies, and particularly in highly structured democracies, we make distinctions between people; and we make judgements based on the categories and differentiations that we have established. For example, employers often use educational qualifications to assess the worth of an applicant for a job. Combined with other distinguishing characteristics, scholastic achievement separates those who have from those who have not. Distinctions, like these, are dividing practices and they operate right across society. Stop and think about the medical profession and its multiple layers of expert involvement. A case in point concerns surgeons. Because of thc nature of the tasks that surgeons are required to perform, and the qualifications that those tasks demand, we tend to think of surgeons as a different breed from general practitioners and other medical professionals. And, more than that, based on the kind of surgical expertise in question, we tend to create hierarchies amongst surgeons themselves.

Expertise and qualifications, of course, are not the only means of categorising people, but they are certainly highly utilised. In schools a wide range of practices are at play to create distinctions between people, and by other institutional standards, schools are highly ritualised. Students are objectified and classified according to intelligence testing, streaming/setting, performance on entry tests, record of achievement on school and national curriculum examinations, learning styles, participation and ability in sports and music, and so on. In keeping with these divisions, schools organise for learning by creating specific curricula and developing means for assessing students. As a complement to their chosen methods for categorising students, schools organise physical space and time in order to support particular kinds of pedagogical approaches, to create particular kinds of provision for 'gifted', 'average' and 'special needs' students, and to nurture particular kinds of relationships between teachers and students as well as between students themselves.

Though these dividing practices are often considered by the schools concerned as undeniably progressive, it is by individual students that their full effects are experienced. The significance of setting up classificatory systems within a school becomes evident when we understand that it is through these systems that specific identities are constructed for students. This isn't to say that other social practices are not involved in developing in students a sense of self, but it is to point out that schools and teachers are tremendously influential in controlling the sorts of self-images students come to create. Knowledge about students' behaviour, their achievements and the like, is developed through these dividing practices—they are instrumental in shaping the way we think about particular students. Students also come to think of themselves in ways that have been shaped for them and begin to act accordingly.

In our involvement in a wide range of social practices, we will often be categorised quite differently from one context to another. Dividing practices that operate across social situations, impact on us in ways that create a different sense of self. To this end, divisions operate not only between people but also within individual themselves. Dividing practices that are at odds with each other are most keenly felt by pre-service teachers as they move from one disciplinary institutional site to another. The school creates specific conditions and forms of control that will shape the teacher's behaviour, her attitudes and her pedagogical practice. It is not an especially obvious procedure on the part of the school but, nevertheless, in its subtlety, it is extremely powerful in establishing the parameters along which pedagogical practice will be defined.

This is a different way of interpreting teaching. It doesn't read teaching as 'natural' and it doesn't take a teacher's identity for granted. As Britzman (1991) has pointed out, it doesn't approach the issue of identity in some *a priori* way, as an outcome of belief change, a measure of content knowledge acquisition, or an aftermath of being there in the classroom community of practice. Such conventional approaches are often taken as getting to the heart of teaching. Though they vary widely in appeal, in remedy, and in theoretical stance, what they have in common is an underlying celebration of first-hand experience. For all their appeal within the literature, what these approaches do, inadvertently, is script identity as synonymous with the teacher's role and function. As a result they tend to overlook other important factors at play.

Foucault (1984) explicitly asks that we give up thinking about the self as a centre of coherent experience. As much as we would want to believe it, we are not masters of our own thoughts and actions. Our identities are historically and situationally produced, always contingent and precarious. This is what Butler (1997) means when she claims that there is no originary moment establishing pure identity which can be rationally unpacked. Putting Foucault to use allows us to explore the construction of teaching identity, paying attention to its contingency and precariousness. Rather than reading teaching as 'natural'—an interpretation that captures the popular imagination—we can interpret teaching as constructed by disciplinary power. The pre-service teacher's sense of self within the 'teaching practice' school, depends a great deal on collegiality and the opportunity to construct and reflect on new self-understandings. Self-understandings are mapped against certain criteria of effective teaching established within the school, and these determine the kinds of activity, behaviour, speech, gestures, and networks that are legitimated. They also endorse the way in which time and physical space will be controlled.

The same thing happens within the teacher education course. An ideological construction of a teacher is advanced within the course and pre-service teachers are shaped to fit the mould. Like the school, the university participates in practices that seek a hold on the teacher. They produce mechanisms that will shape, monitor, and discipline the knowledges, modes of operating, and positionings of pre-service teachers. In so doing, the university operates as a disciplinary technology that, without really being aware of it, attempts to control, classify and delimit the work that teachers do. In the process pre-teachers (usually) become receptive and pliable. Finding out what kinds of contexts and communities of practice support pre-service learning is crucial for pre-service education. In a very real sense, disciplinary institutions create the conditions for certain discourses and not others, in relation to categories of being, acting and thinking, to be entertained. Foucault notes:

> Every educational system is a political means of maintaining or modifying the appropriateness of discourses with the knowledge and power they bring with them.
>
> (Foucault, 1972, p. 46).

Once we shift our thinking about teaching towards the view that it is constitutive of, and by, material and embodied relations of discourses and practices, we can begin to see that identity might not be as much assigned as consented to through constant social negotiation. And talking of negotiation draws us into a context of power relations. Learning to teach could then be viewed as inextricably bound up with relations of power surrounding the pre-service teacher's participation within and her negotiation in the sites within which she is engaged. A view of teaching like this demands an acknowledgment of the tentative and shifting balance between classroom experience and political processes. Taking this a step further, if we wanted to explore teacher's identity, we would need to attend to forms of social control and the teacher's level of compliance. We would need to investigate the interplay between discursive regulation and the subjective investment in and reworking of, and even resistance to those normative practices.

Foucault talks of 'governmentality' by which he means enforced obedience to rules that are presumed to be for the public good. It is the process by which our conduct is controlled in minute detail. The school and the university both perform the function of a technology of power, "determin[ing] the conduct of individuals and submit[ting] them to certain ends or domination, an objectivising of the subject" (Foucault, 1988, p. 18), without, of course, resorting to physical restraint. They train people towards acceptable behaviour, providing "(1) technologies of production which permit us to produce, transform or manipulate things; [and] (2) technologies of sign systems, which permit us to use signs, meanings, symbols, or signification" (p. 18). Those within these institutions guarantee their compliance through "technologies of the self, which permit individuals to effect by their own means or with the help of others a certain number of operations on their own bodies and souls, thoughts, conduct, and ways of being, so as to transform themselves" (Foucault, 1988, p. 18).

We mustn't confuse the fact that individuals create their own selves willingly through subjectification with the fact that individuals are created as docile bodies by others against their own will through subjection. Subjection was a focus of Foucault's middle writing period but in time he shifted his emphasis to his concept of subjectification. Such terms are, undeniably, hard to distinguish between. It is enough to know that subjectification is a positive process that involves the willing development and transformation of selves and usually involves disciplinary power, and with it, surveillance and normalisation. Subjection is a negative process through which individuals are made subjects unwillingly. The change in conceptualisation in Foucault's work marks an extension of his thinking about power and knowledge, and an interest in the potential of self creation.

This is all well and good, but exactly how do certain versions of 'good' teaching, and not others, come to be intelligible to pre-service teachers? There are several good reasons why we might want to pursue these questions, using a Foucauldian approach. Directing our attention to the political and institutional processes central to identity construction is useful in that it, first, opens up other possibilities for teacher education. Second, it offers a more complex and layered notion of the way in which a teaching identity is constructed. Third, it allows us to engage the historically specific relationship between pre-service pedagogical practice and forms of social control and possibility. Assessing how identity is shaped and lived in different sites by the pre-service teacher can provide an insight into understanding contemporary classroom teaching politics in education.

EXPLORING CONTEXT IN IDENTITY CONSTRUCTION

We are going to look at an exploration into the construction of teaching identity, from the perspective of a teacher's own narrative. In it we will be able to see the discursive practices at play in the process of becoming a teacher. It is through an examination of those processes that we begin to observe the political and strategic nature of *modes of operating*, *knowledges*, and *positionings* that are central to identity construction. As you read the account notice how learning to teach is clearly a distinct social activity with particular social relationships, knowledge forms, and associated pedagogic modes. We will analyse identity construction through three moments in the discourse of one student teacher named here as Helen, who is working hard to become a 'good' secondary school mathematics teacher.

In the exploration we will come to appreciate the way in which pre-service teachers' identities are crafted. Pre-service teachers, just like any other individuals, engage with different discourses. We will bear witness to how ideas from one discourse are woven into another. We will see how discourse systematically constitutes versions of the social and natural worlds and, specifically, how discourses create different material effects with regard to the constitution of pre-service teachers' identifications as teachers. And we will see how teaching identity is produced and reproduced through social interaction, daily negotiations, and within particular contexts which are already laden with the meanings of others.

THREE MOMENTS OF IDENTITY

In our first exploration, we read what Helen has to say about becoming a teacher. Helen's story is particularly telling, because it spells out the constant tension experienced in confronting everyday visions of what it means to be a teacher while negotiating visions yet to come. The moments through which we shall grasp that tension are her own history of school mathematics, her involvement in the course work to gain accreditation, and her participation in three practicum experiences at three different schools during her year-long course. The intent of my interview with Helen was to understand how she understood her own process of learning to teach. Through the interview process, the discussion became a significant space for her own theorising.

The context of educational biography

It is impossible to discuss learning to teach in Foucault's terms as the production of discursive practice without taking into account participation in the social practices of schooling. For the student teacher, learning to teach is the initiation into a social tradition, involving experiences within key different contexts. Because each context is chronologically and geographically distinct one from the other, each presents a different set of assumptions and demands. Importantly, each makes available a different range of voices and discursive practices. To that end, learning to teach is an evolutionary process that is responsive to context and the discourses in operation within.

Pre-service teachers bring with them their first over-familiar context, constructed through their own educational biography and through common sense ideas about the roles and functions of teachers in school. The second context is composed of personal student experiences in the university degree course and the postgraduate teacher education programme during which they become privy to aspects of the teaching profession. The third context is given definition by their involvement in teaching practice. During the practicum, new aspects of the teacher's world and departmental and school politics are laid bare to them, and new relationships with teachers, administrators and students are made possible. Precisely because each of the three contexts (prior educational biography, tertiary studentship, and teaching in schools) carves out its own borders, each represents different and competing relations of power, knowledge, dependency, commitment, and negotiation. More importantly, each institutionalises mandates for conformity, authorising particular frames of reference that validate certain ways of doing and being in teaching.

As neither wholly 'student' nor 'teacher' in the classroom, Helen brings all three contexts to bear as she attends to the task of learning to educate others. For as long as she can remember she has wanted to be a teacher and she entered the secondary teaching course with the encouragement from her (now retired) teaching parents. Her undergraduate double major in mathematics and in statistics provided a way to put to use her knowledge of mathematics and her satisfaction in helping other people. Like many of her peers, nearly everything she worked towards as a pre-service teacher was to enable her to make a difference in the lives of students by helping them, and for her that meant in the manner of the teachers she encountered in her own schooling.

Helen's long-term objective as a teacher is constructed, in part, from an internally persuasive discourse which tells her that all students should have the opportunity to learn, even if individual attention necessitates a slower pace. To take up the ideas from this discourse she sought to construct an identity which could celebrate individuality whilst simultaneously pressing for curriculum coverage. In Foucault's terms she had to give due consideration to the way in which constructing a sense of self-as-teacher falls within the rules and conventions of specific discursive formations. For Foucault, the point is that the modes by which, "human beings are made into subjects" (Foucault, in Dreyfus & Rabinow, 1982, p. 208) are systematically governed by a complex groups of relations. Helen had to negotiate her own space, ever mindful of the definitions of schooling mapped out by her own secondary and tertiary experience as a learner.

> There were lots of teachers in my past who I thought I'd really like to be like. Many of them and all in different ways. And there was one lecturer – his teaching style, like, to me, was excellent because he introduced a really difficult concept. Because it was like he was telling you a story. It's not a story really but the way he said it was like he was telling a story. I thought this could be a really good model for me.

The context of the teacher education programme

If, as in Foucault's understanding, teaching identities are constituted and negotiated within contexts that carry their own sets of discursive relations, then those identities are constantly on the move. Within and between different contexts student teacher identifications are marked by competing meanings of experience, circumscribed by differences in time, place, events, and commitment. It makes little sense then to reduce the complexity of pedagogical activity to a technical solution. Yet, as many educators are acutely aware, prospective teachers want and expect to receive practical ideas, formulas, automatic and generic methods that can be applied immediately and successfully to the classroom. Invariably, pre-service teachers seek out mechanical procedures, bringing to their mathematics teaching course a search for recipes for putting across the mathematics content. Such a process sits comfortably within the transmission tradition of teaching and the acquisitionist understanding of learning, institutionalised in traditional classrooms.

> I expected that the teachers' college course would teach me how to teach maths. I didn't know in what way. Maybe the best thing is to give them ten questions to do and then warm up to the main work, like copying down into notebooks, or like how you organise your lesson. Like what's the first thing that you want the students to do and next, how do you set up your notes on the board, and the way you get students to do the exercises. The organisation is really important. Sometimes I feel that students are slack during the period. The teacher might not have the control to deal with that because the whole class won't do any work. So I also wanted to know how to handle the classroom.

In the telling, Helen as collapsed two expectations into one: knowing how to teach and knowing how to gain and sustain classroom control. Helen looked to the course as the source rather than the effect of pedagogy. She expected to acquire 'tricks of the trade'. In common with many of her peers, she worried about classroom control. She sought methods for classroom discipline, presumably, in order to teach with effect and ultimately to gain respect as a competent member of the teaching profession. Creating an identity, in Foucault's understanding, entails more than learning *from* talk about techniques for immediate classroom application; it involves learning *to* talk within and about the practice. Technical approaches, which encourage learning from talk, seriously limit the student teacher's understanding of the relationship between pedagogical practice and theory. They fail to take into account the specificity and political commitments of the pedagogical act. Helen's course work did not provide her with the methods she desired.

MW: Did you think that the course might tell you that this is the best way to do things; that you start with this and then move onto that?

Helen: Yes, that's right. And, like, give you a couple of ways to work through a problem, instead of so many ways.

The course gave consideration to the more messy questions of what to teach and why particular methods might be more suitable than others. It required students to discuss and debate the main terms of the prescribed curriculum and their theoretical underpinnings, and work through the types of practice born out of such theorising. It also focused on the technologies of lesson preparation, computer software evaluation and the critique of the microteaching of peers. In Helen's estimation, those approaches did provide pre-service teachers with an opportunity to unmask their own relationship to mathematics. In the process it offered them a set of global features rather than specific coordinates for teaching. It endeavoured to shape opportunities for the activity of teaching and hence the process of learning to teach.

> One classmate in teachers' college, in the course, introduced Pythagoras with the areas, you know, the squares—the little squares that add up to the big one. And I thought that was a great idea and most of the students would like that idea as well. I thought that if I didn't introduce the idea properly, then I'm going to have a heap of trouble for the following two or three weeks.

The context of teaching in schools

During three blocked weeks of the course year the pre-service teachers worked in schools under the supervision of their assigned associate teacher. The practicum is the time when a sustained structure of support is made available to student teachers. It is founded on the presupposition that school life is the authentic moment for knowing, thinking, and understanding about teaching. Like others in apprentice situations student teachers observe 'experts' and others at work and they evaluate for themselves the 'products' of the experts' labour. Pre-service teachers value the practicum experience as an opportunity to think, act and interact with knowledgeable others. In most schools, the teaching practice phase is carried out with one-off lessons at first, and builds to a much longer set of consecutive and sequenced lessons. A reasonable execution of the various constituencies such as questioning, and facilitation of student engagement is important but it is the overall pedagogical encounter which the student teacher will be developing.

In Foucault's terms, we can speak of the constitution of teaching identities as positioned in relation to the discourses and practices levels operating within the classroom and school community. Those newly inserted into such practices, such as pre-service teachers, work hard to engage with those discourses. Pre-service teachers seeking membership to the category, teacher, attempt to mobilise the discourses of the school community and, in doing that, they mark out distinctions between practices about teaching as established from other relevant and meaningful systems and practices. Generally speaking, they make the best of things, even when what they understand by the category teacher is challenged by the school. In seeking to resolve ambiguous and contradictory meanings, with the expressed purpose to become a member of the category teacher as designated by the school, the pre-service teacher negotiates her position. In the process, the school's ideas, language and practices of teaching may well be modified and adapted. Often a new or hybrid discourse about what it means to be a teacher eventuates. Thus the pre-service teacher's membership in the category teacher is contingent, provisional, and in process.

Access to the school's discourses opens up membership to the category teacher, but it may also obstruct or deny. The practice and its meanings need to be made transparent by the community for mobilisation to take place. Membership of the category teacher represents knowledge. It represents knowledge of information, artefacts, technologies, symbol systems, routines and rituals, language, relationships and opportunities for participation. Such discursive practices are highly significant to the process of learning to teach. Becoming knowledgeable about teaching practice, then, is not an issue of receiving the authoritative once-and-for-all position on the nature of the teacher's work and the identity one must assume. The student teacher is not a static product but enhances category membership by continually shaping and being shaped by the dynamics of the practice, structure and history, and by the way in which the school community makes the meaning of those practices visible. Helen talks of the ways in which the practices of the mathematics department at her school, and the 'inner workings' of those practices, were made transparent for her:

> There were about 1100 students and there are about seven maths teachers, I think, including the junior teachers…In the maths teachers' meeting I felt like I'd come to a classroom, because there was one speaker and I sat at one table and they were looking at assessment and it felt like being in the classroom. But then, after a while, I felt it's great to work with a team. They made me feel part of the group though they didn't talk to me but I knew that they saw me as another maths teacher. Those teachers were really sharing, and my associate maths teacher gave me a lot of help as well. They talked about what they had done in class all the time. So that's really helpful for other teachers to know and try out. They just talked about it as normal talk.

From the student teacher's standpoint, full membership into the category teacher entails knowing the material backward and forward. Theorising about full membership provides the pre-service teacher with a double insight into the meanings of their relationships to individuals, institutions, personal, cultural and institutional values and events, and how these relationships constitute his or her own identity and ideological orientations. This kind of insight is helpful to the new teacher who can, in turn, participate in shaping and responding to the specific forces which impinge and construct teaching identity.

> The teacher is a really caring person. He showed a great interest in his students in the way he explains…Like the way he speaks. I can't think of any examples. He sort of talked to each of them, although he was talking to the whole class but you felt that he was talking to you - only talking to you so that's really good. And he also moved to the centre of the students, or quite close to the students so that the students won't think, oh, he's just so far away from us, so far away. And also he moved around the classroom. When he was introducing a new topic he'd use some activity and he used to involve his students. Once he bought a box of ice cream to share with everyone. They were doing the Poisson Distribution. He had the little lollies in the ice cream—Hokey Pokey. He used this to chat a little bit with the students…I think that another thing is that he tried to make things easy and clear. Say, like, he introduced 'exponential'. He just said it's a special number because he didn't need the students to know exactly so he just made it simple for students and linked it with natural log.

Normative notions of teaching tend to ignore the social basis of pedagogy. In Foucauldian understanding, however, every pedagogy is influenced by the complex social relations between teachers, students, school culture, and the larger social world. Within this compulsory relationship teaching cannot be construed as an extension of one's personality. Rather, contradictions and social dependency are inevitable dynamics, and teaching becomes subject to social negotiation. As Britzman (1991) has noted, teaching then turns out not so much an individual determined product as a dialogic movement between the teacher, the students, the curriculum, the knowledge produced in exchange, and the social practices that make pedagogy intelligible.

> Another teacher was a really old teacher. He was due to retire in two or three years. The way he taught is that he knew whatever things the student knew, you know. Like say, for example, in [the local town] he used the highway that everyone knows. He knows the road names and all that. All the students know where he was talking about and he used this to kind of apply a really difficult formula. The topic was 'making x the subject', and he used this formula. He introduced this by telling them how the highway is built and all the students were focused on it. I'd like to be like this teacher, this older teacher.

The older teacher provided Helen with an entry point to the community of practice which would lead to her own attempts at practice. At first these steps were tentative; they constituted an intellectual and emotional activity. Meanings of and membership within the category teacher constantly changed for her and this shift occurred as particular identities sought attachment. In time she came to replace her desire for a unitary teaching identity to one which better represented teaching as an ongoing process and challenge, demanding and constructing complex social relationships:

> I don't think I managed classroom control until the last about two weeks of my third teaching experience. I suddenly got some idea of how to control students. It's very slow, but at last I know that. At the beginning of the course I didn't expect that teaching would be so hard. And now although I think it's still a hard job I still think I'm capable. I mean I'm quite happy about it. I feel it's still difficult but I think I can do it.

REFLECTIONS ON CONTEXT IN IDENTITY CONSTRUCTION

Constructing an identity as a teacher is not as straightforward as some educators would like us to believe. Specific discursive practices operate on the process of becoming a teacher, with specific political and strategic *modes of operating*, *knowledges*, and *positionings*. They systematically constitute versions of the social and natural worlds which are fundamental to identity construction. And they create different material effects with regard to the way pre-service teachers 'see' themselves as teachers. It makes a lot of sense, then, to think of learning to teach as a distinctly social activity with particular social relationships, knowledge forms, and associated pedagogic modes. From that understanding we can say that an identity as teacher is produced and reproduced through social interaction, daily negotiations, and within particular contexts which are already filled with other's meanings.

Of course pre-service teachers, just like any other individuals, take up some ideas from one or other discourse and modify other parts of those discourses. There is never a once-and-for-all identity out there for us. Rather, identity implies potentialities that signify what we are or might become.

> ...identity is not the goal but rather the point of departure of the process of self-consciousness, a process by which one begins to know that and how the personal is political, that and how the subject is specifically and materially engendered in its social conditions and possibilities of existence (de Lauretis, 1986, p. 9)

ACTIVITY CHECK

Earlier in this chapter you traced the pathway of one teacher over the course of a year.

The transcripts of the teacher were recorded in this order:
(ii), (iii), (i), (iv)

Write a paragraph that explains, in Foucauldian terms, the teacher's sense of self as a teacher.

CHAPTER 7

SUBJECTIVITY AND REGULATORY PRACTICES

IN THIS CHAPTER

- Disciplinary power
- Subjectification
- An exploration into the constitution of teaching
- Transitory positionings
- Regulatory practices
- Technologies of surveillance and normalisation

Structural processes and historical practices make a significant contribution to the kinds of people we become. They open up discourses and practices that are available for us to take up. They shape our identities. Those who are working at becoming teachers are positioned in relation to a range of discourses and practices. Teaching is not simply an extension of a teacher's personality because teachers are continually shaping and being shaped by the dynamics of practice, structure and history. Gaining full membership into the category teacher within a specific institution requires insight into the relationships and processes that the institution endorses. Every pedagogical practice is influenced by the complex social relations that exist between teachers, students, institutional culture, and all are nested within the larger social world. Teaching turns out to be not so much an individual determined product, as a negotiation between these complex relations.

This leads us to wonder how exactly do the discourses and practices of an institution shape the person we become. Among the many interesting mysteries of identity construction is the question as to what it is that makes us want to be shaped. What makes us conform? Do practices of regulation within an institution, such as the school, intrude into the ways in the 'making' of the teachers within them? If so, what regulatory practices can we detect in the making of a teacher? Of course there are any number of rules and regulations with which teachers must comply—their professional competency is dependent upon continual conformance to these prescriptions. Our interest here is not so much in the contractual obligations that are the bedrock of educational governance but in the more covert disciplinary arrangements operating within schools—the ones that have the effect of inducing teachers into becoming a particular 'docile body'. We also look at the flip-side: the capacity that teachers have in responding to the disciplinary mode of domination.

DISCIPLINARY POWER

At this stage, we should be quite comfortable with Foucault's understanding of power. His genius was in conceptualising how modern power operates through two quite distinct strategies. He demonstrated that it functioned through specific techniques of bodily control as well as through forms of self-monitoring of our own subjectivity. And he showed that disciplinary power affects us all. It impacts on and regulates not just every body but every soul. As we know, for Foucault power is distributed rather than centralised, it operates from the bottom upwards instead of from the top down, and it is positive and enabling. It is, however, also negative and coercive. How can we explain this phenomenon? Basically, we can explain it from history. Certain historical events led to a shift in the execution of power. It happens that from the middle of the sixteenth century the art of government was through the laws set down by sovereignty. Around the end of the eighteenth century a series of special circumstances wrought wholesale changes to the way power was conceptualised. Control of the population turned from the imposition of laws to invisible strategies and tactics.

The special circumstances are what Foucault calls a 'historical conjuncture of forces'. Briefly, they involved the management of both people and goods. As far as people go, during the eighteenth century nations had to deal with issues in relation to increasing populations that tended to drift in nomadic fashion. There was also a need to monitor the activities of growing groups in institutions like schools, and an urgency to control crises such as the spread of disease, poverty, and crime. It separately emerged that the Industrial Revolution had brought with it problems that had not been encountered previously—these were problems specific to the growth of production and control over markets. The issues were of such severity that previous approaches to control through feudal power and administrative monarchy proved to be inadequate in dealing with the situation.

In the nineteenth century new indirect forms of management emerged in response to these pressing social concerns. New programmes insinuated themselves in society with the expressed function of executing disciplinary control. It was the modern era of a new disciplinary society—the human science counterpart to the physical sciences of the Enlightenment. And the upshot was that the individual began to be conceived of differently in relation to the whole population. This new conceptualisation, and the schemes that derived from it, were the brainchild of a number of experts and scholars, all of whom promoted control through the operation of the complex strategies and tactics of biopower. Biopower, as a mindshift, developed from the idea that controls would operate at the micro rather than at the macro level, and would target whole populations. Interesting enough, the school and the classroom were among other institutions such as hospitals, asylums, and housing estates, that were to play a part in the regulation and control of people. These institutions exercise power in much the same way but because they operate across groups of people, rather than entire populations, they are said to exercise disciplinary power, establishing particular individualities within their spaces.

It is thanks to people like Jeremy Bentham that a society of individual control and compliance developed. Up until that time it seemed impossible that you could get control of the population without force or violence but Bentham's plan was evident proof that you could. Bentham, a utilitarian philosopher, is famously known for the plan he produced for a design of a prison. His submission showed an advanced understanding of the importance of disciplinary power not simply for inmates, but also for society as a whole. He came up with a plan that was novel in many respects, not the least being that its specific geometric features lent themselves to the exercise of total control of its prisoners. What he envisaged in his drawings for the penitentiary was a structure that had the coherence to provide pervasive and invisible observation.

The Benthamite Panopticon, as the architectural innovation came to be known, consisted of a 12 sided polygon with a central observation tower. From this central point of inspection a superintendent had uninterrupted visibility in all directions and was able to observe the behaviour of all institutional inmates. The specially designed blinds, gave the unseen superintendent all seeing potential. For their part, the inmates resided in solitary cells which were layered in the manner of spokes from a wheel. Each inmate was fully aware of the threat of surveillance from the central tower because each cell was lit by a peripheral light that illuminated the inmate within. Because there was no guarantee at any particular moment that an inmate was not being watched, the fear and intimidation of constant surveillance meant that inmates eventually disciplined and regulated themselves. Instead of being controlled by force, they started to act and behave as though they were being disciplined, regulated and under surveillance.

> Bentham laid down the principle that power should be visible and unverifiable. Visible: the inmate will constantly have before his eyes the tall outline of the central tower from which he is spied upon. Unverifiable: the inmate must never know whether he is being looked at any one moment; but he must be sure that he may always be so.
>
> (Foucault, 1977, p. 201)

Most of what we know about the plan was that it was conceived for the observation of prisoners. Examples of the Panopticon were purpose-built, at cost, for specific numbers of inmates. But Bentham had wider application in mind. He believed the concept would solve other control problems, such as students in schools, the army in the barracks, patients in hospitals and workers in factories, whose institutional practices lent themselves itself open to the self-regulation of the people within them. The important thing was that the design offered the promise of a new vitality and morality, a strengthened and educated society, enhanced production levels, and a growing economy. So it's no surprise that it became a metaphor for the disciplinary mode of domination.

SUBJECTIFICATION

The key point about the design was that control over people no longer depended on observing them directly. People were not simply subjected to processes of objectification. They actively involved themselves in self-forming subjectification. It was this latter aspect—the principle of self-regulation—that marked a turning point in the disciplinary mode of domination. We are really talking about *subjectification* and this is what the design could achieve, where earlier modes of domination had failed. By subjectification we mean a process through which individuals becomes accountable to specific discourses that claim their hold—the way they discipline themselves without any formal compulsion to do so.

> He who is subjected to a field of visibility, and who knows it, assumes responsibility for the constraints of power; he makes them play spontaneously upon himself; he inscribes in himself the power relation in which he simultaneously plays both roles; he becomes the principle of his own subjection.
>
> (Foucault, 1977, p. 202-3)

It's a good idea to remind ourselves at this point that disciplinary power is not necessarily negative. We need not think of it as a series of 'must nots', prohibiting, repressing and discouraging unwanted behaviours and actions. But what agency do we really have? We don't want to make a case here for what Foucault calls in his earlier work 'docile bodies'. After all, we are not passive victims of social oppression; we don't wish to be called 'cultural dopes'. We are *active agents* capable of intervening in and transforming (within limits of course) the settings and institutions within which we live and work.

This intuition is given expression in Foucault's later works where readers can find a more complex and differentiated analysis of disciplinary power. As it happens, it is in his later works that the potential for creativity and agency within social constraints are accounted for. It is worth knowing that Foucault implicitly acknowledged that the emphasis he placed on the effects of power upon the body in his archaeological and genealogical work had an undesirable effect. Take nothing away from this earlier work: it was inspired. But it did conjure up the impression of social agents as decidedly passive bodies. And it did portray power as monolithic and functionalist, subjugating bodies and fixing the circumstances surrounding subjectivity.

Foucault's later writing incorporates the adoption of an attitude of self-critique and the exploration of new positive modes of subjectivity. Subjectification is positive in the sense that it opens up possibilities for us. To be sure, the possibilities are not endless or far-reaching, but we do have certain degrees of freedom. Quite frankly, would we really want the sky to be our limit in our everyday activities? Most of us like order, consistency, and predictability. The thing is that disciplinary power provides us with those conditions by setting parameters around what we do. And in doing that, it contributes to the process of subjectification.

AN EXPLORATION INTO THE CONSTITUTION OF TEACHING

In the following exploration we are going to look at how organisational patterns in schools impose particular rhythms and temporal conditions which induce teachers into a particular programmable order and 'body', and how teachers, in turn, set themselves rules of conduct, but also seek to transform themselves; to change themselves. In brief, our exploration will look at the processes of subjectification and will looks closely at technologies (or practices) of the self that teachers set themselves intentionally and voluntarily. In exploring subjectification we will be able to marry the critical investigation of the individual teacher's institutional situation with a capacity for self-governance. The exploration might also provide a challenge to fundamental assumptions about the powerlessness of people within institutions.

Our focus is centred on what it means to engage in pedagogical work in the context of primary [elementary] school classrooms. There are a number of specific things we will be interested in exploring. In the discussion we will discover how pre-service teachers draw upon the pedagogies normalised in the course work to construct a frame of their view of the routine practices in the classroom. Under investigation is the way in which the practicum functions as part of the technology of surveillance and control. In looking at instances of teaching knowledge in production, we will begin to observe the political and strategic nature of organisational patterns in school that are ordinarily considered to be either relatively independent of power, and if they are not independent of organisational or institutional control, then they are usually thought of as linked only in a vague or inadequate way to power.

Our analysis begins in Foucault's theory of language and social power and takes seriously the discursive constitution of subjectivity. It will show how schools impose conditions and specific regulatory strategies that seduce pre-service teachers (and accredited teachers) into a particular identity and impact powerfully on pre-service teachers' constructions of themselves as teachers. The analysis is grounded in pre-service teachers' own words, generated through questionnaire responses. The pre-service teachers came to the course with varying backgrounds (mathematical and otherwise) but all were in their second year of a three-year primary [elementary] teaching course. They ranged in age from 19 to 53 and most were women. Only a small proportion of the 72 respondents was over the age of 40 and these were, in the main, change-of-career students. The second-year course work was developed by the team of lecturers and showed consistency across classes with respect to design, scheduling, pedagogical approach, and assessment.

I asked the pre-service teachers to respond to a questionnaire about their recent teaching practice experience. During the three weeks prior to the questionnaire, when they had recently been out in schools, they had worked to build up a professional partnership with their associate teacher within the supportive environment formed by links with the university and the school. A few days previous to administering the questionnaire their lectures had provided an opportunity for them to discuss their teaching practice in class discussion. That discussion had created a space for the individual pre-service teacher to name similar and different experiences in relation and reaction to the class.

To give you some background, the questionnaire developed from my involvement with the course during the two previous years. In those previous class discussions, as well as in my conversations with individual pre-service teachers, tensions had surfaced when pre-service teachers spoke their practicum experience into existence. I developed the questionnaire to allow the pre-service teachers currently enrolled in the course to give expression to their experiences. Through completion of the questionnaire each pre-service teacher was given the opportunity to construct a sense of how teaching identity is created in relation to people and practices: how it is socially structured and historically inflected. I was curious to see how "power seeps into the very grain of individuals, reaches right into their bodies, permeates their gestures, their posture, what they say, how they learn to live and work with other people" (Foucault, 1977, p. 28). More importantly, by making those processes visible through the questionnaire, it was hoped that pre-service teachers might see how similar processes could be acted upon, in future practicum experiences.

Because I wanted to understand how pre-service teachers constituted *themselves* as teachers in mathematics and how they constituted *themselves* as moral subjects responsible for their own actions, the observations and reports of associate teachers were extraneous to the analysis. To be sure, associate teachers' views of the practicum might contradict those given by the pre-service teachers but that is not a concern here. What we will be particularly keen to find out is how discourse systematically constitutes versions of the social and natural worlds for pre-service teachers, *not* for associate teachers. We will want to explore how discourses create different material effects with regard to the constitution of pre-service teachers' identifications as teachers. In putting the narratives together I try to make visible underlying structures of power.

TRANSITORY POSITIONINGS

From our previous discussions we have grasped a sense of what Foucault means when he claims that identity is never fixed. In this discussion we will again confront the transitory and mobile nature of the sense of self. At the beginning of the practicum pre-service teachers position themselves in relation to available discourses. During the practicum other discourses come to play which in some ways confirm and in other ways contradict those earlier discourses. Through the following quotes taken from pre-service teachers' responses about how they positioned themselves at the beginning and the end of the practicum, ongoing transitional positionings come to the fore.

Beginning: I was looking forward to teaching. I felt confident and enthusiastic, though sometimes I am unsure about how to explain some maths ideas.
End: I was more confident and able to see students developing understanding.

Beginning: Prior to posting I felt inadequate and concerned in algebra and problem solving.
End: I realise now that teaching any curriculum required me to learn the subject first. Teaching maths made me learn maths.

Beginning: I felt a bit uncomfortable—wanted more in-depth knowledge of how to teach it. How to get it across. How to start and introduce a unit.
End: More confident. Timing and pacing is now more sorted out. I learned which resources, activities, and strategies worked for students.

Beginning: I was lacking confidence.
End: I knew the material well and I was comfortable with maths. However I still lacked management strategies.

Beginning: I felt that I was familiar with the resources and activities but I had no idea how to run the maths lessons.
End: I was still very in the dark with what she did with each group individually. That's because I was always helping the very new group.

Beginning: Scared of teaching maths.
End: Feeling a lot more relaxed. Children really seemed to enjoy the activities, especially using money.

Beginning: I was a bit shaky and nervous about teaching maths as it is not my favourite subject. I feel it is necessary to give children a sound base of understanding in mathematics and mathematics skills so I was therefore skeptical of my own ability.
End: I appreciated being able to teach at different levels and gain strategies for teaching each level. I feel a lot more confident in teaching maths. However I am going to further my maths education by taking maths papers next year [electives].

Pre-service teachers' identity during the practicum is mapped onto a complex grid of formal and informal educational discourses and practices. Steeped initially in the as-yet-still-developing self-constructions produced to some extent by the university course and by their own mathematical background, though they cannot articulate it in these words, many are aware that they enter a new range of discourses and identities which will constitute them as a teacher of mathematics. On the threshold of something new, slightly over fifty percent of the pre-service teachers worried about the development of their teaching voice and how they might constitute the teaching of mathematics within their own subjective experience of mathematics. Many were aware of the difficulties involved in attempting the delicate work of educating others while still being educated oneself.

Pre-service teachers in this study identified and named categories of unknown knowledge: the teacher's mathematical explanations; algebra and problem solving; starting and introducing a unit; how to get it across; how to teach it; how to run the maths lessons; general mathematical knowledge. By naming these categories pre-service teachers established their own personal classificatory grid that would help them develop a teaching identification for mathematics. At the end of the practicum they registered a growing confidence. The categories they identified become less general and more specifically tied to the construction of actual pedagogical practice within the classroom. Variously named as: timing, pacing, resources, activities, workable strategies, management strategies; teaching to groups; teaching different levels; intention to enrol in an elective maths paper—all these knowings became the parameters of what would identify as successful pedagogical work.

Yet these identifications did not have the full measure of pre-service teachers' subjectivity precisely because subjectivity is an interactive weaving together of many complex selves in relation to available discourses and to the complex selves of others. The school, the associate teachers and the students in the classroom are all implicated in the identifications which pre-service teachers assign themselves. Because of that, the way in which pre-service teachers identify themselves as teachers is constantly refashioned, as investments are lived and rearranged within the classroom.

Such thinking may not make much sense to the pre-service teachers themselves. It isn't from lack of interest in understanding themselves as teachers, but because of their long-time investments in the essentialised humanist subject. They see themselves as individuals with a real and essential core, whose outer layers are a series of roles and functions which can be cast off to reveal the true and real self. They use this naming because it gives them an identity. It gives them something 'authentic' about where they come from, where they stand, how they are desired and described, and in what terms. In all probability, they would consider that a teaching identity comes about not by theories, but by actualised practice, and like many pre-service teachers they would view the practicum as an opportunity in which the true teaching self might manifest itself. Given that, it is unlikely that they would hold onto an understanding of themselves as teachers caught up in available discourses and in the working of power. However, putting Foucault to use allows us to consider teaching identities as continuously being transformed, displaced, and extended.

REGULATORY PRACTICES

Pre-service teachers are not only redefining their teaching identities in relation to available discourses in the classroom and to the complex selves of others, they are also learning what is defined as 'regular' practice. One of the avenues for them to do this is through the school's organisational procedures. It is true that institutional practices are measures and techniques which produce identities implicitly rather than by repressive force, yet the rationalities underpinning their specific ways of doing and knowing, have the same purpose of getting the individual teacher to conform. Once we begin to think of the school as a regime of power, it is easy to recognise how it constructs specific regulatory practices whose expressed intent is to normalise individual teachers. Ultimately, the intent is to produce teachers who are able to govern themselves. To try to fathom the part that schools' organisational practices play in governing teaching, I asked pre-service teachers to state the 'Usual time of day for mathematics lessons'; 'Usual duration of lessons'; and 'Total number of mathematics lessons occurring during teaching practice'.

The student teachers in this study stated that mathematics was routinely taught in the morning (89%). For fifty-six percent, mathematics was scheduled for early morning, and for a third, mathematics took place between the morning break and lunchtime. Timetabling arrangements like these, which differentiate curriculum areas, in effect impose temporal conditions through which the pre-service teacher is constructed to perform a designated teaching task and discouraged from teaching any other. Convincingly, the widespread practice of morning mathematics, taken together with commonsense understandings of positive effects of morning learning, would suggest that the social significance of mathematics is not lost on schools.

A third (30%) of the pre-service teachers saw mathematics taught on a daily basis, and only a relatively small number (15%) reported that mathematics took place less than four times per week. Pre-service teachers quickly learned how long each lesson would be programmed, given that the scheduled length of time was consistent from one day to the next. However the expected duration varied considerably from one classroom to another. Whilst the median time spent on mathematics during the school week was three hours twelve minutes, one student came to expect five hours regularly each week. Practices of administration like these entice the pre-service teacher into a particular cyclic order in which specific tasks and functions, by turn, are to be performed. And because these institutional practices fix limits, controlling the 'time' around which pedagogical reality might take place, they foster the development and control of what is to count as the mathematics teacher. Such organisational procedures sanction what Foucault (1977) calls 'normalisation'.

Let's now turn to what happens within the classroom. Within the classroom it is the associate teacher who authorises particularities which regulate minute details of space and time. Those particularities also regulate bodies, deportment, actions, even sometimes regulating style and clothing, reaching into the most intimate private thoughts and desires, to the extent that they produce and normalise movements and observable bodily practices.

> It was amazing to watch her in action. She definitely loves to teach, and maths has a very high profile in her class.
>
> My Associate was the leader of the school maths programme and her knowledge and love for maths definitely helped me.

For these two pre-service teachers the associate's work in the classroom operated through specific movements and gestures, all the while creating a divide, in the minds of the pre-service teachers, in the differential relation competent/non-competent teacher. The production of competency here worked through very situated and continuous micro-practices of power, in the most seemingly trivial details of embodied practice. One of the effects of paying attention to these micro-practices was that systems and regimes of 'good' teaching were produced and reproduced. Foucault has a helpful way of expressing this. He says: "What makes power hold good, what makes it accepted, is simply the fact that it doesn't weigh on us as a force that says no, but that it traverses and produces things, it induces pleasure, forms knowledge" (Foucault, 1984, p. 61). Urged on by this thinking, we can speak of spoken and embodied discursive practices as an artefact of the professional collaboration demanded of the associate/pre-service teacher relation. The associate and pre-service teacher form a mutual interdependency. In discussing this interdependency, Butler points out that not only does subjection signify the process of becoming subordinated by power; it also signifies the process of *becoming* a subject:

> [I]f, following Foucault, we understand power as forming the subject as well, as providing the very condition of its existence and the trajectory of its desire, then power is not simply what we oppose but also, in a strong sense, what we depend on for our existence and what we harbour and preserve in the beings that we are.
>
> (Butler, 1997, p. 2)

To be sure, there are other practices at play with which pre-service teachers are expected to comply. Course work at the university also imposes specific ways of doing things, and it is those understandings upon which pre-service teachers fall back on for what is to count as teaching in the classroom. By the same token, associate teachers in schools invest in their particular discursive codes of mathematics pedagogy, which accentuate particular processes and practices, and these codes shape how they might plan and enact practices in the classroom. I asked pre-service teachers to describe a typical lesson to try to understand the part that course work plays in framing their observations of classroom work. Here I wanted to bring to the fore the kinds of normative judgments against which the work of classroom teachers is assessed by pre-service teachers. In doing this I wanted to understand the ways in which the course work functions as part of the technology of normalisation.

Apart from providing a structure to pedagogical arrangements for mathematics work in the classroom, like many educational practices, the typical lesson establishes a set of institutional and social relations for the teacher and learner in the classroom. According to pre-service teachers' observations, in most classrooms the teacher first maintains prior knowledge; introduces new concepts for the day, making links with prior knowledge; provides explanations; models; poses questions for the students; supplies work and activities to enable practice of these ideas; and finally reflects on the work. In this logic the teacher moves reflexively from talk, to writing on the board, to observing, to talk and questioning, all the while grounding understanding through the process of children's activity and written work.

However, each classroom produces its own truths about teaching practice. For all the outward appearance of consistency across mathematics classrooms, what is taken as 'true' in one classroom is not to be considered as universal, nor indeed even necessary, in others. Teaching practice in any one classroom becomes intelligible through its reliance on certain techniques which are accepted, sanctioned, and made to function as true. *Power, knowledge and truth* become coordinates which constitute relationships in the classroom.

Each classroom has its particular *regime of truth* which legitimises and sanctions a discursive space for certain practices and social arrangements. Pre-service teachers recorded that in most classes, the types of practices frequently observed were teacher talk and exposition, children engaged in whole class discussion and debate, and children working with hands-on equipment. Children often worked on worksheets. Pre-service teachers estimated that group and cooperative activities were assigned for half of the class time. A quarter of the pre-service teachers observed peer assessment and a third of the children marked and corrected their own work.

Decisions about learning like these have important implications for the ways in which pedagogical relations can be conceptualised and enacted. In creating particular modes of activity, ways of being and interpersonal relationships, such decision making makes possible both what can be said and what can be done within the classroom. It is within the tradition of this understanding that it is possible to say that knowledge, including practitioners' pedagogical knowledge, is implicated not only in the practices of administration and normalisation, but also in the production of forms of sociality.

I was interested in finding out to what extent pre-service teachers 'took up' the practices of the associate teachers they had observed. I asked the pre-service teachers to comment on the way their expectations were met regarding the way in which mathematics was taught. Eighteen percent chose not to answer this question. Overall, forty-seven percent claimed that their expectations were not met. Some of those responses follow:

> Worksheets weren't great all the time. I expected to see more hands-on work as well.
>
> No use of equipment
>
> Disappointed that only maths text books and worksheets were used.
>
> I felt that by not having group work that some children were slipping through the gaps.
>
> I didn't like children working through a textbook—this was not my idea of teaching.
>
> I think the Associate sees herself as a facilitator to pass out worksheets.
>
> I almost felt as if I knew more about teaching maths and portraying it effectively.

Other pre-service teachers were more enthused about the practices they witnessed in classrooms. Some thirty-five percent of the pre-service teachers stated that the way in which mathematics was taught had met their expectations:

> HANDS ON! Children did enjoy the practical activities.
>
> Group work went well as children are closer in ability.
>
> [I was interested to see] that concepts were put into real, relevant contexts and that children were able to experience these.
>
> The teacher integrated maths into the morning roll call, as children counted how many children were at school, how many boys/girls, the difference between the number of boys/girls etc.
>
> Teacher always asked 'how did you work that out?' and got children to explain their working out.
>
> Math was very much made relevant and hands on for the children who experienced a lot of different activities, e.g., popcorn (mass/weight), cooking recipes, different food containers.
>
> Of interest was the way many children in my class supported each other in their work, or were willing to tutor each other.

Teacher education institutions that offer mathematics courses promote particular mathematics knowledge and particular pedagogic modes of operating. Through the knowledges and modes of operating that it advocates and promotes, the university course establishes a benchmark for what will count as 'doing mathematics'. Through explicit engagements with the official curriculum statement and taking on board the way in which the official curriculum document represents development, cognition, pedagogy, assessment, and the learner, pre-service teachers, before too long, come to learn what counts as evidence of acceptable practices. They very quickly learn what particular pedagogic modes are legitimated in the course and the types of classroom arrangements that are privileged and said to be conducive to knowledge facilitation.

In this study, the symbolic and material resources privileged in course work included the use of *apparatus and technology*. The resources recognised *difference*, and validated *problem solving*, *group activities, integrated learning*, and *collaboration*. The teacher's role was to create a supportive learning environment, facilitating and empowering. The teacher was not to posture as the authoritative validator of thinking. Thus the teacher was expected to provide an inclusive and supportive environment and to offer tasks of a suitable mathematical challenge. She was to press for understanding, knowing when to intervene and when not to interfere, in whole class and small group discussions.

By producing the terms of school mathematics and thus the parameters of school mathematical practice—the possibility and effectivity of classroom teaching—the university course had powerfully created a desirable identity for the mathematics teacher. It is no surprise then, that the pre-service teachers read the concrete classroom practice of the associate teacher through the terms and parameters made available by the course. Those terms established normative judgements about what could pass as teaching mathematics. Knowledge from the course regulated their minds to the extent it coloured their observations.

Although it is difficult to produce conclusive evidence of the fact, most of us would not hesitate to agree that the evaluations we make are often made without our full awareness. For the moment it is enough to know that observations often operate below conscious awareness. The pre-service teachers were evaluating the practice of their associate almost without their full awareness. Yet what they saw, they viewed to some extent from their own vested interests in their university course. In creating knowledge and modes of operating for future teachers of school mathematics, the course worked as a powerful cultural institution, positioning, defining, enabling and regulating its prospective teachers. In Foucauldian jargon, by normalising particular pedagogical practices, the course operated as part of the technology of normalisation.

> [power]...applies itself to immediate everyday life which categorizes the individual, marks him by his own individuality, attaches him to his own identity, imposes a law of truth on him, which he must recognize and which others have to recognize in him. It is a form of power which makes individuals subjects.
>
> (Foucault, in Dreyfus & Rabinow, 1982, p. 212)

TECHNOLOGIES OF SURVEILLANCE AND NORMALISATION

Like practitioners in other fields of professional practice, prospective teachers are confronted with the task of learning the discursive codes of practice. As they move from the university course into the school they enter a different network of political and social discursive practices. In a way that is difficult to imagine, the identity positions which the course's discourses offer often provide pre-service teachers with access to a differential engagement and positioning in relation to the regime of 'knowledgeable' practice operating in schools. The discourses available to them ran in "different and even contradictory" (Foucault, 1984, p. 101) mode. For reasons that escape the novice teacher, the classroom discursive codes of practice are not always made explicit to the novice: "Maths just seems to happen in this classroom. It just arrives along like all the other curriculum areas" [respondent]. On the other hand, for the associate teacher, teaching constitutes a closely scripted strategy of how teacher's work is to be enacted in the classroom.

Lacking the full credentials to live in the world of teaching, pre-service teachers try to carve out a teaching voice in a setting already created by others. They work hard at embodying the classroom practices. The reason for this is that gaining better access to this 'knowledgable' practice may well elevate their subordinate and less influential position. Perhaps it will make them feel part of the classroom community. Whatever the reason, embodying the classroom practices demands attention to those strategic practices and orientations in schools which, taken together, signify the subject position of the teacher. But attention to detail is not enough: that attention to detail must be monitored, and the pre-service teachers' practice must be assessed against the associate's standards.

Practices of surveillance are critically important to consistency and continuity within the pedagogical site. In short, there isn't a great deal that goes on in relation to the pre-service teacher's classroom practice that the associate teacher won't find out about if she seeks consistency for her students. It goes some way to explaining why pre-service teachers prefer to copy and adapt ideas for planning and teaching, that have been suggested by their associate teachers, rather than drawing on their own knowledge. The point to remember is that practices of surveillance, regulating and sanctioning the work of the pre-service teacher, are going on all the time, which is why it is so remarkable that they are interpreted frequently by the pre-service teacher with such positivity. We can see glimpses of their operation in the next transcripts.

> My associate was very well organised and supportive. She shared all her plans and resources with me. She provided quality feedback with positive ideas for me to improve on.

> She [the associate] gave me a lot of freedom to use my ideas. She supported me and asked if I needed anything and shared resources.

> Full of ideas, very supportive of new approaches. Happy to share information. Associate happy to learn herself.

Not only are pre-service teachers working at developing the technicalities of mathematics practice, they are also, among other things, exploring their mathematical teaching positionings in someone else's classroom. It doesn't take much to realise that in the associate/pre-service teacher relation, the pre-service teacher is one of the primary effects of disciplinary institutional power. Now the thing to point out is that the most pervasive disciplinary practice is the panoptical gaze (Foucault, 1977). Whereas the 'gaze' is delicate and seemingly intangible, its networks have the capacity to determine the very texture of teaching and its possibilities. For some of the pre-service teachers in the study, subtleties within the networks of power were shaping a love of and passion for teaching mathematics. Such alliances, however, were not always apparent:

> [At the end] I was disillusioned at the lack of encouragement I received from my A. T. [Associate Teacher]. Nice enough person but I think that I made her feel I was taking her class away as they were so responsive to all the new ideas that I brought into the classroom. I could have used some help in developing new ways for the children to think and try things but the A. T. had tried and true methods of working and that was the way it was.
>
> After slowing down I got the hang of taking a maths lesson. I tried doing more exciting activities with the class which they enjoyed, but I found after a couple of days it was best for them to go back to the structured routine of book work...The lessons should not be structured so much so that children can't handle change.
>
> I was enthusiastic and ready to put ideas to practice about how to be an effective teacher, but the topic based maths programme didn't allow for it.
>
> I wanted to introduce new ideas but did not have enough confidence. I just followed my Associate's plans. I felt I could not try new things as my Associate was set in the way things were done.
>
> At first I was very enthusiastic and full of ideas but found that due to the teaching style of my associate it was difficult to implement my plans. [At the end] I had adjusted my personal style to fit the class culture. It is difficult to force your way. You really just have to fit the class as it already is.
>
> I was forced to follow her methods of teaching in maths as that is what she had planned and wanted maintained. I am confident in maths but was given little opportunity to express my confidence. Could not go outside the square.

Typically for these pre-service teachers, the transfer from the university course into the school brought specific dividing practices sharply into focus. For them, the classroom space was fraught with ambiguous and sometimes painful negotiations to produce a teaching identity. It is certainly true that the pre-service teacher who invests in the discursive practices of the associate tends to engage fully with the technologies and practices through which mathematics teaching is managed in the associate's classroom. It is an engagement made with a glance towards the pre-service teacher's desire for regulated pedagogical practice—a glance oriented prospectively to continued and future placement within this classroom. Pre-service teaching, then depends as much on embodied relations of power between people in the practicum as it does on choosing which material resources or any underpinning educational philosophy.

It seems stretching things to say that teaching practice is a strategic political activity, but this is certainly the case. Once you imagine the pedagogical relation between pre-service teacher/associate as one fused with networks of power, it all makes a lot of sense. What follows from this perspective, is that it is impossible for pre-service teachers to practise disinterestedly in schools, and that it because their practice in schools always works through vested interests—both their own and the rhetoric of others.

We must be careful not to take this line of thinking to what might seem an obvious linear conclusion. Let's be clear that there is no causal link between the determining structures (associate's practice) and the action of individuals (pre-service teaching practice). It is worth noting that Foucault criticises the cause-effect tradition on two counts: the mode of the essential human subject which it employs, and the practices which it projects and regulates about the individual. Although we cannot claim linearity between associate practice and pre-service teaching, that is not to suggest that there is complete disunity between the levels of action. By virtue of her mere presence in the classroom, the pre-service teacher engages with, negotiates, and contests the cultural logics of the associate's practice. Most of what we knew previously, or believed we knew about teacher education, comes from classic studies that talk about pre-service teaching in social and cultural terms. Many of us have latched on to these explanations because they seemed to deal with aspects of practice traditionally overlooked. Such social and cultural studies, regrettably, fail to take into account the way in which the novice teacher is simultaneously inscribed within and refashions classroom existence in relation to others.

Unexplained elements exist in many authoritative arguments about learning to teach. Some researchers have tried to explain the lack of perfect fit between practices advocated by course work and actual teaching practice as a problem of the school setting. Others have set some score on the idea of pre-service teachers' varied engagements with course work. These explanations derive from and sustain conceptions of instrumental rationality: that people and circumstances can be matched up. Within this conventional paradigm there is no place to consider the pre-service teacher in any terms other than in a model of normality/pathology. In drawing attention to a set of issues which commonly have remained outside the scope of analyses, Foucault maintains that a perfect fit between self and society, and between social relations and psychic reality is an impossibility. Perfect fits are impossible between the associate and the novice teacher, between the ideal or imagined teacher and the real teacher, and between course work and classroom practice. Practices always place both parties within circulating and competing relations of knowledge, desire, and power.

CONCLUDING THOUGHTS ON THE CONSTITUTION OF TEACHING

Our exploration has focused on the constitution of teaching identity and its complicity within structures of power, privilege and subordination. The point was to show whose experiences and what knowledges count or are withheld during the process of establishing pedagogic authority. The account revealed that teaching mathematics in primary [elementary] school involves processes of normalisation and surveillance, in which the spoken and the unspoken becomes intricately linked both to the production of teaching knowledge and to the subjectivity of teachers. In the spaces shared by the pre-service and associate teachers, issues of power and privilege feature prominently, contributing in no small way to the shaping of teacher identification.

The analysis took as its starting point the politics of identity construction. Working with Foucault has allowed us to conceive of pre-service teacher identity as fractured and fragmented, and conceive of the classroom as a site of negotiation over the real and its meanings. It is a way of thinking about the concept of teacher identity as complex and multiple, developed in response to other identities which are sometimes held in opposition. Teaching experience then becomes much more than an issue of content knowledge and technical skills; it is, above all, a source of (micro)political engagement. Developing a sense of the pedagogical grows out of a history of response to local discursive classroom codes and wider educational discourses and practices, all of which interrupt, derail, and elide the best intentions of the pre-service teacher.

ACTIVITY

1. Note down features, in relation to the following, that are characteristic of an educational institution familiar to you:
   - its information processes
   - its artefacts
   - its routines and rituals
   - its technologies
   - the language it uses
   - the relationships it engenders
   - the opportunities it provides for participation

2. Now consider another familiar educational institution.
   Compare and contrast its structural and interrelational processes with your first institution. Write about your identity in these two different institutions.

CHAPTER 8

GIRLS DISCIPLINING OTHERS

IN THIS CHAPTER

- Normalisation
- Stories about girls (and boys) in schooling
- The study
- Girls monitoring boys in the classroom
- Girls monitoring other girls in the classroom

Disciplinary power is diffuse. It works through processes and through networks of relationships to control people right across contemporary society. The greatest of all amazements is that we don't normally tend to think of ourselves as being controlled and under surveillance as we go about our day-to-day activities. Most of us feel comfortable in the knowledge that large-scale disciplinary measures are necessary for society's safety and security, but not many of us would have spared a thought about the hold power has over our lives. But that's the thing about disciplinary power: it makes us want to conform and comply. In fact, without often knowing it, we make sure that what we do, think, and say, is in line with what is expected of us in our normal existence.

If disciplinary power influences the way we carry out our everyday tasks, it also affects the way we see others. It works through networks of relationships that involve others. If we 'toe the line' then we make sure that others do also, even to the extent of assessing their reading, writing and the way they do mathematics. We are constantly weighing up others' behaviour in relation to what we take as normal, often without knowing we are actually doing this. It's as if we want everything to be 'normal' in the particular places and times we happen to be. We are continually assessing that what we and others do, never strays too far from the realm of the acceptable and sanctioned and that it's never too close to the wildly aberrant or eccentric.

NORMALISATION

Normalisation is an instrument of disciplinary power. It goes hand-in-hand with surveillance. You can't have one without the other. Think back to what you already know about the practice of surveillance, and recall the Panopticon with its all-seeing yet unseen surveillance operations designed to render compliance and put a stop to unwanted behaviour. It involved the inspection and monitoring of individual actions and bodily behaviour without the individual's full awareness that he or she was actually being observed at any one moment. It influenced what people did. Surveillance is like that: it influences us and affects the choices people made. It tends to make us make 'normal' choices. It normalises being, thinking and doing to the extent that we begin to 'watch ourselves', matching our behaviour against the standards and control established. This is an unparalleled achievement, yet so scarcely appreciated, that it is worth exploring further.

The thing about normalisation is that it opens up membership to social entities that have a sense of cohesion about them. Yet there is something perplexing about this idea. Part of the problem is that we tend to think of normalising processes as coercion. But the coercion that goes alongside our membership in particular groups extends only so far as we readily accept it as legitimate. It's difficult to imagine that institutions such as the Bridge club, the needlepoint group, or the gardening circle, for example, are coercive. We fairly quickly learn the norms of practice as members within these institutions but we don't tend to consider our practice as coerced. Coercion is disguised from us in these and in all the social institutions within which we participate.

Education is one such social institution. It provides a perfect demonstration of how easy it is to be seduced by its emancipatory rhetoric. Membership to its services is through practices and understandings that measure up to the norms is sets. Its norms are many and varied and have the effect of regulating us while simultaneously constituting us as individuals. The norms, in their capacity as standard-settings and, in keeping with the trappings of an influential governing body, mark out hierarchies, classifications and ranks, more often than not, through examinations and tests. Tests and examinations are primary instruments of disciplinary power because their functions include both surveillance and normalisation. It is these dual strategies that become the means by which students can be appraised by others and by which they can assess themselves without resorting to formal rules. Just to be sure that they keep themselves in check, there are rewards, as well as penalties.

It makes a lot of sense to think about the school as one of the modern apparatuses of social regulation. It performs a normalising function—and does it admirably well, by the way; disciplining intellect through remedial classes and extension groups, setting/streaming, repeat testing and examination, and so on. It's not just intellect that is the focus of the school's attention. Students every actions and interactions, and their understandings of their place in the school, are just some of the aspects of their subjectivity that come under the constant gaze of teachers, principals, other students and so on. The gaze differentiates and compares. The tiniest deviation from normal practice is noticed. Gaps, omissions, and extremes—all these are held up for inspection. To give some examples, the practices that the school gaze focuses upon are lateness, absences, inattention, disrespect, lack of enthusiasm, failure to complete homework, impropriety, offensive language, and so on.

Within and between the school's wide normalising gaze, the student's whole body and soul is open to scrutiny. Even the most seemingly insignificant features of the student's life become subjected to analysis. It is not simply the school itself that performs the normalising function: scrutiny doesn't tend to stop at the school gate. Beyond the school, but still part of the wider educational process, the student becomes an object of surveillance and normalisation from a whole battery of services, such as school counsellors and educational psychologists, and even the courts and social services. These services perform the tasks of controlling, policing, managing and transforming forms of behaviour, character and attitudes. Once you begin looking for it, disciplinary power over students is pervasive. It appears in:

> ...the multiplicity of force relations immanent in the sphere in which they operate and which constitute their own organisation; as the process which, through ceaseless struggles and confrontations, transforms, strengthens or reverses them; as the support which these force relations find in one another, thus forming a chain or a system, or on the contrary, the disjunctions and contradictions which isolate them one from another.
>
> (Foucault, 1984, p. 92)

It is little wonder that students learn to monitor their own being, and they do this by practices of self-regulating, ever mindful of the gaze of others. Their success within their classes and at school is a measure of the level with which they embrace and perform the practices of the institution. What happens is that they become normalised into the school's practices. But more than that: they begin to monitor others. Students, themselves, become part of the disciplinary machinery intent on meticulous inspection to ensure conformity and compliance within the whole school body. They search for deviations from the norm, and describe, evaluate and compare. The deviant student becomes a case to tell a story about.

STORIES ABOUT GIRLS (AND BOYS) IN SCHOOLING

As you will be aware there's been many a story told about girls in mathematics. Traditional studies told us that girls had inferior spatial skills (Maccoby & Jacklin, 1974); that they asked fewer and more lower level thinking questions in class than do boys (Fennema & Peterson, 1986); and that they received less attention and less praise and criticism than the boys in their mathematics classes (Fennema & Peterson, 1986). Victory narratives circulating at the current time tell us about girls' changed participation patterns and enhanced achievement levels. In sharp contrast to the focus of research a few decades ago, it is girls' enhanced performance that is preoccupying a growing body of international work. In many countries girls are excelling in their chosen subjects and completing university courses with more success than boys.

Now we don't want to downplay these successes, but we do need to be aware that success does not come to every girl. Scholastic achievement is influenced more by ethnicity and social class than by gender. The hard reality is that students from low-skilled and unemployed families are much less likely than students with higher professional origins to perform well at school or participate in university courses. It is worth considering, too, that traditional roles are still fixed for girls in some classrooms. In a number of classrooms, boys still tend to dominate classroom space and teacher time and, just as they have always been, girls' contributions tend to be marginalised. This fact is of interest to us here and we want to see if these practices operated in the social space of a low socioeconomic classroom.

Valerie Walkerdine (1990) has argued that the school is a site of production and regulation of subjectivities—it is a site of specific practices whose primary objective is the covert regulation of young people. Nairn (1997) described that regulation by exploring how male and female students learn the differential cultural meanings attached to silence and talking in the classroom. Kehily and Nayak (1997) focused on the specific practice of humour and the part it plays in positioning young men within peer groups at school. In their study of working-class heterosexual masculinities, they reported that "humour plays a significant part in consolidating male peer group cultures" (p. 69) and "structuring the performance of masculine identities" (p. 84). These researchers propose that the young working-class men in the study were posturing heterosexuality and using humour to discipline others with a view towards building a 'proper' social world. Boys, just like girls, in their day-to-day moment-to-moment social worlds, work at constructing social orders.

One of the ways gendered subjectivity has been explored in recent scholarship is through spatial metaphors that model the classroom as a site for practices of exclusion and inclusion—the classroom is a *space* that seeks to define and monitor subjectivities. Spatiality, in this kind of thinking, is neither opaque, transparent, nor independent of power. Pink (2001) elaborates: "the gendered self is never fully defined in any absolute way,...it is only in specific social interactions that the gender identity of any individual comes in to being *in relation to* the negotiations that it undertakes with other individuals" (p. 21). The idea of the classroom as a gendered space—a space constituted of, and by, material and embodied discursive relations and practice—suggests that the classroom is deeply implicated in power. "[A]ll spatialities are political because they are the (covert) medium and (disguised) expression of asymmetrical relations of power" (Keith & Pile, 1993, p. 220).

Like all other institutional structures the classroom, in a sense, is a closed system, with its own rules governing beliefs about ways of operating. Those disciplinary operations not only normalise practice, they also, through subtle coercion, mark out social relations and create positionings amongst the people within the classroom space. "The gentle efficiency of total surveillance" (Foucault, 1984, p. 217) ensures that the classroom becomes part of a wider educational regime whose central mission presupposes conforming and obedient individuals. But surveillance and normalisation are not only fundamentally political, they are also highly gendered. Femininities and masculinities are shaped by the powerful practices of surveillance and normalisation that operate within the classroom. The notion of the female gaze goes some way to explaining how disciplinary social power operates locally and strategically right across members within the classroom setting.

THE STUDY

The exploration that follows tracks normalisation processes at work within a group of school girls. Reading what girls have to say about everyday classroom life will give us insights about negotiations that take place around femininity and masculinity in schooling. Through the girls' stories we can appreciate how femininities and masculinities are normalised in the classroom. The specific group under investigation here is made up of a cohort of four girls all of whom attended a small urban school whose students were from families of low socioeconomic status (SES). The following year, as is the custom in New Zealand where this study took place, the girls all moved as Year 7 students to an Intermediate school for the next two years in the same locality. The latter school's roll was approximately three times the size of their primary [elementary] school. Like the primary school, it attracted students from an ethnically mixed urban area.

With the consent of the school and the Principal a group interview was conducted in a committee room in the school's administration block before the lunch break during a regular day at the bigger school. The interview was part of a larger data set that included observations over a period of time in the girls' classrooms. The girls [aged 11] familiarised themselves with the audio recording equipment before the interview by asking each other questions and playing the recording back to the group. They had a lot of fun in doing this. I had prepared an interview schedule, asking what the classroom was like for them. I told them that what I was interested in the group interview were the students in the classroom—the boys and the girls. What do the students do and how do they behave? Most of the prepared questions became redundant because the girls took the lead in the conversations.

It needs to be pointed out that because only four students were involved, we can't make sweeping generalisations that speak on behalf of all school girls. Nor can we make comparisons with girls from other social classes. But what we can do is pay attention to the diversity amongst the girls themselves, and find out how each girl constituted herself in the classroom and sought to contribute to the subjectivities of others.

Transcriptions notes:

(i) The quotes appear in the same order as they were recorded during the interview.

(ii) Occasionally a student repeated herself or another student's words. Repetitions that do not contribute further to the discussion have been edited.

(iii) The names used are not the girls' given names.

GIRLS MONITORING BOYS IN THE CLASSROOM

Shanaia Well, the boys, they're just like the most disgusting boys I've ever met on the earth 'cause you know last year at primary school the boys were a lot more behaved, but the ones in my class they're just disgusting, farting on peoples' desks, throwing bugs in your hair and doing everything.

This was not exactly what I had expected to hear. My observations in the classroom led me to suggest that Shanaia spoke with exaggerated effect. For reasons that can only invite wondered speculation, she spoke with high levels of emotion. What we can say, however, is that her views do capture a heightened sense of loss: she is, like all students who move to a new school, confronted with the discursive codes of a new environment. Lucey and Reay (2000) have explained how transitions from one school to another place the student "on the threshold of momentous changes in their lives" (p. 194). As she shifted from her small primary school to the larger school, Shanaia entered a different network of political and social discursive practices. The identity positions and politics which these discourses offer, provided her with access to a differential engagement and positioning in relation to the regime of 'knowledgeable' practice operating in schools. And the interesting thing about the interview was that it provided her personally with a power and a voice to oppose masculinities confronted in the classroom and to assert herself as "more mature and educationally focused than the boys" (Reay, 2001, p. 157), legitimating the expression of moral judgments.

A complex family history of low socio-economic status also came into play. In relation to that history, she was also learning what is defined as 'normal' and 'not normal' practice through the available discourses in the classroom. Through her words it is easy to read the same critical assessment of young people's behaviour as "out of control and a threat to the moral order" (Lucey & Reay, 2000, p. 193), that are aired in the public arena. Equipped with her own gendered and classed understandings of appropriate behaviour, Shanaia was exploring her own gendered positioning in relation to her image of the normal, conforming male student, naturalised by wider social commentary and her previous classroom experiences.

In Shanaia's words we find evidence of what McLeod (2000) names as her "self-conscious struggle with new forms of identity" (p. 505). "Rooted in the spatial home of the body" (Pile & Thrift, 1995), she is constituted by a "federation of different discourses" (p. 11) one of which she presents to us as the 'disruptive boys' behaviourial code. The popular media discourse of female power might also signify in her "negotiations around masculinity and femininity" (Lucey & Reay, p. 192). To address the question of how codes of behaviour, as developed by the classroom, are implicated in the production of gendered individuals, I continued:

Margaret:	Lisa, do you want to say anything?
Lisa	Most of the boys in the class I think are really annoying, because they don't listen to the teacher and one of the most annoying ones is Hayden 'cause he's always yelling and playing around and he's always writing on people's desks.
Margaret	Meriana, did you want to say anything about the boys in the classroom?
Meriana	Oh yeah, I'll say one thing. There's these boys Teno and Aaron and Johnny they're—no one in our class likes them because every time we like do something they back chat the teacher and they get smart and all that, and none of us like it.
Shanaia	I know something. Because of the boys in our class, when the teacher's trying to teach us she has to like deal with them like she has to go over to them and tell them off and it takes a long time. So it disrupts the learning of us. So she's been pretty much mostly all of her time telling them off instead of teaching us....For the boys in my class, they always call out and our teacher has to always stop what she's doing and stuff and it's really annoying 'cause when all the boys are talking we have to stay in at lunch times and play times and umm, it's like really annoying 'cause we lose some of our play time and lunch time.

In the classroom students are one of the primary effects of disciplinary power. Gaining better access to that disciplinary power requires exploring those strategic practices and orientations in classroom which, taken together, signify the subject position of the female and male learner. It involves investigating how particular surveillance procedures, exercised in relation to gendered practices, monitor the work of the male student in the classroom. Lisa, Meriana, and Shanaia suggest that male students in this classroom are regulated through a covert set of standards and value systems associated with classroom behaviour and attitude to work. These standards are sustained in subtle and diffuse ways. Differences, deviations, peculiarities, and eccentricities of male students' practice are placed under the female gaze and assessed against her standards.

Surveillance practices are important here because they suggest practices of monitoring that are, simultaneously, practices for defining and potentially regulating subjectivities. The classroom, construed as a regime of power, constructs specific regulatory practices for the normalisation and ultimately the production of the self-governing individual student. Even as those watchful practices operate covertly rather than by repressive force, the rationalities underpinning their specific ways of doing and knowing, have the same purpose of 'securing' the conforming individual. It is the practice of surveillance that contributes to gendered continuities within the pedagogical site.

In their descriptions of classroom life, Lisa, Meriana, and Shanaia reveal both "a limited and a limiting discourse" (Reay, 2001, p. 158) of conventional classroom masculinities, based on their knowledge of the 'normal' male student. For them, in Foucauldian terms, assessing others is "a surveillance that makes it possible to qualify, to classify and to punish. It establishes over individuals a visibility through which one differentiates them and judges them" (p. 184). In order to adjudicate on normality, they need to be able to name benchmark acceptable practices and states of being. Those practices invariably implicate them directly, as indicated in the excerpt below:

Lisa	Connor - he sits beside me and he's sometimes nice and he asks for things before he takes them.
Patrice	There's one boy in our class. His name's Matthew. He's kind of cool sometimes.

The two girls' explicit normalising practices are predicated on their own knowledge of the target object (the male student) and, for them, being a student in this classroom constitutes a closely scripted strategy of how that presence is to be enacted. They mark out that presence by identifying and naming what they consider appropriate behaviour and presences: "nice," "asking for things before taking them," "kind of cool." By naming these categories, the girls have established their own personal classificatory grids for normalising other students in relation to practice within the classroom, strategically fashioning identifications for the boys in the class. It is through the practice of differentiation and judgment that the parameters of what will qualify as gendered patterns of behaviour are named, sanctioned and against which the performance of others will be assessed. It is those fashionings that will be both sustained and contested in the dynamics of everyday classroom life.

The students' narratives trace out 'laddish' practices and behaviour, and might be read as knowledge about *other* texts that prescribe meaningful and acceptable thinking about students as learners within this particular classroom. Reay's (2002) working-class exploration illustrates extreme laddish behaviour of "classroom and intermittent eruptions of violence," a "classroom context rarely conducive to learning" (p. 227). Shaun, the subject of the investigation, "tough in the playground and scholarly in the classroom" (p. 226) is caught between a rock and a hardplace.

Recent scholarship that attempts to map the subject has emphasised the fluid and fragile nature of subjectivity: a shifting ground formed from spatial coordinates. Important questions that we might ask about the nature of the subject are "dependent on the kind of map on which we place these coordinates" (Pile & Thrift, p. 5). Those maps allow us to experience ourselves as gendered, classed, and so forth—the object we appear to have become. Gendered subjectivity is experienced through a range of different maps, for example, diligent scholar, helpful daughter, financially disadvantaged family. Varying degrees of movement are available within and between each map. In Reay's study, movement was restricted by the culture of male aggression that operated as a "fixing mechanism" (p. 224). That culture became a coalition that put tight constraints around the effects of the male student's self-fashionings as a diligent learner. Becoming aware of the limits of one's effectiveness is a task fraught with feelings of powerlessness, as indicated in Patrice's comment below:

Patrice	Most of the boys, they throw things around and since I'm Pupil Counsellor [classroom rep] I can do something but they don't listen, cause, yeah, I'm only, I'm only little and yeah.

Davies (1997) reports on the difficulty encountered in constructing new subject positions for children. In Davies's study, positions of dominance provide meaning and definition to what is 'ordinary' and taken for granted. Within other discourses and at other times, there is more space for manoeuvre, and subjectivity is able to be acted upon by the subject as well as the social collectivity. As in a number of other explorations (e.g., Connolly, 1998; Martino et al., 1999; Skelton, 2001) male subjectivity in this study is displaced and extended as the boys engage in resisting the girls' practices and discourses that centre the girls' ideal of masculinity in the classroom. The boys do this by using the spaces opened up for them to sustain their current configurations. Subjectivity in this classroom exists in multiple differentiations emerging "in a space of difference and tension–between potential and possibility" (Hayes, 2003, p. 9).

GIRLS MONITORING OTHER GIRLS IN THE CLASSROOM

The girls in the study spoke about the behaviour of male students in the classroom and from their views, the political and strategic nature of classroom life emerged. Although there was some consistency in their viewpoints, not all discourses had the same pull for each of the girls. Variously they positioned the boys in the class, constituting some in one discourse and some in others. The forms of subjectivity they validated, respectively, were sanctioned in accordance with their own networks of scrutiny and coercion. From their surveillance came a general conclusion that many of the boys in the class did not measure up. How do the girls in the class measure up?

Margaret	You've said lot of things about the boys. What about the girls in the classroom?
Shanaia	The girls, some of the, like a few of the girls in the classroom they're sometimes chatty like Julia and Victoria. And they always play around and Julia, like, talks a lot and she does really long stories and she's sometimes annoying and talkative.
Margaret	Okay, anybody else like to say anything?
Shanaia	Well. Pretty much me and my friend, Lisa, we hang out with all the girls in our class 'cause we all play tackle, rugby and netball…. Well, there's this girl Judith, she's like the craziest girl in class. She acts sort of, okay this is kind of mean, but she does act sort of a little disabled and she writes a real lot. Victoria, she thinks she's God. She threatens to beat us up if we tell anyone, if she tells us something or anything. What else does she do? Today I saw Lisa trying to put her desk up but Victoria had her head back like that and Victoria—she tries to be like as mean as Hayden and all that.
Lisa	She tries acting like she's cool. She's really annoying 'cause she acts like she's the boss of everybody.

All students, both female and male, are subjected to the female gaze. To some extent there is evidence of "the emergence of a group identity" (Lucey & Reay, 2000, p. 199) outside the classroom; a solidarity formed from playing the same sports. Within the classroom, however, the research students gave voice to particularities that attempt to regulate minute details of inappropriate actions: writing "really long stories;" "being annoying;" "being talkative;" "threaten[ing] to beat us up;" "boss[ing] everybody." In labelling Judith as *the craziest girl in the class* Shanaia appeared to wrestle momentarily with the conflict between whether or not to risk naming disability. On one level, classifying Judith as "a little disabled" would have the effect of setting Judith apart from the other girls in the class: she is different and hence not like the rest of the girls. On another level, educational discourses that abound in the community argue for a more politically correct inclusive standpoint in which difference and diversity are not to be shunned. Difference wins out and Shanaia attempts to normalise movements and gestures: "had her head back like that;" "as mean as Hayden;" "acting like she's cool." In the way I read it, for these girls being 'cool' takes on different meanings for the girls and the boys in this classroom.

In this classroom, the gaze upon other girls, rather than being erased, was, in many ways, brought into sharper focus. It was more hypercritical. Highlighting the trivial and marginalising the idiosyncratic, it operated to facilitate the production of the ideal conforming female student. Reay (2001) described how the 'girlies' and the 'nice girls' in her study of a working-class classroom were the object of intense critical observation by other members in the class. The 'nice girls' were criticised as 'boring' and 'not fun to be with', whereas the 'girlies' were 'stupid' and 'dumb'. (p. 159). The 'tomboys' criticised all other girls: "Girls are crap, all the girls in the class act all stupid and girlie" (p. 161). Denigration fell to the 'spice girls' who were criticised heavily by both students and teachers alike for failing to comply with the conventions of traditional femininity.

Through very situated and continuous micro-practices of power, the girls' gaze in this study worked to equalise behaviour and actions in the most seemingly innocuous details of embodied practice. Directly linked to systems of knowledge, subtleties within the networks of power determined the texture of 'female student'. What obtained was a construction of 'female student' that appeared natural and inevitable, but that was in effect, shaped by others' ideas and intentions. It is by naturalising particular constructions and excluding all others that do not comply, that regimes of female practice and constructions of identity were produced and reproduced. Some girls embodied the 'naturalised' practices; others lacked the commonalities, at least at the time, to access the subjectivity expressed for them.

Margaret	Did you want to say anything Meriana?
Meriana	When I hang out with my friends, Mariah and Micheala and Hayley, every time I go out for PE, Tapuae, there's always Stephanie and Melissa and heaps of other people that, like at least one person ruins our PE time and then we have to stay in. Mostly all my friends have to tell Stephanie or another person why they spoilt our game Tapuae.
Margaret	Is that sometimes a boy, or it could be a girl as well?
Meriana	It's mostly girls.
Shanaia	There's these three girls in my class and they really, they talk all the time. Like, 'cause there's only one [large] desk and, like, those three girls, oh not three but one of them, Lulu, she's on there. Loreisha, she's on that desk with two other girls Laura and Lesley, they always talk and they get us in trouble. It's really annoying when they talk. And but even though they say sorry, they still do it. And one time we had a student teacher and Laura and Lesley were talking and our student teacher told Laura off and she back ch..., oh whatever. And she talked back to the teacher like angrily and then he was getting, he didn't growl her really bad, he just stood there, just told her off and she just kept on back chatting. And then, well that's what I don't like about them.
Margaret	So it's not just the boys in the class who are annoying, there are some girls?
All	Yeah.

The practices of surveillance that Shanaia, Lisa, Meriana, and Patrice have spoken into existence map onto a complex grid of wider formal and informal educational and social discourses about female and male identifications in schooling. Girl power in this classroom operated as a set of highly coercive articulations through strategic disciplining practices that focused on both attention to trivia and seriously disruptive practice claiming classroom space and teacher time. These practices seldom left a stone unturned, targeting gestures, behaviour, and practices of both male and female alike. It was these that were used by the girls to differentiate from what they believed counted as gendered patterns of behaviour. It was sparked by their own idiosyncratic understandings of classroom behaviour and their understandings of gendered and classed positionings within wider social discourses.

CLOSING COMMENTS ABOUT DISCIPLINING PRACTICES

Truths about gendered subjectivity are produced in all classrooms. Each classroom cohort of students operates within its particular regime of truth, all the while legitimising and sanctioning gendered practice. Once students in the classroom are subjected to surveillance and normalising measures by other students, their subjectivity is continuously transformed, displaced, and extended. We have seen how this played out in the study. The girls' classroom observations had the effect of homogenising experiences and in restricting others' efforts in daring to be different. The result was a view of the political and strategic nature of classroom life—a decidedly frank look at how power infuses the 'reality' of classroom life. It is safe to say that educational experience in any classroom becomes much more than participation and performance; it is an issue of micropolitical engagement with discursive classroom codes, all of which are set upon providing the student with a sense of self-in-schooling.

Differential access to normalised female classroom subjectivity may have implications for students' current and future participation and performance. Those students who 'read' correctly the practice-specific meanings and tools of the learner will assume an identity that associates them with membership of the classroom student community. Those students who cannot or refuse to identify with the patterns of 'normal' studentship will be marginalised to some extent from the practices of classroom learning. And the thing is, the classroom becomes a space that has the potential to set cognitive limits both now and for future educational chances.

ACTIVITY

A teacher is talking to her Year 12 class during a unit on calculus.

(i) *If we start with y equals x to some power, which we will call n, then the instantaneous rate of change, which we are going to call y dashed, for a start–there are other notations too–is n times x to the power of n minus one. So whatever this number is, we put it in front and we reduce this by one. So this is a rule which you've got to learn.*

(ii) *Please don't use this sort of 'd'. Use that sort [pointing to the whiteboard]. Some of you write fancy 'd's' like that. They look very nice but they mean something entirely different.*

(iii) *Make sure it's set out properly, not just a whole jumble of numbers with an answer at the end. Clearly distinguish between your original function and your derived function. Make this DASH clear.*

(iv) *X to the power negative two, is one over x squared. Are you all happy about this? If you have one over 'a' to the power negative three, it's the same as 'a' cubed. If you have one over 'm' to the power four, it's going to be 'm' to the power negative four.*

Using the transcripts and drawing on the concepts of normalisation and surveillance, describe the ways in which mathematics teaching features as a mode of disciplinary domination and discuss the part it plays in shaping subjectivities.

CHAPTER 9

RESEARCH

IN THIS CHAPTER

- Knowing others
- Research traditions
- Rethinking research
- Constructing reality
- Breaking away from convention
- Rachel's story

We are all consumers of research. We read what researchers are doing. We hear about research on tv and the radio. Friends and family occasionally tell us about this or that fascinating finding. In fact, barely a day goes by when 'research has found' or 'science says' doesn't hit our radar. Whether we like to admit it or not, we thrive on research, in much the same way that some people thrive on living vicariously through the lives of celebrities. A few of us simply can't get enough of research. As if to emphasise its special place in our lives, we attend conferences to hear or talk with others about latest trends and to be assured that what we are doing is on the right track.

Most of us tend to accept what we read or hear about research without any reservation. We don't usually question it. After all, science has come up with any number of important facts, solutions and figures. To us it all seems highly credible. But is it? The mystery of research is that it is not necessarily all it seems. This is hardly a radical observation because some of us can recount stories of opinion polls contradicting each other. Others caution us about the use of statistics, pointing to cases where number crunching has actually fudged the truth. But there's more to research than skewed statistical figures and contradiction. As it happens, there's more to discovering the truth than meets the eye.

> **ACTIVITY**
>
> Enlist the assistance of a friend.
>
> Together observe a teacher, a public speaker, or a tv personality for a short period of time.
>
> Independently both write down your assessment of that person.
>
> Compare your respective characterisations of the person observed.

KNOWING OTHERS

How do we know one another? On the surface this question seems all too flippant. After all, we know people by interacting, working, and sometimes living with people. It's no effort for us to characterise members of our families: we know the kinds of things they like and are attracted to, just as well as we know their dislikes. We can speak knowledgeably about their kind and caring nature, their style, their strengths and their weaknesses. The same is true with people with whom we regularly come into contact. We can speak of how easily they are distracted or how they persevere to the bitter end. In our minds, they are logical, hotheaded, or somewhere in between. We can be fairly sure which of our friends, family or workmates would remain calm and collected, seemingly unfazed, in the same way as we could predict who would fly off the handle in face of catastrophe.

We think we know others well. But do we? How do we actually construct knowledge of other people? This is not a superficial question. It raises epistemological issues about how we know. Patti Lather, an eminent researcher, raised this same question. In one of the most thought-provoking questions directed at educational researchers, she asked: "How does a researcher work to not see so easily in telling stories that belong to others?" (1994, p. 44). It seems a strange question to ask of researchers—people who are usually preoccupied with finding out what ideal researchers ought to be doing. The question was so startling that it served as a wake-up call about the way things had always been done. Not only that: it brought with it, literally and metaphorically, an epistemic air, an invitation to probe more deeply into a whole range of epistemic issues in relation to research. The monumental effort for researchers in doing this made things much less comfortable than the certainties and absolutes of their traditions.

RESEARCH TRADITIONS

Before we open up that less comfortable space we will explore the research traditions which provide a frame for most of the investigative work in the field. We will look at how we customarily construct knowledge of other people. As we plunge into traditional ways of doing things, we will investigate how some research models limit and regulate epistemological legitimacy.

Let's begin by stating the obvious: research is about making a difference through science. Science cultivates the means by which research make the classroom and the wider communities of knowers, a better place. This is hardly new news because science has been an important social force from around the time when Bentham was designing his Panopticon. It is when you read Foucault's *The Archaeology of Knowledge and the Discourse of Language* that you start to get a keen sense of how science, invested with the multiple interests of regulation, control, progress, and redemption, became an important social force. And it still is. The ideas of truth, to which the scientific project subscribes, still play a major role in the structures and processes of education. They play a critical role in research. In fact, these ideas are so entrenched that, to some extent, they serve to organise and regulate our research practices. In Foucauldian language, they operate as a regime of truth and they do that by telling us what can count as valuable knowledge and who has access to the production, the distribution, and the legitimation of that knowledge. As if to emphasise its standard-setting position, the scientific model stakes out a certain space for establishing true and accurate accounts about others.

There are some things we need to know about the scientific model. It is helpful to know that science is built around a grand design of systematic order and tidy partitioning in the world. Almost at once, the idea of a universal explanation of the world comes into focus. With that kind of thinking under the belt, it is a small step to observe facts about an individual's life. Fitting into the grand scheme of things, these facts are to be classified, categorised, and ordered systematically and linearly as, using Foucault's term, positivities. Once categorised, these facts are ready to be interpreted. And they must be interpreted because it is only then that one is able to discover the truth in human terms. If we can discover the truth then we can normalise the individual's experiences, understandings and even desires, all with a view towards making the world a better place.

How does science do this exactly? It does it by making a number of far-reaching assumptions. First of all, it is worth contemplating that if you engage the idea that it is possible to make a difference to the world through a grand design of systematic order, then you necessarily make an assumption of a coherent and transparent reality. It's as if reality exists 'out there' waiting to be captured. In other words what you are doing is attributing evidential status to reality. In this way of thinking, reality is the site *par excellence* of a metaphysics of presence, and by that we mean that reality takes on a fixed character and exhibits certain qualities, regardless of who is observing. The second point follows naturally from this assumption and it is that it doesn't matter who is looking or observing: they will see the same thing, no matter what their circumstances. Summarising these two points: observers are interchangeable spectators; objects of knowledge are inert items that are distinctly different from observers. These were the understandings that allowed those doing research to put themselves in another's place and know his or her circumstances and interests in exactly the same way as she or he would know them. Truth was guaranteed by the interchangeable observer whose stories about others could be spoken from nowhere and everywhere.

These two interconnecting assumptions were seldom queried a few decades ago. They had phenomenally important implications for the way research came to be conceptualised and undertaken. Like other disciplines, education abided by the rules that 'good science' demanded. Those rules, and the principles that propped them up, informed conceptions not simply in quantitative research but also in research of a more qualitative nature, about what it means to know and what it means to know others. Our researchers worked long and hard to ensure that their research was objective. They kept their distance, taking care to maintain a separation between themselves and what they were observing. They believed that creating distance meant that the object of study would not be contaminated by their own world views and understandings and neither by their feelings.

There is something truly noble and righteous about following the dictates of science. Yet there is something overwhelmingly naïve too. If you accept the logic that accurate research accounts are researcher-neutral, then wouldn't research be made even more accurate if we heard the stories of researched from the participants themselves? If truth and certainty are the objective, then it seems odd that the research subjects' views are not given an airing. And this is the point that many people started to make. The point they were making, incidentally, is not as recent as one might imagine; it was proposed long ago by people like Nietzsche. The reason that people have been paying attention to it recently is because researchers started questioning their own research practices. The thing many people believed would enhance research was the voice of the research participant—the person being studied.

Once in a while something catches the imagination of the research community and this happened with the concept of 'voice'. It seemed to carry with it infinitely rich connotations and looked like it would take care of concerns raised about the scientific method. If you had to select a process that opened up the research tradition yet still maintained its integrity, then the celebration of voice would be the one. As often happens, before too long, the concept of voice and the inclusion of people's experiences as research data came under fire. A number of people asked: Isn't the concept of voice (or experience) entrapped in the very logic which it seeks to subvert? Isn't it still imprisoned within the very same parameters of sameness/difference from which it wishes to escape? Is there any view from nowhere?

RETHINKING RESEARCH

Objectivity is simply not possible. It seems strange to say, but that's the truth of it. Partly we can say this because things have moved on a bit in the education research world. Where not so long ago science stood for all there was to know about research, today research is not so narrowly defined. Researchers in education share with others a new awareness about the knowing subject and a new understanding of contextual lived experience. It's not merely by chance that this rethinking has coincided with moves for a wider critique of the nature of knowledge and representation. Those wider epistemic shifts have had profound effects on the way we think about education, not just about its pedagogical, curricular and evaluative practices, and the politics that drive them, but also about its inquiries—and about them all as socially and culturally constituted.

When we say that objectivity is not possible we are not saying that it's not possible to capture a sense of ongoing movement. And we are not suggesting that we don't have the capacity to grasp complexity. Movement and complexity are still imminently achievable–thanks to today's technology. Aside from all those remarkable achievements, however, is the question about the kind of knowledge claim that we can make. The nub of the issue is that what we see, and the knowledge we derive from those obervations, will be made with a view from somewhere, from some location, from some perspective. And, of course, we will miss some things that others might not overlook. They, in turn, may not see what we see. The point is that what we all see will be from our individual perspectives, and creating a distance in research, between ourselves and the researched, is not going to add to objectivity.

Now, you might say that's all very well for researching people, but this argument doesn't apply in the hard sciences, where real scientists work with data under microscopes. It must be said, after all, that there is something incomparably reassuring about the notion of objectivity in their work: it has the much the same virtues as truthfulness and honesty. But let's be honest about this: it is a rarefied understanding of research. The argument against objectivity actually does apply in this field in just the same way as it applies in others. It started with a number of eminent scientists advancing the novel premise that there is no view from nowhere. They subsequently convincingly demonstrated that no matter how careful scientists might perform the tiniest of measuring tasks, the sheer fact of being there in the measuring activity will inevitably distort their observations. They found that the observer is not as disengaged as was originally thought. This idea was revolutionary, to say the least, and not good news for those people whose research was founded on the assumption of non-interference from people.

But it was good news for a wider definition of research. Foucault realised that the kernel of the problem with knowledge lay with the claims that we make about it. His ideas explained so many things for researchers. Among a great deal else he showed us how the scientific model stakes out certain spaces for establishing credibility and demonstrated how it limits and regulates epistemological legitimacy. The fact is that these traditional methods of reality construction are no longer adequate nor desirable when we try to make sense of our contemporary world. Had we not had the benefit of these new theories, then research in education might well have gone down a very narrow track. Of all that Foucault had to say, nothing had greater impact on researchers than his critical interrogations of familiar ideas about knowing. He showed how the conventions of research practice are staked out in such a way as to preclude it from even and equitable possibilities of knowledge construction. It's a sobering thought that truth and knowledge claims are intimately tied up with strategies of normalisation that set the parameters of right and wrong, true and false.

Put bluntly, knowledge claims are intertwined in a power-game. No researcher can claim to be the bearer of universal Truth any more than knowledge can be sourced from the depths of individuals. In his interrogations, Foucault encouraged a scepticism about the possibility of true and accurate research findings, and, moreover, about the very possibility of knowing others and of telling their stories honestly and accurately. The point he made was that, irrespective of our efforts to contain it, knowledge will always escape our grasp. How reality is constructed depends on who is constructing it. Nobody, no matter how credentialed they are, has access to a 'God's eye view'. To drive this point home, read through the transcripts following of views about a student.

Knowledge claims also depend on the conditions and practices that make that reality possible. Constructing the truth or not telling it, is a much lesser problem than the problem of shifting perspectives, for we all see things from different vantage points. It's as though we are all observing the same landscape but we are all located at different points on it. And then there's the problem with the landscape itself. Why do you see this feature and not that? How is it possible to recall an entire area on the landscape and none of another? Can you be sure that what you remember is more significant than what you don't? These are deep epistemological questions that have no right answer. If that's not enough, there's the issue of time. Things on the landscape are constantly moving—but not in a linear fashion. They're rather like reflections of raindrops on the office window, dotted across the desk beneath. As the sun moves the mirrored dots change their shape and form. Even though all the raindrops are there for all to see, sometimes you notice this shape, sometimes that.

Transcripts of journal observations made by two researchers of the same student over the same period.

I was scared of Joanne – she was so forceful and so angry. The first month or so she was often in tears with frustration because she couldn't sort out some problem and she kept asking whether we thought she should be on this course. She had strong ideas about what ought to happen at university and what our teaching sessions should be like. Joanne challenged me to think hard about my teaching because if I was going to contradict and disappoint her expectations then I had to be sure I was doing it for good reason and offering appropriate support. I found out very quickly that she had children and was worried about childcare and finance. I remember thinking that she would be the student who would be most changed by the course because she was so thoroughly engaged in the debate around what learning is. I remember offering her reassurance and encouragement but at the same time seeking it myself from other tutors. This was the first time I had taught an undergraduate cohort – would students like Joanne really cope and get through? She seemed to have so little mathematical experience to draw on. Listening to her now I realise that she must have sensed my doubts more strongly than she 'heard' my reassurance. [Corinne]

Teaching an honours level pure maths module, I found Joanne to be a competent and engaged mathematician. She was prepared to hold her own corner and worked well with the group of co-learners from another cohort that I had designated for her. She showed greatest affinity for Ray from her own cohort who was also in her group and who had a similar general and mathematical background, but she made it clear that she had decided not to be intimidated by the others. She knew that she hated being assessed by formal examination, that exams led her to panic and underachieve. Nevertheless, she worked hard to overcome these difficulties. She rang me on at least two occasions during the revision period to check out and explore the meanings she was making of the module topics; the conversations were mathematically mature and informed. She managed to complete the exam satisfactorily although she probably achieved at a class lower than her usual performance. Despite this she seemed secure and confident about herself and her relationship with mathematics. [Hilary]

Transcripts used with kind permission from Hilary Povey,
Sheffield Hallam University, England

CONSTRUCTING REALITY

Some have called the problem of objectivity, and all that goes with it, the disintegration of the classical *episteme* of representation. It would helpful if we could construct a plausible research practice that is responsive to the disintegration by accommodating the limits of knowing. Foucault's ideas, at least, are something that researchers can make practical use of. You won't find much about applying 'correct' research procedures. And you won't find that research has been dumped in the too-hard basket and abandoned wholesale. Quite frankly, it's irresponsible of researchers to retreat from engaging in research, on the grounds that they can no longer exert significant influence.

Those of us committed to understanding the implications of knowing others well, will find a potential vantage point here from which to rethink the way we do research. Research informed by Foucault's ideas necessarily invokes political deliberation. The reason for this is simple: objectivity and representation are not politically neutral and innocent activities. Researchers ask critical questions about the implications for the way they construct reality. They emphasise how it is historically situated and strategically practised. They work hard to offer "less false stories" (Harding, 1991), questioning not simply the methodological process, but the discourses operating on their preliminary decisions in the research process. In a nutshell, they have become more aware of themselves in the research process. They pay more attention to their responsibilities in decision making than to 'getting it right'. That is because they are well aware that being right is, for all intents and purposes, a position within a regime of truth. They reflect on the conceptual baggage that makes it possible (or not) to contemplate a particular research area and to derive particular research questions. This is the conceptual baggage that comes with the rules and conventions of a particular discursive formation:

> By system of formation, then, I mean a complex group of relations that function as a rule: It lays down what must be related, in a particular discursive practice, for such and such an enunciation to be made, for such and such a concept to be used, for such and such a strategy to be organised. To define a system of formation in its specific individuality is therefore to characterise a discourse or a group of statements by the regularity of a practice.
>
> (Foucault, 1972, p. 74)

The thing to remember is that a researcher's own knowledge always privileges particular interests. That is because what the researcher sees or hears must pass through the filter of biography, and social determinations, such as race, class, gender, ethnicity, and so on. Researchers have no way of telling if their construction of reality is actually what is really 'out there'. And because of that, the stories they create are in a sense, imaginings of what is happening, and are just as much about the researchers as they are about the research participants. The stories might even include these imaginings, as it did in the story about Joanne, an undergraduate mathematician, reported by Hilary Povey and Corinne Angier (2006). Researchers can't say without absolute conviction that their particular construction hits the nail on the head simply because their own subjectivity shapes the observational, interpretive and organisational choices that are made. As if to complicate things further, the researchers' own knowledge, along with the research landscape, is continually shifting which makes it all the more important to say that the researcher is a key player, and hardly an innocent bystander, in the production of educational knowledge.

What strikes home is that if there is no unmediated access to a transparent reality, then all our categories, identities, and processes in education are historically and locally emergent rather than naturally given. They are also multivalent rather than unified in meaning. But more than that: they are the frequent result and possible present instrument in struggles of power. By that is meant that all our categories and concepts of educational practice are the effects of specific relations of power, and all produce some dissonance between and within individuals. It is worth mentioning that once we start thinking along these lines then it becomes pointless to search for common denominators, such as categories and homogeneous networks of causality and analogy, in specific practices—all of which are part of the trappings of scientific practice.

Foucault was not interested in causality. He was more taken with ideas of complexity, circumstance and indeterminacy. From conceptualisations of people that are premised on the indeterminacy, circumstance and complexity, it is a small step to propose that reality is fluid in nature, forever in process, continually being reshaped by the changing categories individuals use to understand themselves, others, and the spaces they share. Of all the things that we could apply this understanding to, none has more influence than research practice. Once you accept that reality is constantly mobile, then our interest in research moves from establishing truth onto an understanding of how meaning is produced and created and in how these productions factor into larger decisions concerning power and privilege. Let's look at how Foucault himself explains it:

> Truth isn't outside power, or lacking in power: contrary to a myth whose history and functions would repay further study, truth isn't the reward of free spirits, the child of protracted solitude, nor the privilege of those who have succeeded in liberating themselves. Truth is a thing of this world: it is produced only by virtue of multiple forms of constraint. And it induces regular effects of power.
>
> (Foucault, 1984, p. 72-3)

Pushing traditional boundaries in terms of how we know others and how we tell their stories, calls for a different set of strategies, protocols, and conventions for research. Among the things to be considered is shifting the research participants from original presence, to one in which they are decentred, relational complex processes. This might seem an odd notion but it does get us around the problem of fixed identity and universal experience. Making the shift in thinking involves "changing the subject" (Henriques et al., 1984). With that in mind, the focus moves away from a true and accurate account of participants in education to one that constitutes them within practices and discourses. Among a great deal else, Foucault has told us that in order to understand the truth about people, we need to examine discursive practices, paying attention to how they limit what is possible to say and do. At his urging, then, we need to look at the effects of power and give up the search for causes and absolute certainty. By and large, the things that stand tall in these kinds of analyses, are the effects of power.

As a case in point, if we were interested in exploring how students are constituted in everyday schooling, then we might look at how discourse systematically constitutes versions of the social and natural worlds and how students are positioned by discourse in relations of power. With that focus we would then be able, if we had a mind, to investigate how students negotiate contestation and conflict in their self- and world-concepts and attempt to solve these dilemmas through language. And if we felt so inclined, through our investigation into lived moments of classroom practice, we could unmask the ways in which the teaching and learning is intimately tied to the social organisation of power—how power informs, constrains, and implicates classroom work. Most of all, we could account for the different degrees of coherence between subject positions and educational practice.

Let's emphasise again that what we won't find in such research accounts are claims to an empirically verifiable real truth. Compelling though the desire for coherency and truth may be, it is simply not possible. We need to be absolutely clear about that. Truth, in these forms of research, demands attention to historical specificity, and within that focus, such truth inscribes limits discursively, epistemically, and strategically; it is always provisional, open-ended, and relational. Once-and-for-all answers are out of the question. Rather, the intent is to capture how meanings that inscribe subjects are made and allowed to make sense.

BREAKING AWAY FROM CONVENTION

In an effort to emphasise the point about the limits of knowing, a small number of researchers are currently experimenting with different textual forms in their research reporting. Hilary Povey and Corinne Angier (with Michelle Clarke) (2006) worked with a different writing format, doing away with conventional signposts such as subheadings. Their account works both within and beyond convention. Their particular format introduced other kinds of texts to help with the story telling. These other texts were used as raw data, gathered during the process of the research with a student they named Joanne. The data set included extracts from Joanne's assignments, journal notes from the two researchers, extracts from transcripts of interviews with Joanne, assignment feedback to Joanne, Joanne's diary records of a project assignment, and emails.

Literature reviews that break with customary practice might take the form of a short list of findings that are relevant to the object of attention. The chart below is an example of a different kind of review. It represents a set of claims to truth about girls and mathematics. You'll notice that it crosses decades, scholarly thinking and interests. My decision to opt for the chart in preference to discussing findings that showed some synergies with the points that I wanted to make about the research at hand, was quite deliberate. I didn't want to impose my own meanings but hoped that the reader might grasp an understanding of the complexity and the multiple forms that gendered identifications in mathematics have taken over recent decades. It worked as a useful backdrop for the analysis of an interview with a young woman studying mathematics. As it happened, certain entries in the chart contradicted the student's story.

According to educational research and commentary on mathematics and gender:

- Girls have inferior spatial skills when it comes to visualising movements of geometric figures (Maccoby & Jacklin, 1974; Fennema & Tartre, 1985).
- Cooperative activities are preferred by many girls in mathematics whereas many boys prefer to work in a 'traditional' competitive environment (Forgasz & Leder,1996; Fox & Soller, 2001).
- Teachers often describe girls in their mathematics classrooms as nice, kind, and helpful. Girls sometimes take on the role of 'subteacher', in order to help their peers (Walkerdine, 1990).
- Teachers tend to initiate 'analytical models of instruction which tend to favour males more than females' (Fox & Soller, 2001, p. 16).
- In class girls ask fewer questions than boys, and a small percentage of those questions that are asked demand higher-level thinking (Fennema & Peterson, 1986).
- Girls receive less attention from their teachers and are less likely than boys to receive either praise or criticism for their work (Fennema & Peterson, 1986).
- Girls are less confident in their mathematical ability and do not perceive mathematics as useful as do boys (Fennema & Peterson, 1985).
- Girls attribute their mathematical success to effort whereas boys attribute their success to ability (Walden & Walkerdine, 1986; Meyer & Koehler, 1990).
- Girls are connected thinkers whose ways of mathematical knowing are quite different from boys who tend to view mathematics in terms of their separate autonomy (Becker, 1995).
- Boys who consider themselves weak at mathematics are more likely to view mathematics as a female domain, whereas girls who rate their mathematical achievement highly are more likely to view mathematics as a female domain (Leder & Forgasz, 2003).
- Mathematics is 'imbued with an almost mystical power' (Kenway et al., 1998, p. 38) and operates as a 'critical filter' (Sells, 1978), controlling entry into many high-status areas of academia and employment. Girls' history of nonparticipation in mathematics limits their post-school opportunities (Kenway et al., 1998).
- Boys assume control of technological apparatus when mathematics classes are working at computers. Boys tend to distract others from their computer work and receive more help from the teacher during the lesson (Forgasz, 2002).
- Girls' characteristic experiences are different to boys' and hence those experiences do not provide equal grounds for reliable knowledge claims (Burton, 1995).

- Girls 'seem to be more concerned than boys in trying to remember what the teacher has said and following her instructions' (Lucey, Brown, Denvir, Askew, & Rhodes, 2003, p. 53).
- The claim that boys are currently underachieving has been challenged widely in many western countries (Skelton & Francis, 2003).
- There is a 'conspicuous lack of discussion about the usefulness of mathematics in everyday life or to students' future' (Forgasz & Leder, 1996, p. 168).
- A 'disproportionate number of girls opt out of powerful areas of curriculum' (Mendick, 2003, p. 169).
- A contradictory relation exists between doing mathematics and stereotyped female gender roles (Ernest, 1995).
- 'Regardless of how mathematically competent a woman becomes she can never escape discursive practices that reify the idea that mathematics is, indeed, a male domain' (Damarin, 1995, p. 25).

A break from usual protocols provides a creative means for dealing with the problem of telling other people's stories. In the following discussion a different strategy helps deal with that problem. The top part of the page is a commentary recorded from single interview of a young woman student, known here as Rachel, in a secondary school. The transcript is included almost in its entirety, omitting only those sections that were repetitive. The lower section underwrites the interview through a Foucauldian analysis of mathematical identity. As you read it you will notice how it is multilayered with the student's own narrative of classroom experiences and affiliations, and with learning and teaching.

The textual design turned out to be a way to give structure to a constantly changing identity that moved forward, even as it folded back onto itself. It gave form to how Rachel produces a narrative of her successes, her difficulties, her hopes, and her frustration in mathematical work. At the time of the study she was an 'extension' student, working alongside students who were one year senior to her. The analysis represents my efforts to engage with her story. I tried to take into account competing stories and times as they worked through and against the stability of meanings and experiences. I looked at differences within and among the stories of mathematical experience Rachel had structured, the discourses at play and the way in which they layered themselves about her. In linking all these discourses together I examined how the production of mathematical knowledge is tied in complex ways to particular historically specific trajectories and how it is strategically practised, and constantly in process. The overriding objective was to explore "the different modes by which, in our culture, human beings are made into subjects" (Foucault, in Dreyfus & Rabinow, 1982, p. 208).

RACHEL'S STORY

My dad's a computer technician and my mum works in an accountant's office. And I've got an older brother who's seventh form [Year 13] this year and he's doing calculus. So he sometimes helps me a little bit if I need it. My parents encourage me to do whatever I want to do and if that means working really hard and getting me through my maths then they're quite happy for me to do that. They didn't want me to sit there being really bored. My mother would love me to be an accountant. That's one that I've thought about. Tourism or something would be good. Lawyer. I'm interested in law. I'm definitely looking at university first.

[MW: What's it like being the youngest?] I hate being the youngest because I'm totally different to what my brother was. And I find school easier than my brother did and they think I should spend as much time studying as he did but I can't be bothered. There's always little things that annoy my parents because I'm so different to my brother. They could cope with it with him but they want me to be the same because they know what to do if I behave that way, but I don't. But it's a constant thing to try and do well so they'll be happy with what I do because I can go home and, because I find things easier than my brother, I could go home and say that I'd got, like, ninety per cent on a test and my brother could go home and say that he got sixty but they'll be more happy with him, because they just assume that's what I'll get anyway. So it doesn't matter, it doesn't matter how hard I work for it.

****

Rachel's story cannot escape her contradictory mathematical experiences; nor can it escape the effects of her own desire to relate a coherent and compelling account that allows me, the listener, to know from the inside what is on the outside. The interview is a vehicle for Rachel to disclose her story; to face the task of producing her own subjectivity for someone else. At one level the story is a construction of a personal mathematical biography that develops, through a series of static controlled moments, a set of themes to do with success, boredom, familial relations, peer and teacher-student conflict. And, at another level, the account registers disruptions and tensions that have the effect of undermining the coherent and cohesive story. The continuously running narrative evokes traces of other events and interpersonal relations that create a counter story to the one related to me at this moment in time. Together these two 'stories' open up important aspects of her subjectification as it relates to being a female senior mathematics student. Brown, Jones and Bibby (2004) have noted that personal accounts of mathematics are construed from past, present and future experiences in a multiplicity of sites. All of these aspects weave through Rachel's story. Her identification with mathematics is produced through a convergence of a number of often competing discourses and practices, each vying for her attention, and all of which position and designate her in some way. What is important to us is how they enter into her

[MW: Tell me a little about your earlier school experiences] Relatively good experiences there. Had lots of friends. Got picked on a lot because I was short. I still do. It's just a constant battle over that, but it gets a bit old though!
I remember my Standard Four class [Year 6] and I was doing extension maths and everything and I know that there was one question in my Standard Four maths book and my teacher didn't know the answer to it. And I worked out the answer and it was different to the one in the book and I had to go round all the teachers to tell them what it was. But it was a big shock when I got to Third Form [Year 9] because suddenly you had to understand this stuff. But I didn't find it too hard or anything. It all goes back to the really basic stuff that you do in primary school and that. But doing School C [School Certificate: national examination] last year— that was a bit of a thing. Because I missed two months of school, something like that last year. I was off sick for six weeks and then for a month I was overseas and so I was cramming two years of stuff into less than a year. Such a rush! I learned most of that by teaching myself because I couldn't understand what Mr E was getting at. It was just going right over my head. It went right past me so I had to do it all by revision to get School C…

[MW: How would you sum up your personality?] I'd sum it up as *dizzy.* At the beginning of the year I decided that I didn't want to be as boring as I was last year. I didn't enjoy what I was doing. So that's probably when I started not working and stuff, actually.

[MW: Why do you think you managed to skip Form 4 [Year 10]?] I wanted to do School C because I was finding Third Form really easy and so I thought that Fourth Form would just follow on from that and be really

****

subjectivity. Let me tell you about my own impressions. In conversation with me, Rachel presents as lively and fun-loving. Her own assessment of her personality is not the same. Dizziness she equates with enjoyment. For her, a personal change this year—a 'makeover'—will enable a more enjoyable school life. "The concept of the 'makeover'," Walkerdine (2003) notes, "has been the staple of women's magazines for many years" (p. 252) and it is those cultural discourses that, consciously or otherwise, make real for Rachel a new positioning. Intersecting those cultural discourses is the gendering of school mathematics, that is, the ways in which mathematical work is enacted on a gendered basis. Thus Rachel saw and ordered her subjectivity in relation to the discourses about what it means to be a female learner in mathematics. As Ernest (1995) has argued: "Women must choose to be feminine or choose to be successful at mathematics. If they opt for both, they have to live with the contradiction mathematics ≠ feminine" (p. 456). It is within this contradictory discursive positioning that Rachel names herself as 'dizzy'.

easy and I would just get bored and give up. And I wouldn't want to do it when I came to Fifth Form [Year 11]. I wouldn't want to be working on it, because I'd be so sick of it and so I wanted to do something last year that sort of extended me a bit because Fourth Form tends to be a bit of a wasted year. It seemed to be at the time but you look back now and it's not, because all the stuff you did last year is really valuable. I just wanted something to aim for, for that year otherwise I wouldn't have got anywhere.

I got 81% for School C, which I was really happy with at the time, yea, especially considering I taught most of it to myself. But now if I went and did it now I would do so much better because the stuff I'm doing this year is so much harder. I could pick the other stuff up so much easier now.

[MW: What do you think has contributed to your past success in maths?] I don't know. I just seem to be good at doing exams. I've got a lot of friends—they know the stuff in class and I could sit there and it goes right over my head. But I get into an exam and I'm surprisingly clear-headed and lot of people just get stressed out about it and I don't. It doesn't worry me because I think if I go in there and I don't know it then I don't know

****

'Giggly,' is how Mrs S described her. My observations note that she always entered the mathematics classroom full of smiles and sat at the same desk in the middle of the front row of paired seating arrangements. Kate, her friend and only other Year 10 female student in this class, always sat next to her. Her liveliness contrasted with the 'sophistication' and 'poise' of the older girls in this class. So, too, did her school uniform—the two friends and the two boys who sat behind them, were the only students in this class who were not eligible to wear 'mufti.' I could not find myself completely in her giggly disposition, yet I could identify with being an 'exotic other' in a mathematics classroom—an object of curiosity in a senior mathematics classroom. It is with regard to 'being different', as a researcher rather than teacher or student in the mathematics classroom, that I felt a powerful empathy with her story.

But competing discourses work through her words and I will try and look beyond the literal reading of what she said in order to tease out those opposing categories within which she structured her dialogue. In the context of earlier mathematical experiences Rachel's desire to aim high is not formed from any perception of teacher as role model. Nor, indeed, has it anything to do with an accessibility to mathematics enabled by the teacher, although she does concede that her Year 9 teacher 'moved quite a few of us on.' Neither internalised learning nor role model theory works here: rather, psychic and social intersect to fashion her mathematical aspirations.

it. There's nothing I can do about it so there's no point in worrying. But I did, *I worked quite hard last year.* I spent ages going through the pink Mathematics Workbook and I was going over and over and over it. Trig [Trigonometry] was the worst bit. I couldn't do trig last year, and then like two days before the exam I was looking at it and it finally clicked. I spent about six hours just on trig that day and right at the end I just got it, and my parents were trying to make me go to bed and, No, I'm really understanding this. I'm not giving up now. I just did a lot of study. Always read and do examples. Working out answers, checking them and making sure, and if I don't get it I go back and try and figure it out and if I still don't get it I get my brother to have a look at it or I ask someone at school the next day. Things like that.

I do this a bit this year. Kate and I study a lot together and we help each other because she understands, she seems to understand a lot more of it than I do. I don't get much of it at all this year. *It's just going straight past me.* But she's understanding it so she helps me out with that.
We help each other and if she doesn't understand it then I'd ring one of the guys who are friends. Martin would help. He got like 94% in School C. So I'd ring him. My older brother would help but he's not hugely good with maths. I mean, he just scraped through last year, so he sort of helps me with what he can but he gets to a point where it's beyond him and he can't cope with it so I have to turn to friends who I know will be able to help me with it. And it's fresh in their minds rather than for him trying to think back to last year's work.

[MW: How would you describe a typical maths lesson?] Boring. I don't know. It's like, it's really hard to explain. I don't do much work. I'm really lazy in class. I can't be bothered. Spend most of my time talking to my friends.

****

Rachel gives us her own justification for her desire to succeed: 'I wanted to do something last year that sort of extended me a bit because Fourth Form tends to be a bit of a wasted year'. Overlaying this explanation is a more powerful intent. She was keen to progress, to come out career-advantaged at the end of her schooling. Woven into this desire is another discursive strategy, one that is reactive to (apparent) parental disenchantment: 'it's a constant thing to try and do well so they'll be happy with what I do.' The personal investment here lies both in pleasing her parents and in the possibility of enjoying the success which Rachel feels is her due. Taken together, these discourses point to, at least at Rachel's level of awareness, the striving for success in the national examination as both desirable and inevitable.

[MW: Is that because you find the work easy?] Some of it. Yea. Most of my other classes. But maths I find hard and I tend to give up really if I don't get it straight away. I can't be bothered with it. And it's really easy to say, yea, OK, I'll go home and look at my revision book and I'll figure it out tonight or my brother will help me but I never do. Never get around to it. If I have any homework that I can be bothered doing, I do it. But I very seldom do any maths homework. I don't know. I seem to be able to get away without doing it. If I have other stuff, I always seem to put maths last…

****

What is of major interest in this exploration, is the part that mathematics itself plays in the discursive pull of Rachel's desires. Mathematics, and in particular abstract reasoning, was itself produced within highly specific practices. Davies (1994) has argued that "[i]n our education systems we tend to valorise abstraction as a higher, purer form of knowing, to treat it as if it is separate from the concrete" (p. 5). The concept of abstraction has been such a successful discursive strategy that most people "experience mathematics as pure and uncontaminated by the real world" (Apple, 1995, p. 333). Ernest (2004) makes a similar claim. He argues that the modernist face of mathematics as an abstract, logical, and unquestionable certain body of knowledge is sustained by the privileging of rational and scientific knowledge in our social practices as pure and true. "Mathematics becomes a social filter to sort out those who gain access to the high status, wealth and power associated with certain professions and those who can not" (Zevenbergen, 1994, p. 1). Willis (1990) elaborates the point to argue that "the reality of school mathematics is that it is used...for intimidation, socialisation and selection" (p. 192).

On entering her third year of secondary schooling there was never a moment of doubt in Rachel's mind that she would be selected for the Year 12 academic mathematics course offering at her school. There was no hesitation by the mathematics department either since her national examination result had assured her position. Whilst in Mrs S's class Rachel had learned powerful lessons from classroom discourses which provided her with cultural meaning systems about doing mathematics. In the weeks she had been in this class, she had learned what did and did not count as gendered mathematical performance. Specific pedagogic practices, Martino and Meyenn (2002) contend, relate closely to the teacher's assumptions and beliefs about gender. It is through Mrs S's pedagogic practices that she has learned the regulative measures and normative positions produced for her as a student in this classroom. In addition to the academic labour required, she was also beginning to learn, for the first time, the emotional costs of that labour, involving what Reay (2002) names as the "intolerable burden of psychic reparative work" (p. 222) in maintaining her gendered and promoted position in this class.

[MW: Could you describe for me what you do when Mrs S is explaining at the board?] I'm usually drawing pictures in my book. I try to understand her but she goes too fast and she sort of works at the board and starts up there and gets down to there and I'm still trying to understand the bit that's up in the corner. Because she just goes really fast. She does examples on the board and so we start on them and we've finished half, like the first couple and then she's answering them already and we're trying to block out what she's said so we can do it ourselves, so then match it to what she's done.

Sometimes I think if she slowed down a little we'd do, we might have to do less work, but we'd actually understand it the first time so we wouldn't have to keep going over and over. It's really frustrating. I feel like saying slow down, but the thing is there's a lot to get through in one year as well. She's got to move on.

Most of the time I get all the important notes and everything she writes up and a few of the examples. What I can get down before she rubs it off, I mean…

****

Precisely because psychic conflict plays out in Rachel's views I do not think we can explore her homework discussion without recourse to her past and current self. Setting the 'dizzy' self-reinvention alongside the past 'boring' and conscientious individual, allows us to understand why Rachel might at one moment say she rarely does mathematics homework, and at another moment, why she might present as a diligent out-of-school worker. She paints a picture of see-sawing perceptions, and underlying those, we glimpse momentary switches of self production: 'Kate and I study a lot' and 'If she doesn't understand it then I'd ring one of the guys who are friends'. And by way of contrast, she says: 'I very seldom do any maths homework'. To understand how meanings are made here for Rachel we need to consider what she perceives her "imagined transformation of status" (Walkerdine, 2003, p. 254) requires of her. It is useful to consider that perception together with her acknowledgement of what her own mathematics work out of school time in the past has allowed her to achieve. And in all this her current difficulties with mathematics play a part. Engaging with that complexity enables us to see Rachel in a transitory state, in which neither her transformed nor past self have her full measure.

At the moment, maths is *very boring*. But, see I've got one friend, my best friend, in that class and I don't have any other classes with her so I tend to spend most of the time catching up with her, talking to her. It would be lonely if Kate wasn't there. I don't know. I'd probably do more work, most likely. Either that or I'd be turning round and talking to other people instead of talking to her. I'd probably get a bit more done. Because I did last week when she was at photos and she was away for most of the period. We check against each other. We do that a lot and we race against each other and see who can get it down quicker. It's not a conscious thing. I mean, we work through it faster. I mean if I wasn't checking against her answers I'd be checking against someone else's answers. Most likely. And if I don't get it I start asking questions…But Mrs S, she tends to go right over my head and I don't tend to ask questions from her because last time I did that she tried to explain and it just went, well, I sort of understood half when I asked the question and by the time she'd finished I understood none of it! I don't know. But I don't have a very good relationship with her, because we've had a few arguments in the past.

My aunty works in the music block and she really likes Mrs S but, the guys, they know that I laugh really easily and they keep making me laugh in class and she just gets really frustrated with me because when I start laughing I can't stop and so she starts to get really angry at me. And apparently no-one has ever heard her raise her voice before she met me. So it's a bit stressed there. I'm just trying very hard not to let the guys get to me now. Then I don't have to laugh.

[MW: The boys who sit behind you?] Yea. Mostly, Blair and Richard, he's one of the bad ones as well.

[MW: The girls in the class don't stir you up?] No. Because the only one I really talk to is Kate. Blair—he just likes really to get me in trouble and he has done for the last three years and he'll just keep on doing it and there's nothing I can do so I just try not to sit in front of him. And hope that he doesn't sit in the row behind me…

****

Thus it is possible to note the complex interplay of relations between mathematical identification as constructed by Mrs S for her students, the reading of this practice by Rachel, and the subversion of it for her by the boys. On the one hand Rachel is clear that enjoyment is all-important; on the other hand, controlling non-permissible classroom behaviour is highly desirable. After her 'falling out' with Mrs S, she could not, at least while Mrs S was the holder of surveillance power, be fully reactive in this way again. As she says: 'I'm just trying very hard not to let the guys get to me now. Then I don't have to laugh.' In defending her current position, Rachel was endeavouring to "deconstruct old patterns and speak into existence new ones" (Davies, 1997, p. 12).

[MW: What do you think maths is really about?] It's a bit hard to say, I don't know. I doubt if I would think in the same way in another subject. Maths just seems to have its own logic. It's all the little rules. Sometimes it seems logical to me but sometimes I'm so slow picking up what she's saying that I don't see the patterns that are going through it. It's definitely my hardest subject, especially this year because it's so much ahead of everything else that I'm doing. It does seem to be totally different. I walk into maths and I'm in a different mood to when I walk out again. Go to the next class and it's totally different. I sort of walk out of maths and I try to forget about it because it's so confusing. I don't know if I'm going to do any maths next year. Because this work this year seems to have gone over my head completely. But I know that maths is something you really need but I don't know if I'm going to be wasting my time sitting in maths, not understanding any of it.

****

Rachel's mathematical identity is lived as her own experience, but is not an analysable experience on her part, since it is discursively produced. She tells us that she is having difficulty understanding some of her work this year. To explore her lack of understanding without falling back on pathologising discourses, requires a perception of the mathematics classroom as a site in which certain meanings, and not others, can be made. What I want to suggest is that Rachel's understandings (or lack thereof) are produced in part in the complex history of the mathematics classroom in which she is already inscribed, and by which her very actions, needs and desires are made to signify. That suggestion requires that we look at the conscious and unconscious processes and meanings as they crosscut her lifeworld. It would be easy to suggest that responsibility rests with both parties in the pedagogical relation and that Rachel's mathematical problems could have been solved if she had asked Mrs S for help. However the work of Foucault has warned that such interpretations are too simplistic. Mathematical understanding is a complex phenomenon, in which gender and history play a major part. So too do issues of power, regulation and surveillance.

To this end I am suggesting that Rachel's private talk here be taken together with her previous conflict with Mrs S, her reasons for this conflict (in which the boys seated behind her are implicated), her avoidance of dialogue and future conflict with Mrs S. I want to suggest that this complexity might be conceived of in terms of a psychic/social relation, produced in historically specific regimes of meaning and truth. This is not an essentialist narrative about a female student's nature or 'inner' mental capacity in relation to school mathematics, but about a complex construction of gendered mathematical identification in which important issues of familial, cultural and pedagogic regulation and surveillance are involved. What her learning problem points to is the power of pedagogic practices and discourses operating in the family, within cultural forms, and in the classroom.

As I see it, Rachel is caught up in discourse through which she was not able to exercise agency. She did not have the theoretical resources to look at the discourses in which she was trapped to see how they each both constrain and enable things to be done and said. She was not able to see where power lay in each discourse and by which means she could decide which practice could be refused and which could be sustained. If she had been able to do so, she might have reworked those discourses towards personal enablement. In Davies' (1994) words: "In removing the site of the problem from herself to those structures…it is possible to see both the power of the structures and the inevitability of bowing to their pressure and to contemplate the ways in which those structures might be worked on to change them such that they do not in the future exert such intolerable pressures" (p. 24).

ACTIVITY

Put Foucault to use in Rachel's interview.
Identify the specific discourses through which she constructs her identity.

1. Identify the ways in which she negotiates the categories imposed on her within the everyday patterns of her classroom life.
2. Identify the different time periods that intersect through, and are constitutive of her present.
3. Examine how her meanings of herself spiral back and forth as her investments and desires change during the interview.

REFLECTIONS ON RESEARCH

Given the epistemic shifts of recent years, the issue is not about getting the analysis right: rather, it about recognising that hidden forms of social relations lie behind what we see and what our research participants tell us. What Foucauldian research is able to do where conventional research stories have failed, is tell us about the social and political motivations in the stories told to us. It is not so much interested in understanding and controlling better, as it is about conducting research in a more interactive way and capturing the dynamic between and within what we study. Interesting things will emerge such as competing stories working through and against the stability of meanings, identities, experiences, as well as the treacheries of language.

But research is more than finding out interesting things: it is about critically engaging with those narratives and being accountable to what those narratives tell us about education. Here's the point: research is less about establishing researcher authority, and more about questioning the very construction of that authority. No explanation can ever be universally authoritative simply because there is no privileged position from which anyone can speak without one's own discourses being itself put under question. Foucauldian research is about a commitment to thinking about research data as a site of political struggle over meanings, and being accountable to those whom we research. The question we should be asking is not 'is this research objective enough', but rather 'if this research is authenticated and validated, what motivates it? What are the political effects?'

CHAPTER 10

ENDINGS MARKING NEW BEGINNINGS

IN THIS CHAPTER

- Looking back
- Looking forward

> This work done at the limits of ourselves must, on the one hand, open up a realm of historical inquiry and, on the other, put itself to the test of reality, of contemporary reality, both to grasp the points where change is possible and desirable, and to determine the precise form this change should take.
>
> (Foucault, 1984, p. 46)

We have now arrived at the final chapter of the book. It's time to take stock, reflect on our reading, and contemplate the future. Our treatment of Foucault's work has been through both exposition and application. We have sketched out Foucault's ideas in broadstrokes, introducing a new way of thinking and a new conceptual toolkit for exploring the practices and processes in education. Despite best intentions, new ideas have the annoying habit of sliding out of reach. Some concepts are simply too hard to grasp. In an effort to prevent this happening we have applied Foucault's ideas, putting them to use in very real everyday practices and processes in education so that, irrespective of the starting points and interpretations we bring to the reading, we may engage fruitfully with Foucault's exacting scholarship. In this book, thinking and doing–theory and practice–are two of a kind.

One thing that this book has avoided is a critical evaluation of Foucault's arguments. In my view, readers have difficulty enough coming to terms with ideas that operate at a high level of abstraction. Instead, we looked at a tapestry of Foucault's diverse ideas. Much more could have been said. Other authors are filling the gaps and you will find a selected list of additional sources, following, to enhance your understanding. What this book does offer is a beginning appreciation of the depth of Foucault's insights and the way they offer an alternative approach to thinking about education. It is an approach that differs from its predecessors not only in the vision it provides but also in the method it advocates. The point in doing this has been to suggest how it might be possible to gain new perspectives and produce new knowledge about education through exploration and critical reflection on the processes of education in contemporary society.

LOOKING BACK

Let us summarise our investigations. Our investigations have allowed us to describe and explain the world of education from various points of view. These investigations have been conducted in the belief that Foucault's ideas have the potential to make a substantial contribution to the formation of particular forms of socio-political organisation. Why is that so? Quite simply, ideas really do matter. An idea whose moment has come is stronger than tenacity. Foucault's ideas for education are ripe for development in the material conditions and the intellectual circumstances of our discipline. Yet his critique of inherited structures of belief and convention profoundly disrupts what we have come to know and needs to be taken seriously.

Our investigations introduced us to new concepts that led us to new meanings about power knowledge, discourse and subjectivity. In the course of that exploration, although our predispositions may have been challenged, we saw how Foucauldian methodology could trace the educational world in a different way. We used discourse analysis to explore underlying meanings in curriculum documents. In turn, we theorised identities as complex and unstable, as well as historically informed, despite the categories we assign them. We noted how power inserts itself, when we least expect it, in practices in the classroom and other educational institutions. And we pulled together Foucault's ideas to look at the practice of research.

The chapters work with different concepts and there is no one methodology that takes precedence. Yet while the different analyses have few common themes, they all rely on the underlying assumption in the usefulness of Foucault's work for exposing aspects of practices previously situated beyond our vision. To be more specific, we employed the following Foucauldian strategies to our educational interrogations:

- *An historicisation project* to trace understandings of how people learn. We looked at the discourses that made it possible for understandings to take seed during different times and places over the past decades. In this project the specific terms history of the present, and archaeology, provided the conceptual language to enable us to think about knowledge about learning as a discursive event. Our account of learning did not flow seamlessly. It was governed by chance and within different power blocks.
- *An analysis of discourse.* Our analysis interrogated a policy text as a medium of knowledge creation about school mathematics and as a means for constructing forms of social organisation. The interrogation demonstrated the historical contingency of learners in school mathematics. It demonstrated the enormous authority and control wielded by policy documents, in the way that they order, measure, categorise, normalise, and regulate people, processes, and knowledge. And it showed us how discourse analysis has the potential for initiating change.

- *A critical inquiry into the constitution of subjectivity.* Our analysis looked beyond commonsense interpretations of students-in-class to examine the way power infuses itself within and operates through the discourses and practices of classroom life. It unpacked the role that power has in the constitution of subjective experience. We noticed the effects of teacher, peer- and self-regulatory practices on one student, and how it impinged on thinking and acting.
- *A revisioning of identity, taking on board cultural dimensions.* Cultural discourses bring a powerful dimension to the way we take up our identity. Our analysis showed that for female students from different socio-economic backgrounds, issues associated with femininity, family, academic progress, and history claimed attention. Through those particular categories we developed an understanding of class-based practices of subjectification that contribute not only towards the production of one's life chances but also the continuation of one's social class positioning.
- *A denaturalisation project.* The focus was on the ways in which a teaching identity is constituted differentially across sites. Three moments that contribute to teaching—history, course work, and practicum experiences—all contribute to the making of a teaching identity. Yet they each have different practices and different systems that seek to normalise pre-service teachers' ways of thinking and ways of doing things. For the pre-service teacher, agency requires coming to terms with one's intentions and values, as well as one's knowing and being, in a setting of contradictory realities.
- *A critical investigation that reconfigures learning to teach.* An identity as a teacher develops within structures of power, privilege and subordination. Our account challenges the *a priori* subject, revealing that teaching in classrooms involves processes of normalisation and surveillance, through course work and teaching practice in schools. Issues of power and privilege feature prominently, contributing to the shaping of teacher identification.
- *A classroom exploration into gendered surveillance.* Every classroom cohort of students operates within its own particular regime of truth, all the while legitimising and sanctioning student practice, and, above all, setting cognitive limits both now and for future educational chances. Those students who cannot or refuse to identify with the patterns of 'normal' studentship will be marginalised or excluded to some extent from the practices of classroom learning.
- *An inquiry into knowing others through research.* The inquiry sought to reconstruct what we do in research. It pointed to the social and political motivations in the stories told to us. It was not so much focused on understanding and controlling better, as it was about conducting research in a more interactive way and capturing the dynamic between and within what we study. Research is about being accountable to what those

narratives tell us about education and about questioning the very construction of researcher authority.

These are different kinds of inquiries. And they use language differently. Incidentally, none will produce knowledge in any enduring sense. In producing knowledge differently, what they do is make the point that all knowledge claims are inherently unstable. What is more, the analyses did not offer holistic accounts, modelled on the orderly relationships that seem to be inherent in a rational world. They used Foucault's conceptual tools as a framework, not with the promise of total vision, but to examine relations of power and knowledge which structure the educational discursive field. The approach allowed us to unearth and question taken-for-granted meanings and values.

We found in Foucault's conceptual language a useful way to understand lived experience. Of course lived experience is a temporary fixing but the analyses put Foucault's concepts to use to investigate the 'making' of social subjects, not in the sense of capturing their reality, but of trying to understand the operations of the complex and changing discursive processes by which identities are taken up or resisted and of the ways in which these processes achieve their effect. Teachers and students are historically variable social subjects. They are constituted as subjects in discourses, and disciplinary practices and knowingly or not, contribute themselves to the process of turning themselves into particular kinds of subjects. We explored what modes of subjectivity are available to them and what power/knowledge implications those modes of subjectivity carried. This sounds easier than it actually was. It involved thinking of a subject as a place or location, constructed in complex and multiple ways over time. Simply giving voice to subjects did not suffice. To add to the difficulty, it involved hearing what wasn't being said, and reading the unsaid against what was said.

The chapters were not focused on demonstrating causality. They were more set on exploring the particular effects of specific practices, and, particularly, the ways of being that those practices effect. The important idea we can take from this is that power seeps through all educational communities and all educational processes. It is exercised in discourse through the production of social agents, structuring collective life and shaping individual identity. The thing is that Foucault's framework will assist us finding out where meanings and values are legitimated. It will show us whose investments they favour, and how they are sustained. It will allow us to discover why our interests are sometimes silenced, how we are caught up in constraint or empowerment and where we might find weak points to imagine a space for creative change.

LOOKING FORWARD

Education is not a closed category, and that's because it is interwoven with a host of socio-political conditions and variables. The structures and power and dominance of these multiple locations intersect with and play into the discipline. With that in mind, Foucault's conceptual language is a useful toolkit for understanding its practices and processes. To put matters in perspective, it can create a politically constructive moment for education. One thing we need to keep at the forefront is that we won't be able to find out the real truth about educational practices or processes. Quite frankly, truth in any final or transcendental sense has never been within grasp. It's more about asking questions about which we have not previously thought to ask. The types of questions we might ask are: What formative events have brought this present situation about? How are individuals constituted as subjects of their own knowledge? How are they constituted as subjects who exercise and/or submit to power relations? This new way encourages us to think of education as a *political resource*, as constructed through the intellectual and cultural conditions of our times.

But if new knowledge is to be produced, then we must also be willing to rethink education with a new attitude. A new attitude is one that envisions new possibilities. It is a sobering thought that inequities in schools and other educational institutions do persist even when structural barriers are removed. From a Foucauldian point of view, this is *not* the result of flawed interventionary practices by those seeking more equitable practice but because the prevailing educational discourse lacks the analytic power to change existing historical formations. A strategic politics for education, putting Foucault to use, unearths those regulatory practices and processes that seek to normalise and regulate in education. It's not their explanation but the exposure of the power/knowledge relations within education that sets this kind of investigation apart from others. Devoted in large part to exploring how power is exercised, the investigation allows us to see whose voices are excluded, and how this might be open to change. We would carry this out with an experimental and cautious pragmatism towards the ways in which these practices are interpreted in particular contexts.

Rereading the practices and processes in education through the conceptual language offered by Foucault means that the rules and practices of education are held up for scrutiny. Trying to get a grasp on all this, it helps to think that the scrutiny focuses widely, both on the relationship between education and society, as well as the tensions and contradictions between current educational practices. Quite a lot might be exposed—and some of it unexpected and even disturbing. The investigation might reveal how education imposes categories that situate individuals, themselves, as being the site of the problem.

One of the really useful aspects about putting Foucault to use like this is that it allows us to make choices about how to speak, and write, and teach in ways that move toward the kind of arrangements in education which are more desirable. Any changes are always limited, of course, because there are institutional relations of power in place which serve to constrain (without fully defining) what is possible. But it can help create a space in which knowledges, roles, and relationships are questioned, where new possibilities are envisioned; a space in which we reflect on what we are today in education, and how we have come to be this way, and the consequences of our actions.

As you will have gathered by now, putting Foucault to use is not to argue against the idea of agency, so long as we redefine the term. The Foucauldian trick is to reformulate agency beyond its purely descriptive category to one that situates education in relations of power. In the shift we stop asking 'what can be done?' to focus on examining the constituting social relationships in operation. Once we start thinking of agency as contingent and 'multi-centred', then it is possible to question even the most firmly held assumptions about the world of education. Teachers, learners, educators and policy makers, curriculum writers and other educationally-minded individuals *can* resist discourses. They have the wherewithal to transform political relations through new discourses and new forms of power and new forms of educational practice.

The intellectual task of the agentic professional is to understand the way in which education is managed, crafted, extended and controlled—to understand how it is determined within the dense web of power regimes and to distinguish between disciplinary modes of power and the kinds of resistances that they occasion and spawn. To engage actively with issues in education means being prepared to challenge the configurations of power that traditionally have existed between teacher educators, teachers, pre-service teachers, educators, policy workers, students, and so on. Articulating the possibilities for change in education is to construct educational practices that do not impose a rigid and disciplinary set of values. It is to make a commitment to engage in political struggle in the meaning of education itself, while simultaneously acknowledging that to speak of transformative social change is to question the very meanings of empowerment. But above all, the task of professionals is to question the practice by which they willingly accept questionable limits of knowing and acting, and to replace this acceptance with a sense of their own power to make decisions—and all this in the face of the educational apparatus and its discursive regimes that seek to deny them any sense of agency. It is to create a practice that transgresses and exceeds a knowable order.

From the perspective of education a whole new space for critical reflection on the scope and limits of freedom becomes available. What it means is that every practitioner in the discipline of education can produce new knowledge that, in its own small way, can envisage new possibilities and make them realisable. Points can then be grasped where change is possible and desirable, and the determination of the precise form this change should take. For in a perspective in which the individual practitioner is seen as not simply constituted but also invested and traversed by often uneven and inequitable relations of power-knowledge, then what becomes possible is something more than a 'construction': it is rather the possibility of an intervention through a commitment to social and educational change.

> The essential political problem for the intellectual is not to criticise the ideological contents supposedly linked to science, or to ensure that his own scientific practice is accompanied by a correct ideology, but that of ascertaining the possibility of constituting a new politics of truth. The problem is not changing people's consciousness - or what's in their heads - but the political, economic, institutional regime of the production of truth.
>
> (Foucault, 1980, p. 133)

BIBLIOGRAPHY

Althusser, L. (1971). *Lenin and philosophy and other essays*. London: New Left Books.

Apple, M. (1995). Taking power seriously: New directions in equity in mathematics education and beyond. In W. Secada, E. Fennema, & L. Adajian (Eds), *New directions for equity in mathematics education* (pp. 329-348). Cambridge: Cambridge University Press with NCTM.

Bauersfeld, H., Krummheuer, G., & Voigt, J. (1988). Interactional theory of learning and teaching mathematics and related microethnographical studies. In H. G. Steiner, & A. E. Vermandel (Eds.), *Foundations and methodology of the discipline mathematics education* (pp. 174-188). Antwerp: Proceedings of the Theory of Mathematical Education (TME) Conference.

Becker, J. (1995). Women's ways of knowing in mathematics. In G. Kaiser & P. Rogers (Eds.), *Equity in mathematics education: Influences of feminism and culture* (pp. 164-174). London: Falmer.

Blake, N., Smeyers, P., Smith, R., & Standish, P. (1998). *Thinking again: Education after postmodernism.* Westport: Bergin & Garvey.

Blumer, H. (1968). *Symbolic interactionism: Perspectives and methods.* Englewood Cliffs, NJ: Prentice Hall.

Britzman, D. (1991). *Practice makes practice: A critical study of learning to teach.* Albany: State University of New York Press.

Brown, T., Jones, L., & Bibby, T. (2004). Identifying with mathematics in initial teacher training. In M. Walshaw (Ed.), *Mathematics education within the postmodern* (pp. 161-179). Greenwich, CT: Information Age.

Brownell, W.A. (1928). *The development of children's number ideas in primary grades.* Chicago: The University of Chicago.

Burton, L. (1995). Moving towards a feminist epistemology of mathematics. *Educational Studies in Mathematics, 28*, 275-291.

Butler, J. (1997). *The psychic life of power: Theories in subjection.* Stanford, CA: Stanford University Press.

Butler, J. (2004). *Undoing gender*. New York: Routledge.

Carr, W. (1995). Education and democracy: Confronting the postmodern challenge. *Journal of Philosophy of Education, 29*(1), 203-209.

Connolly, P. (1998). *Racism, gender identities and young children*. London: Routledge.

Damarin, S. (1995). Gender and mathematics from a feminist standpoint. In W. Secada, E. Fennema, & L. Adajian (Eds.), *New directions for equity in mathematics education* (pp. 242-257). Cambridge: Cambridge University Press with NCTM.

Davies, B. (1994). *Poststructuralist theory and classroom practice.* Melbourne: Deakin University Press.

Davies, B. (1997). Constructing and deconstructing masculinities through critical literacy. *Gender and Education, 9*(1), 9-30.

Davis, B., & Simmt, E. (2003). Understanding learning systems: Mathematics education and complexity science. *Journal for Research in Mathematics Education, 34*(2), 137-167.

Davydov, V. V. & Radzikhovskii, L. A. (1985). Vygotsky's theory and the activity-oriented approach to psychology. In J. V. Wertsch (Ed.), *Culture, communication, and cognition: Vygotskian perspectives* (pp. 66-93). Cambridge: Cambridge University Press.

Department for Education and Employment (DfEE). (1999). *The National Numeracy Strategy: Framework for teaching mathematics from reception to Year 6.* London: Department for Education and Employment.

Derrida, J. (1973). *Speech and phenomenon.* Evanston: North-Western University Press.

Derrida, J. (1976). *Of grammatology.* Baltimore: The John Hopkins University Press.

Dewey, J. [1916] 1963. *Democracy and education.* New York: Macmillan.

Dreyfus, H. L., & Rabinow, P. (1982). *Michel Foucault: Beyond structuralism and hermeneutics. With an afterword by and an interview with Michel Foucault.* Brighton: Harvester.

Engestrom, Y. (1987). *Learning by expanding.* Helsinki: Painettu Gummerus Oy.

Ernest, P. (1995). Values, gender and images of mathematics: A philosophical perspective. *International Journal of Mathematical Education in Science and Technology, 26*(3), 449–462.

Ernest, P. (2004). Postmodernism and the subject of mathematics. In M. Walshaw (Ed.), *Mathematics education within the postmodern* (pp. 15-33). Greenwich, CT: Information Age.

Fairclough, N. (1992). *Discourse and social change.* London: Polity Press.

Fairclough, N. (1994). *Critical discourse analysis: The critical study of language.* London: Longman.

Fennema, E., & Tartre, L. (1985). The use of spatial visualisation in mathematics by boys and girls. *Journal for Research in Mathematics Education, 16*(3), 184–206.

Fennema, E., & Peterson, P. (1985). Autonomous learning behaviour: A possible explanation of gender-related differences in mathematics. In L. Wilkinson & C. Marrett (Eds.), *Gender-related differences in classroom interactions* (pp. 17-35). New York: Academic.

Fennema, E., & Peterson, P. (1986). Teacher-student interactions and sex-related differences in learning mathematics. *Teaching and Teacher Education, 2*(1), 19-42.

Forgasz, H., & Leder, G. (1996). Mathematics classrooms, gender and affect. *Mathematics Education Research Journal, 8*(2), 153-173.

Forgasz, H. (2002). Computers for learning mathematics: Equity considerations. In B. Barton, K. Irwin, M. Pfannkuch, & M. Thomas (Eds.), *Mathematics education in the South Pacific* (Proceedings of the 25th Annual Conference of the Mathematics Education Research Group of Australasia, pp. 260-267). Sydney: MERGA.

Fox, L., & Soller, J. (2001). Psychological dimensions of gender differences in mathematics. In J. Jacobs, J. Becker & G. Gilmer (Eds), *Changing the faces of mathematics: Perspectives on gender* (pp. 9-23). Reston, VA: NCTM.

Gagné, R. (1965). *The conditions of learning.* New York: Holt, Rinehart, & Winston.

Garfinkel, H. (1967). *Studies in ethnomethodology.* Englewood Cliffs, NJ: Prentice-Hall.

Gutting, G. (Ed.) (2005). *The Cambridge companion to Foucault* (2nd ed.). New York: Cambridge University Press.

Hardy, T. (2004). 'There's no hiding place': Foucault's notion of normalisation at work in a mathematics lesson. In M. Walshaw (Ed.), *Mathematics education within the postmodern* (pp. 103-119). Greenwich, CT: Information Age.

Hartsock, N. (1983). The feminist standpoint: Developing the ground for a specifically feminist historical materialism. In S. Harding & M. Hintikka (Eds.), *Discovering reality: Feminist perspectives on epistemology, metaphysics, methodology, and philosophy of science* (pp. 283-310). Dordrecht, Netherlands: Reidel.

Hayes, D. (2003). Mapping transformations in educational subjectivities: Working within and against discourse. *International Journal of Inclusive Education, 7*(1), 7-18.

Hekman, S. (1990). *Gender and knowledge: Elements of a postmodern feminism*. Cambridge: Polity Press.

Henriques, J., Hollway, W., Urwin, C., Venn, C., & Walkerdine, V. (1984). *Changing the subject: Psychology, social regulation and subjectivity*. London: Methuen.

Hoy, D, (Ed.) (1986). *Foucault: A critical reader*. Oxford: Blackwell.

Kehily, M. J., & Nayak, A. (1997). 'Lads and laughter': Humour and the production of heterosexual hierarchies. *Gender and Education, 9*(1), 69-87.

Keith, M., & Pile, S. (1993). *Place and the politics of identity*. London: Routledge.

Kenway, J., Willis, S., Blackmore, J., & Rennie, L. (1998). *Answering back: Girls, boys, and feminisms in schools*. Sydney: Routledge.

Kristeva, J. (1981). Women's time. *Signs, 7*, 13-35.

Kristeva, J. (1984). *Revolution in poetic language*. New York: Columbia University.

Kristeva, J. (1986). *The Kristeva reader*. Oxford: Blackwell.

Krummheuer, G. (2000). Mathematics learning in narrative classroom cultures: Studies of argumentation in primary mathematics education. *For the Learning of Mathematics, 20*(1), 22-32.

Lacan, J. (1977). *Ecrits: A selection* (Trans: A. Sheridan). London: Tavistock.

Lakoff, G., & Núñez, R.E. (2000). *Where mathematics comes from: How the embodied mind brings mathematics into being*. New York: Basic Books.

Lather, P. (1994). Textual strategies and the politics of interpretation in educational research. *Australian Educational Researcher, 21*(1), 41-62.

Lather, P. (2006). Paradigm proliferation as a good thing to think with: Teaching research in education as a wild profusion. *International Journal of Qualitative Studies in Education, 19*(1), 35-57.

Lauretis de, T. (1986). Feminist studies/critical studies: Issues, terms, and contexts. In T. de Lauretis (Ed.), *Feminist studies/critical studies* (pp. 1-19). Bloomington: Indiana University Press.

Lave, J. (1988). *Cognition in practice: Mind, mathematics and culture in everyday life*. Cambridge, UK: Cambridge University Press.

Lave, J. (1996). Teaching, as learning, in practice. *Mind, Culture, and Activity, 3*, 149-164.

Lave, J., & Wenger, E. (1991). *Situated learning: Legitimate peripheral participation*. Cambridge: Cambridge University Press.

Leder, G., & Forgasz, H. (2003). Achievement self-rating and the gender stereotyping of mathematics. In L. Bragg, C. Campbell, G. Herbert, & J. Mousley (Eds.), *Mathematics education research: Innovation, networking, opportunity* (Proceedings of the 26th annual conference of the Mathematics Education Research Group of Australasia, pp. 476-483). Sydney: MERGA.

Leont'ev, A. N. (1978). *Activity, consciousness, and personality*. Englewood Cliffs, NJ: Prentice-Hall.

Lucey, H. (2001). Social class, gender and schooling. In B. Francis & C. Skelton (Eds.), *Investigating gender: Contemporary perspectives in education* (pp. 177-187). Buckingham: Open University Press.

Lucey, H., & Reay, D. (2000). Identities in transition: Anxiety and excitement in the move to secondary school. *Oxford Review of Education,* 26(2), 191-205.

Lucey, H., Brown, M., Denvir, H., Askew, M., & Rhodes, V. (2003). Girls and boys in the primary maths classroom. In C. Skelton & B. Francis (Eds.), *Boys and girls in the primary classroom* (pp. 43-58). Buckingham: Open University Press.

Lucey, H., Melody, J., & Walkerdine, V. (2003). Uneasy hybrids: psychosocial aspects of becoming educationally successful for working-class young women, *Gender and Education, 15*(3), 285-299.

Maccoby, E., & Jacklin, C. (1974). *The psychology of sex differences.* Stanford: Stanford University Press.

MacNaughton, G. (1998). Improving our gender equity 'tools': A case *for* discourse analysis. In N. Yelland (Ed.), *Gender in early childhood* (pp. 149-174). London: Routledge.

Martino, W., & Meyenn, B. (2002). 'War, guns and cool, tough things': Interrogating single-sex classes as a strategy for engaging boys in English. *Cambridge Journal of Education, 32*(3), 303–324.

Maturana, H., & Varela, F. (1987). *The tree of knowledge: The biological roots of human understanding.* Shambhala: Boston.

McLeod, J. (2000). Subjectivity and schooling in a longitudinal study of secondary students. *British Journal of Sociology of Education, 21*(4), 501-521

McNay, L (1994). *Foucault:* A *critical introduction.* Cambridge, MA: Polity Press.

Meaghan, M., & Patton, P. (1979). *Michel Foucault: Power, truth, strategy.* Sydney: Feral Publications.

Mehan, H. (1979). *Learning lessons.* Cambridge, MA: Harvard University Press.

Mendick, H. (2003). Choosing maths/doing gender: A look at why there are more boys than girls in advanced mathematics classes in England. In L. Burton (Ed.), *Which way social justice in mathematics education?* (pp. 169-187). Westport: Praeger.

Meyer, M., & Koehler, M. (1990) Initial influences on gender differences in mathematics. In E. Fennema & G. Leder (Eds.), *Mathematics and gender* (pp. 60-95). New York: Teachers College Press.

Ministry of Education (1992). *Mathematics in the New Zealand Curriculum.* Wellington: Learning Media.

Nairn, K. (1997). Hearing from quiet students: The politics of silence and voice in geography classrooms. In Jones, J. P., Nast, H. J., & Roberts, S. M. (Eds.), *Thresholds in feminist geography: Difference, methodology, representation* (pp. 93-115). New York: Rowman & Littlefield.

Nash, R. (1999). Social capital, class identity, and progress at school: Case studies. *New Zealand Journal of Education Studies, 34*(2), 267-280.

National Council of Teachers of Mathematics (2000). *Principles and standards for school mathematics.* Reston, VA: NCTM.

Nunes, T., Schliemann, A. D., & Carreher, D. W. (1993). *Street mathematics and school mathematics.* New York: Cambridge University Press.

O'Brien, M. (2003). Girls and transition to second-level schooling in Ireland: 'Moving on' and 'moving out', *Gender and Education, 15*(3), 249-267.

Piaget, J. (1959). *The language and thought of the child* (Trans: M. & R. Gabain). London: Routledge & Kegan Paul.

Pile, S., & Thrift, N. (1995). *Mapping the subject: Geographies of cultural transformation.* London. Routledge.

Pink, S. (2001). *Doing visual ethnography*. London: Sage.

Povey, H., Angier, C., & Clarke, M. (2006). Storying Joanne, an undergraduate mathematician. *Gender and Education, 18*(5), 459-471.

Reay, D. (1998). Engendering social reproduction: Mothers in the educational marketplace. *British Journal of Sociology of Education, 19*(2), 195-210.

Reay, D. (2001). 'Spice girls', 'nice girls', 'girlies', and 'tomboys': Gender discourses, girls' cultures and femininities in the primary classroom. *Gender and Education, 13*(2), 153-166.

Reay, D. (2002). Shaun's story: Troubling discourses of white working-class masculinities. *Gender and Education, 14*(3), 221-234.

Saussure, F. de (1983). *Course in general linguistics* (Trans: T. Harris). London: Gerald Duckworth and Co.

Sells, L. (1978). Mathematics: A critical filter. *The Science Teacher, 45*, 28–29.

Skelton, C. (2001). *Schooling the boys: Masculinities and primary education*. Buckingham: Open University Press.

Skelton, C. B., & Francis, B. (Eds.) (2003). *Boys and girls in the primary classroom*. Buckingham: Open University Press.

Skemp, R. R. (1976). Relational understanding and instrumental understanding. *Mathematics Teaching , 77*, 20-26.

Thomson, R., Henderson, S., & Holland, J. (2003). Making the most of what you've got? Resources, values and inequalities in young women's transitions to adulthood. *Educational Review, 55*, 33-46.

Usher, R., & Edwards, R. (1994). *Postmodernism and education*. London: Routeldge.

Von Glasersfeld, E. (1996). Aspects of radical constructivism and its educational recommendations. In L.P. Steffe & P. Nesher (Eds.), *Theories of mathematical learning* (pp. 307-314). Mahwah, NJ: Lawrence Erlbaum Associates.

Vygotsky, L. (1978). *Mind in society: The development of the higher psychological processes*. Cambridge, MA: Harvard University Press.

Walden, R., & Walkerdine, V. (1986). Characteristics, views and relationships in the classroom. In L. Burton (Ed.), *Girls into maths can go* (pp. 122-146). London: Holt, Rinehart & Winston.

Walkerdine, V. (1988). *The mastery of reason: Cognitive development and the production of rationality*. London: Routledge.

Walkerdine, V. (1989). and the Girls and Mathematics unit. *Counting girls out*. London: Virago.

Walkerdine, V. (1990). *Schoolgirl fictions*. London: Verso.

Walkerdine, V. (2003). Reclassifying upward mobility: Femininity and the neo-liberal subject. *Gender and Education, 15*(3), 237-248.

Walkerdine, V., Lucey, H., & Melody, J. (2001). *Growing up girl: Psychosocial explorations of gender and class*. Hampshire: Palgrave.

Weedon, C. (1999). *Feminism, theory and the politics of difference*. Oxford, UK: Blackwell.

Willis, S. (1990). Some beliefs about girls, mathematics and the early childhood years. *Australian Journal of Early Childhood, 15*(1), 47–48.

Wolin, R. (1992). *The terms of cultural criticism: The Frankfurt school, existentialism, poststructuralism*. New York: Columbia University Press.

Zevenbergen, R. (1994). *The construction of educational inequality: A critique of dominant discourses in mathematics education*. Geelong: Deakin University Press.

SUGGESTIONS FOR FURTHER READING

Cousins, M., & Hussain, A. (1984). *Michel Foucault.* London: Macmillan

Fillingham, L. A. (1993). *Foucault for beginners.* London: Writers and Readers Ltd.

Gordon, C. (Ed.) (1980). *Power/knowledge: Selected interviews and other writing 1972-1977 by Michel Foucault.* Brighton: Harvester.

Gore, J. (1995). *Foucault's poststructuralism and observational education research: A study in power relations.* London: Falmer Press.

Gutting, G. (Ed.) (2005). *The Cambridge companion to Foucault* (2nd ed.). New York: Cambridge University Press.

Hoy, D. (Ed.) (1986). *Foucault: A critical reader.* Oxford: Blackwell.

Martin, L. H., Gutman, H., & Hutton, P. H. (Eds.) (1988). *Technologies of the self.* London: Tavistock.

McKinlay, A., & Starkey, K. (Eds.) (1998). *Foucault, management and organizational theory: From panopticon to technologies of self.* London: Sage.

McNay, L. (1992). *Foucault and feminism: Power, gender and the self.* Cambridge: Polity Press.

McNay, L. (1994). *Foucault:* A *critical introduction.* Cambridge, MA: Polity Press.

Meaghan, M., & Patton, P. (1979). *Michel Foucault: Power, truth, strategy.* Sydney: Feral Publications.

Popkewitz, T. S., & Brennan, M. (Eds.) (1998). *Foucault's challenge: Discourse, knowledge and power in education.* New York: Teachers College Press.

Strathern, P. (2000). *The essential Foucault.* London: Virgin Books.

FOUCAULT'S BOOKS: A Selection

Foucault, M. (1961). *Madness and civilization: A history of insanity in the age of reason.* (Trans: R. Howard). New York: Random House.

Foucault, M. (1962). Mental illness and psychology. (Trans: A. Sheridan). New York: Harper and Row.

Foucault, M. (1965). *Madness and civilisation: A history of insanity in the Age of Reason.* (Trans: R. Howard). New York: Random House.

Foucault, M. (1970). *The order of things: An archaeology of the human sciences* (Trans: A. Sheridan). New York: Vintage.

Foucault, M. (1972). *The archaeology of knowledge and the discourse of language* (Trans: A. Sheridan Smith). London: Pantheon.

Foucault, M. (1973). *The birth of the clinic: An archaeology of medical perception* (Trans: A. Sheridan Smith). New York: Pantheon.

Foucault, M. (1975). *I, Pierre Riviere, having slaughtered my mother, my sister, and my brother...: A case of parricide in the 19th century* (Trans: F. Jellinek). Lincoln: University of Nebraska Press.

Foucault, M. (1976). *Mental illness and psychology* (Trans: A Sheridan). New York:

Foucault, M. (1977). *Discipline and punish: The birth of the prison* (Trans: A. Sheridan). Harmondsworth: Penguin.

Foucault, M. (1977). *Language, counter-memory, practice: Selected essays and interviews* (Trans: D. Bouchard & S. Simon). Ithaca, NY: Cornell University Press.

Foucault, M. (1977). *The history of sexuality, Volume 1: An introduction* (Trans: R. Hurley). New York: Pantheon.

Foucault, M. (1980). *Power/knowledge: Selected interviews and other writings 1972-1977* (Trans: C. Gordon et al.) New York: Pantheon.

Foucault, M. (1981). *The order of discourse.* (Trans: R. Young). London: Routledge.

Foucault, M. (1981). *This is not a pipe* (Trans: J. Harkness). Berkeley: University of California Press.

Foucault, M. (1984). *The care of the self.* (Trans: R. Hurley, 1986). Harmondsworth, UK: Penguin.

Foucault, M. (1984). *The use of pleasure.* (Trans: R. Hurley, 1985). Harmondsworth, UK: Penguin.

Foucault, M. (1984). Complete and austere institutions. In P. Rabinow (Ed.), *The Foucault reader: An introduction to Foucault's thought* (pp. 214-225). Harmondsworth, UK: Penguin.

Foucault, M. (1985). *The use of pleasure, Volume 2 of the history of sexuality* (Trans: R. Hurley). New York: Pantheon.

Foucault, M. (1986). *The care of the self, Volume 3 of the history of sexuality* (Trans: R. Hurley). New York: Pantheon.

Foucault, M. (1987). The final Foucault (J. Bernauer & D. Rasmussen, Eds.). Cambridge, MA: MIT Press.

Foucault, M. (1988). *The ethic of care for the self as a practice of freedom.* Cambridge: The Massachusetts Institute of Technology Press.

Foucault, M. (1988). *Selections. Politics, philosophy, culture: Interviews and other writings, 1977-1984.* (L. Kritzman, Ed.) (Trans: A. Sheridan et al.). New York: Routledge.

Foucault, M. (1989). *Foucault live: Interviews 1966-84* (S. Lotringer, Ed.) (Trans: J. Johnston). New York: Semiotext(e).

Foucault, M. (1991). *Politics and the study of discourse.* In G. Burchell, C. Gordon, & P. Miller (Eds.), *The Foucault effect: Studies in governmentality* (pp. 53-72). Chicago: University of Chicago Press.

Foucault, M. (1991). *Remarks on Marx: Conversations with Duccio Trombadori* (Trans: R. J. Goldstein & J. Cascaito, Eds.). New York: Semiotext(e).

COPYRIGHT ACKNOWLEDGMENTS

A number of extracts used in the book have appeared in other publications of the author's work. Acknowledgment is made to the following journals for permission to reprint the extracts.

Chapter 2:
For the Learning of Mathematics, 24(3), 4-11, 2004.
A powerful theory of active engagement.

Chapter 3:
New Zealand Journal of Educational Studies, 35 (2), 145-155. 2000.
The emperor(ess)'s new clothes: Deconstructing gendered constructions within MiNZC.

Chapter 4:
Journal for Research in Mathematics Education, 32 (5), 471-492. 2001.
A Foucauldian gaze on gender research: What do you do when confronted with the tunnel at the end of the light? (Reprinted with permission, copyright 2007, by the National Council of Teachers of Mathematics. All rights reserved.)

Chapter 5:
British Journal of Sociology of Education, 27(5), 555-567. 2006.
Girls' workplace destinations in a changed social landscape: Girls and their mothers talk.

Chapter 7:
Journal of Mathematics Teacher Education, 7(1), 63-86. 2004.
Pre-service teaching in the context of schools: An exploration into the constitution of identity.

Chapter 8:
New Zealand Journal of Educational Studies, 41(1), 69-84. 2006.
The classroom as a space for the production of subjectivities.

Chapter 9:
Cambridge Journal of Education, 35(1), 19-34. 2005.
Getting political and unraveling layers of gendered mathematical identifications.

INDEX

A

agency
  as awareness of discursive restrictions and enablements, 71
  as located within games of truth, 92
  as examined by discourses in action, 76
  as situated in relations of power, 169-170
  as the capacity to intervene and transform practice, 114
Althusser, 4, 5
Angier, 150, 152
Apple, 159
archaeological analysis, 28-36
archaeology
  as a methodological approach, 9, 27
Aristotle, 6, 11
Askew, 154
autonomy, 15

B

Bacon, 11
Barthes, 4
Bauersfeld, 33
behaviourism, 2, 28
Becker, 153
Bentham, 113
Benthamite Panopticon, 113
Bibby, 155
biopower
  as control at the microlevel of practice, 112
Blake, 92
Blumer, 33
Britzman, 100, 108
Brown, 154, 155
Brownell, 30
Burton, 153
Butler, 101, 120

C

Carr, 5
Carreher, 35
classroom experience
  as engagement with discursive classroom codes, 140
cognitivism, 29
concepts
  deriving a theory from, 7
  tracking the history of, 3
Connolly, 137
constructivism
  as a theory of knowing, 2, 31, 54
  radical, 31
  social, 33
critical race theory, 2
critical theory, 2
culture
  and formulations of learning, 32

D

Damarin, 154
Davies, 137, 159, 163
Davis, 35
Davydov, 34
Denvir, 154
Derrida, 4, 5
Descartes, 6, 11
Dewey, 30
Discipline and Punish, 21
disciplinary power
  as diffuse, 129
  as insinuated within society, 112
  as making us want to conform, 129
  as working through networks to control people, 12
discourse
  as a key concept, 6, 39
  as competing ways of organising meaning, 82
  as constituting individuals as subjects, 19, 66
  as constituting subjectivity, 79
  as creating material effects, 103
  as historically variable ways of specifying knowledge and truth, 40
  as human conversation, 19,
  as implying forms of social organisation, 19
  as structuring areas of knowledge, 19
  as the means by which reality is read, 42
  bumping, 83
  colliding, 82
  cultural, 84, 93
  hybrid, 107
  markers, 49

discourse analysis
as a tool to unmask power relations, 54
as revealing how discourses position people, 45
critical discourse analysis, 44
for understanding how texts produce the people they target, 62
discursive construction of subjectivity, 42
discursivity
as a way of organising people and systems, 41
distributed cognition, 2
dividing practices
as operating across society, 99, 100
docile body, 24
Dreyfus, 7, 15, 104, 123, 154

E

education
and rethinking it with a new attitude, 169
as a political resource, 169
Einstein, 3
Engestrom, 34
enactivism, 2
episteme, 10
Ernest, 154, 156, 159
essentialism, 6, 80
ethics of the self
as promoting new forms of subjectivity, 9, 15
as politically optimistic, 15
Everybody Counts: A Report to the Nation on the Future of Mathematics, 47

F

Fairclough, 44
feminist theory, 2
femininity, 83, 132
Fennema, 153
Forgasz, 153, 143
Fox, 153
Francis, 154

G

Gagné, 28
Garfinkel, 33
gender
gendered selves, 80
gendered subjectivity, 77, 140
performing gender, 81
genealogy
as a methodological approach, 9, 13
exploring power/knowledge interactions, 13
girls
and achievements, 75
and presumed deficiencies, 56, 57
as a problem, 56
as produced and subjected to systems of regulation, 56
governmentality
analysis of, and key contribution to social theory, 6
as an interpretation of individual experiences, 23
as enforced obedience to rules, 102
Gutting, 7

H

Habermas, 6
Harding, 150
Hardy, 13
Hayes, 137
Hegel, 6
Heidegger, 6
Henderson, 92
Henriques, 151
hermeneutics, 2, 5
historian of the present, 7
Holland, 92
humanism, 6, 17

I

identity
as a social construct, 93
as created at the intersection of discourses, 81, 93, 162
as fashioned and contested through systems of power, 98
as fixed, 11
markers, 80
of teachers, 95
as constituted within different sites, 98
information-processing, 2
interactionist approaches to learning, 33
interpretation
and no objective truths, 6
separation between knowing subject and objective world, 6
interpretivism, 2
intersubjectivity
in sociocultural formulations of learning, 32

J

Jacklin, 137

Jones, 155

K

Kant, 6
Kehily, 132
Keith, 132
Kenway, 153
knowledge
  as a key concept, 6
  systems of discursive events, 10
Koehler, 153
Kristeva, 4, 5
Krummheuer, 33

L

Lacan, 5
Lakoff, 36
language
  as constituting social reality, 5
  as playing a key role in identity formation, 12
Lather, 2, 144
Lave, 36
learning
  theory of, 27
  to teach, 96
Leder, 153, 154
Leont'ev, 34
liberalism, 17
Lucey, 90, 92, 134, 154
Lyotard, 4

M

Maccoby, 153
MacNaughton, 45
Madness and Civilisation, 8
Martino, 137, 159
masculinity, 132
Mathematics in the New Zealand Curriculum, 46, 47, 51
McLeod, 134
McNay, 4
Meaghan, 8
Mehan, 33
Mendick, 154
Mental Illness and Psychology, 8
Meyenn, 159
Meyer, 153

N

Nairn, 132
Nash, 88
naturalism, 2
Nayak, 132
Newton, 3
New Zealand Curriculum Framework, 47
Nietzsche, 6, 13, 14
normalisation, 132
  as naming acceptable practices and states of being, 136
  as political and gendered, 132
  as opening up membership to social entities, 130
  as predicated on knowledge of target object, 136
Nunes, 35
Núñez, 36

O

objectivity
  as problematised, 5, 146-7
O'Brien, 91
ontology of the present, 7

P

participatory approaches to learning, 33
Patton, 8
pedagogical relations, 50, 52
Peterson, 153
phenomenology, 2, 17
Piaget, 29-30, 31
Pile, 132, 134
Pink, 132
Plato, 11
policy text
  as an apparatus of social regulation, 54
  as identifying specific categories, 50
  operating with political interest, 46
  where subject positions are created, 45
postmodernism, 4
poststructuralism, 4, 5
Povey, 150, 152
power, 6, 20
  as an integral part of our lives, 68
  as coercive, 20
  as constituted through discourses, 20
  as exercised within the social body, 21, 68
  as fusing the pre-service teacher/teacher associate relation, 126
  as constituting the reality of classroom life, 140
  as knitting the social fabric together, 67
  as negative, 9, 20
  as the essence of classroom life, 70
  as possessed, 21, 75
  disciplinary, 22, 112
  effects of, 73

in networks continually shifting, 68
Marxist version of, 20, 67
micro- practices of, 139
positive aspects of, 9, 20, 70
power/knowledge
analyses, 6
and its debut, 8
as Foucault's signature statement, 22
as integral to policy text, 56
power/knowledge/truth, 22
practices of the self
as an aesthetics of existence, 16

R

Rabinow, 7, 15, 104, 123, 154
Radzikhovskii, 34
rational autonomous subject, 5
rationality, 10, 49, 50
reality, 1, 3
Reay, 134, 136-137, 138, 159
research
and different textual forms, 152-154
and knowledge claims caught up in power-games, 148
and the problem of shifting perspectives, 148
and the issue of causality, 151
and the issue of time, 148
as being accountable, 163
as conducted in a more interactive way, 163
as questioning researcher authority, 163
as invoking political deliberation, 150
objectivity, 146-150
scientific model, 145-147
reason
as problematised by poststructuralists, 5
local, 6
logic of, 49
universal, 6
regime of truth
as at the heart of power-knowledge effects, 23
as in early gender research, 56
as sanctioning specific practices and social arrangements, 121
legitimising stage-wise development, 59
regulatory practices
as establishing institutional and social relations, 121
Rose, 87
Rhodes, 154

S

Saussure, de, 5, 19
Sartre, 6
Schliemann, 35
science
as an important social force, 145
as assuming a transparent reality, 145
as assuming observers are interchangeable spectators, 145
as built around systematic order, 145
as invested with interests of regulation and control, 145
self
an analysis of, 6
as a centre of coherent experience, 101
as opening up new possibilities for education, 102
decentred, 5
'one true self', 9
Sells, 153
Semiotic mediation theory, 32
Simmt, 35
situated knowing, 2
Skelton, 137, 154
Skemp, 30
socioculturalism, 2
sociocultural formulations of learning, 32
socio-economic status, 134
Soller, 153
structuralism, 5
students
as an effect of disciplinary power, 135
subject positions, 45
subjectification
as the transformation of selves, 102
as active involvement in self-forming, 114
subjectivity
as a site of control, 42
as circumscribed by place, time and specificity, 77
as created in a number of practices, 74
as produced within discourses, 70-71, 79
associated with respectable feminine activities, 91
surveillance
as contributing to gendered continuities, 135
as defining subjectivities, 135
as important to consistency and continuity within sites, 124
as involved in processes of subjectification, 102
as political and gendered, 132
symbolic interactionism, 2

T

Tartre, 153

teaching identity
as complex and multiple, 127
as constituted by material and embodied relations of discourses, 101
as negotiated within context, 104
as produced through social interaction, 103, 109
teaching practice
as intelligible through techniques, 121
technologies of power, 102
technologies of the self, 24, 102
The Archaeology of Knowledge, 10, 40, 145
The Conditions of Learning, 28
the gaze, 125, 130, 131, 135, 138, 139
the learner
as a fiction, 60
as an object of surveillance and normalisation, 131
as a product of discursive practice, 67
as generated by structural rules that govern discursive formation, 60
as the origin of meaning, 60
The Order of Things, 10, 17, 40
theoretical frames
emancipatory, 2
interpretivist, 2
positivist, 2
theories of learning
activity/situativity/social practice
behaviourism, 28
cognitivism, 29
complexity, 35
constructivism, 31
embodied, 36
enactivist, 35
interactionist, 33
participatory, 33
sociocultural formulations, 32
social constructivist, 33
theory
as a lens to improve insight, 1
the importance of, 1
the school
as an apparatus of social regulation, 130
as performing a normalising function, 130
the subject
as a fiction, 11
as an effect of discursive relations, 18
as generated by discursive rules, 11
as the origin of knowledge, 18
autonomous, 6
death of, 17
decentred, 6
Thomson, 92
Thrift, 134
truth
as a construction, 9
as provisional, open-ended and relational, 81

U

utopianism, 6

V

Voigt, 33
von Glasersfeld, 31
Vygotsky, 32

W

Walden, 153
Walkerdine, 35, 59, 75, 132, 153, 156
Wenger, 36
Willis, 159
Wolin, 5

Z

Zevenbergen, 159
zone of proximal development, 32

Lightning Source UK Ltd.
Milton Keynes UK
UKOW05n1007041216
289093UK00001B/63/P